CORE TAX ANNUALS
Trusts and Estates 2009/10

Matthew Hutton MA (Oxon) CTA AIIT TEP

Series General Editor: Mark McLaughlin CTA (Fellow) ATT TEP

Bloomsbury Professional

Bloomsbury Professional Limited, Maxwelton House, 41–43 Boltro Road, Haywards Heath, West Sussex, RH16 1BJ

© Bloomsbury Professional Ltd 2009

Cover illustration © Marcus Duck 2009

Marcus Duck is a Brighton-based graphic designer and photographer.
Contact:marcus@marcusduckdesign.com

Previously published by Tottel Publishing Ltd

A CIP Catalogue record for this book is available from the British Library.

ISBN: 978 1 84766 329 0

Typeset by Phoenix Photosetting, Chatham, Kent
Printed and bound in the UK by CPI William Clowes Beccles NR34 7TL

Preface

This is the 9th edition of a book which now forms part of the Core Tax Annuals series from Bloomsbury Professional, comprising a set of six titles. The thinking behind the Tax Annuals series is to develop the user-friendly practical theme of the previous 'Tax Essentials' series, so as to provide for accountants, lawyers and other professional advisers (and, indeed, for taxpayers themselves) a core set of tax annuals from which they can easily find initial guidance on the mainstream areas of UK tax law.

A revolutionary pricing structure, both for individual books in the series and for the series as a whole, makes them easily affordable for both professionals and taxpayers and thus will enable everyone (from the interested lay person and the sole practitioner) to keep their library up to date each year.

As in previous editions, this book aims to illustrate with examples and tables the primary points of legislation and practice. A book of this length can do no more than deal with the basic tax system as it relates to trusts and deceased estates (though it does also introduce the reader to some of the more complex aspects of the UK tax system). The introduction on page 1 explains how the book is structured, dealing in turn with the tax aspects of:

- starting a trust;
- running a trust;
- ending a trust; and
- deceased estates.

Matthew Hutton
Chedgrave
August 2009

Contents

Contents

Table of statutes

Table of statutory instruments

Table of cases

[All references are to paragraph numbers]

Abbreviations and references

Abbreviations

The following abbreviations are used in this book.

A&M	Accumulation and maintenance trust
AIM	Alternative investment market
App	Appendix
APR	Agricultural property relief
BPR	Business property relief
CA	Court of Appeal
CGT	Capital gains tax
ChD	Chancery Division
Col	Column
CTT	Capital transfer tax
DTR	Double taxation relief
EIS	Enterprise Investment Scheme
ESC	Extra-statutory Concession
FA	Finance Act
FOTRA	Free of tax to residents abroad
HL	House of Lords
HM	Her Majesty's
HMRC	Her Majesty's Revenue and Customs
ICTA 1988	Income and Corporation Taxes Act 1988
IHT	Inheritance tax
IHTA 1984	Inheritance Tax Act 1984
IRPR	Inland Revenue Press Release
ITA 2007	Income Tax Act 2007
ITTOIA 2005	Income Tax (Trading and Other Income) Act 2005
NI	National Insurance
para	paragraph
PET	Potentially exempt transfer
Pt	Part
PR	Personal representative
QB	Queen's Bench Division
RAT	Rate applicable to trusts
s	Section
Sch	Schedule
SDLT	Stamp duty land tax
SI	Statutory Instrument

SP   Inland Revenue Statement of Practice
SpC   Special Commissioners
TCGA 1992   Taxation of Chargeable Gains Act 1992
TMA 1970   Taxes Management Act 1970
TSEM   HMRC Trusts Settlements and Estates Manual
TSI   Transitional serial interest

References

AC   Law Reports, Appeal Cases
All ER   All England Law Reports
STC   Simon's Tax Cases
STC (SCD)   Simon's Tax Cases, Special Commissioners' Decisions
STI   Simon's Tax Intelligence
TC   Official Reports of Tax Cases

NB: The masculine gender, wherever it appears, includes the feminine.

Chapter 1

Introduction

1.1 *Trusts and Estates 2009/10* is a quick reference guide for trustees, personal representatives and their professional advisers to the tax aspects of dealing with trusts and deceased estates, specifically in satisfying their various compliance responsibilities to HMRC. To this end, the book adopts a compliance-based approach, though within its pages are numerous suggestions both for mitigating tax liabilities and for simplifying the administration involved in trusts and deceased estates. The book deals only with UK-resident trusts. The taxes covered are income tax, capital gains tax, inheritance tax and stamp duties (ie stamp duty on shares and stamp duty land tax on land).

This book is designed specifically for ease of use, enabling the reader to find the information required quickly and without having to wade through a mass of detail, which may be irrelevant to him. It is not (and cannot be) a complete guide to the tax aspects of UK resident trusts and deceased estates, however.

The introductory chapter discusses the concept of a trust and distinguishes trusts from estates. Chapters 2 to 9 deal with trusts: specifically the tax implications of starting, running and then bringing them to an end. Chapters 10 to 14 of the book are concerned with deceased estates.

Wherever the spouse exemption from inheritance tax is mentioned, this should be taken as including a reference to the corresponding exemption for gifts or bequests to the surviving member of a registered civil partnership from 5 December 2005 (see for example **2.5, 9.18, 9.21** and **11.19–11.23**).

Reference is made throughout the book to various HMRC forms, which may be accessed from the HMRC's website at www.hmrc.gov.uk.

Compliance responsibilities within HMRC may be summarised as follows. Income tax and capital gains tax are dealt with by HMRC Trusts (formerly IR Trusts) through one of three specialist districts: Edinburgh, Nottingham and Truro. Inheritance tax in relation to both trusts and deceased estates is managed by HMRC Inheritance Tax in Edinburgh and Nottingham. Income tax and capital gains tax in deceased estates are generally handled by the tax district that dealt with the affairs of the deceased when he was alive. Only in a 'large' estate will compliance fall to be dealt with by a specialist division of HMRC Trusts in Edinburgh.

A brief word about tax years used in this book. For compliance (especially income tax and capital gains tax) purposes, the tax rates, allowances and exemptions mentioned are generally those for 2008/09. For planning purposes, that is, especially inheritance tax (but also to an extent capital gains tax), thresholds and reliefs are for 2009/10.

A consultation exercise was launched by HMRC in December 2003 on the modernisation and simplification of the income and capital gains taxation of trusts. From tax year 2004/05 the rate of income tax and capital gains tax paid by trustees was aligned with the marginal rate of individuals (with income tax of discretionary and accumulation trusts payable at 32.5% for dividends and otherwise 40%: to rise to 42.5% and 50% respectively from 2010/11. These rates are subject to the proviso that the first £1,000 of income in any tax year attracts the standard rate of 20%). Two new rules were introduced by *FA 2005* (from 2004/05 and 2005/06 respectively) and further substantive changes were introduced by *FA 2006* from tax year 2006/07 and (for CGT residence of trusts) 2007/08. These changes are summarised in the Appendix, which concludes with a summary of the one outstanding issue.

A reform of capital gains tax took effect for 2008/09, introducing a uniform rate of tax of 18% for all taxpayers, including trustees. Indexation allowance and taper relief have been abolished and entrepreneurs' relief (see **5.32–5.34**) has been introduced. The above said, however, the most significant recent tax reform within the context of this book remains the 'alignment' of the inheritance tax regime for trusts which took effect from 2006/07 (see, generally, Chapter 6).

Chapter 2

Background

WHAT IS A TRUST?

Types of ownership

2.1   A trust or settlement is a long-established creature of the English legal system. Ownership of property may be divided into two categories; legal and beneficial (or equitable). A trust makes use of this distinction by giving to trustees the legal ownership of property, to hold that property for the enjoyment of the various beneficiaries. Legal ownership implies the registration of property eg land or company shares, so that HM Land Registry or the registrar of a company would consider the trustees to be the owners of the trust property (and would not be concerned with the trusts of the particular settlement). Note that a 'settlement' can be wider than a trust for tax purposes, as including a joint bank account which is funded by gift in certain circumstances.

The beneficiaries

2.2   All the persons who may benefit under the trust should be described in the trust deed, either by name or by reference to a class, eg the children of the settlor (viz the person making the settlement).

Trustee powers

2.3   A person who, typically with others, owns property as a trustee is treated in relation to the trust quite separately from his own or beneficial property, both under the general law and for tax purposes. Being a trustee implies a power, and indeed duty, to manage the trust property (ie not just to 'sit on it') for the benefit of the beneficiaries. These powers of management may be found under the general law, eg the *Trustee Act 1925*, the *Trustee Investments Act 1961* and most recently, the *Trustee Act 2000*, all as amplified or extended by the provisions of the trust deed.

Trustee decisions

2.4 Ideally a trust will have at least two trustees (and in relation to land there must under English law be at least two). Trustees must generally act unanimously, though the trust deed may give power to act by a majority. Generally, the terms of the deed should be followed strictly; otherwise, the trustees may be personally liable for 'breach of trust'.

Sometimes a trustee may also be a beneficiary, though in that event the trustee must be very careful about exercising trust powers for his own benefit; typically the trust deed will require him not to be involved in any decisions that benefit him. The same could apply also where a trustee (not being a beneficiary) can benefit in relation to trust property, eg where the trust fund includes shares in a private company and the trustee also owns shares himself.

A standard legal definition of a trust

2.5 'A trust is an equitable obligation, binding a person (called a trustee) to deal with property (called trust property) owned by him or a separate fund, distinct from his own private property for the benefit of persons (called beneficiaries or, in old cases, *cestuis que trust*), of whom he may himself be one and any one of whom may enforce the obligation: any act or neglect on the part of a trustee which is not authorised or excused by the terms of the trust instrument, or by law, is called a breach of trust.' (Underhill and Hayton, *Law of Trusts and Trustees*, 17th edition, page 2).

A trust (or settlement) will have:

- A settlor, ie the person who makes the settlement. Ideally, each settlement will have only one settlor, though some might have husband and wife as joint settlors. Any person who adds property to a settlement by a gift will be a settlor in relation to that settlement (which may involve anti-avoidance rules for the various taxes, discussed at **4.24–4.29** for income tax, **5.22–5.23** for capital gains tax – albeit repealed from 2008/09 – and **6.16–6.21** for inheritance tax). *FA 2006*, in introducing generally conformed definitions for both income tax and capital gains tax purposes, specifically defines the term 'settlor' for these two taxes. Regulations made pursuant to *FA 2005, s 103* ensure that for all tax and other legal purposes members of a registered civil partnership are treated as a married couple. It may be that, after 4 December 2005, the members of a registered civil partnership together make a settlement, though as with husband and wife it is considered preferable for each settlor to have their own settlement.

- A trust deed, setting out the terms of the trust, including identification of the beneficiaries.

- Trustees, who manage the trust property and accept responsibility for the trust.

- The trust fund. This may be an initial nominal sum, eg £10 followed by a transfer of the substantive trust property; alternatively, the substantive trust property may be transferred to the trustees at outset. Other property may be transferred in future.

- A trust period (except for charitable trusts), eg 80 years, within which the trust must come to an end: see **9.1–9.3**, especially for the effect of the *Perpetuities and Accumulations Bill 2009* once enacted. Ideally, the trust deed will specify the 'default beneficiaries' who will enjoy such capital as may remain at the end of the trust period.

- A governing law, assumed in this book to be the law of England and Wales (Scottish law rules, in particular, being different).

DIFFERENT TYPES OF TRUST

Discretionary trusts

2.6   A discretionary trust gives to the trustees a discretion as to how to pay the income between a class of income beneficiaries. Alternatively, the trust deed may allow the trustees, instead of paying out income for a particular tax year, to 'accumulate' that income. Such power of accumulation can operate only within a particular period of time, eg 21 years from the date of the trust deed. This statutory restriction will be removed by the *Perpetuities and Accumulations Bill 2009* once enacted: see **9.1** for the impact on existing trusts. Accumulations of income are added to capital, though the trust deed may allow past accumulations to be paid out as income of the current year.

Discretion over capital is different; the capital beneficiaries may be other than the income beneficiaries.

Accumulation and maintenance ('A&M') – before 22 March 2006

2.7   The A&M is a special type of discretionary trust, broadly for the benefit of children under the age of 25 or, from 6 April 2008, 18. For income tax and capital gains tax purposes it is treated exactly like a discretionary (or 'relevant property') trust. However, for inheritance tax it does not suffer the special exit and ten-yearly charges imposed under the discretionary regime (see **6.30–6.43**). To qualify for this special inheritance tax treatment (see **6.45–6.51**), two sets of conditions must be satisfied (under *IHTA 1984, s 71*):

- there must be no interest in possession (that is right to income) in the settlement; the income must be accumulated in so far as it is not applied for maintenance, education or benefit of the beneficiaries; and one or more beneficiaries will become entitled to income or capital before reaching a specified age not exceeding 25 years or, from 6 April 2008, 18; and

- broadly no more than 25 years have elapsed since the creation of the settlement or all the beneficiaries have a common parent or grandparent.

Following *FA 2006*, no new A&M trusts can be created after 21 March 2006. Transitional rules apply, until 5 April 2008, to A&M trusts in being at 22 March 2006: see **6.49–6.52**. While the transitional period came to an end at midnight on 5 April 2008, the traditional beneficial treatment of A&M trusts for IHT purposes continues after that date, provided that the beneficiaries become absolutely entitled to capital at age 18.

Strictly speaking, the expression 'A&M trusts' is something of a misnomer, albeit in widespread use. This is because it was never the case that a trust was within the A&M regime, rather that from time to time capital held on the trusts of a particular settlement might have been within the regime, whether in whole or in part, subject to satisfying the above two conditions. Increasingly, however, the protection of the A&M regime is being consigned to history.

Life interest trusts

2.8   An interest in possession trust has one or more fixed interests in income. The right to income may be for the life of the beneficiary (called the life tenant), or it may come to an end at an earlier stage, eg on his marriage or remarriage, or indeed it may be for a fixed period. It may also be 'defeasible' – that is the trustees can exercise a power (called a power of appointment) diverting the income to another beneficiary.

What happens on the death of a life tenant or earlier termination of the life interest will depend on the trust deed. There could, for example, be successive life interests to his children or they might benefit outright at, say, age 25. For more detailed discussion, see **6.56–6.62**.

Following *FA 2006*, most interest in possession trusts created on or after 22 March 2006 will, for IHT purposes, be treated in the same way as discretionary trusts as 'non-estate' interests in possession: see **6.59–6.62**. Exceptions to this principle are 'transitional serial interests' (see **6.58**), trusts for a disabled person (see **2.10**) and 'immediate post-death interests' arising under a will (see **6.61–6.62**).

Example 2.1—Discretionary trust

Albert made a trust on 1 January 1998 for the benefit of his four children: Charles, Debbie, Edward and Fiona and their various spouses and children. The trustees are Albert, his wife Betty and their family solicitor. Income and capital may be divided between any of the beneficiaries as the trustees decide, with a power to accumulate income for 21 years from 1 January 1998. At the end of the 80-year trust period the capital, if it remains, is to be divided equally between Charles, Debbie, Edward and Fiona (or their respective estates in the event that they have died).

Example 2.2—Accumulation and maintenance trust

Adrian and Belinda together made a settlement on 1 January 1999 for their two children, Caroline, aged five and David aged two together with any future children. The children become entitled to income in their *pro rata* share of the settlement on reaching the age of 25. Capital is to be held for their children, ie the grandchildren of the settlors, on attaining the age of 25. It was open to the trustees to continue the benefit of the A&M regime beyond 5 April 2008 by changing the terms of the trusts so that capital vests absolutely in Adrian's and Belinda's children at age 18. Failing this, the capital then in the settlement will have entered the 'relevant property' regime on 6 April 2008 (see **6.45** to **6.51** and specifically Examples **6.15, 6.16** and **6.17**).

Example 2.3—Interest in possession (or life interest) trust

Alistair's father made a settlement for him on his twenty-first birthday on 1 January 2006, transferring 200 acres of farmland and a farmhouse to the trustees. Alistair is entitled to the income from the trust fund, though the trustees have power to appoint the income away from him. They also may advance capital to him at their discretion. On termination of the interest in possession, the income of the trust is to be held for such of Alistair's children, if any, surviving on his death in equal shares (or if none, for Alistair's brother Ben absolutely). If Alistair leaves children, they become entitled to the capital at age 25.

Note that the traditional IHT treatment of a life interest trust under which the capital is deemed to be owned absolutely by the beneficiary, as an 'estate' life interest (see **6.53**) applies only in general terms where the trust was made before 22 March 2006 (or where there is an 'immediate post-death interest'

7

under a will trust (see **6.61**). Had in this example Alistair's father made the trust for his son on 1 January 2007, the capital would have fallen into the relevant property regime, albeit possibly not so material in this case insofar as 100% agricultural property relief applies.

Some other types of trust

Charitable trusts

2.9   Income and capital must be applied exclusively for 'charitable purposes'. A charitable trust will normally continue in perpetuity, that is, it is not required to come to an end after any particular time. See Chapter 8.

Disabled trusts

2.10   This is, traditionally, a discretionary trust which exists for the benefit of a disabled person. While discretionary, it is treated for IHT as an interest in possession trust even though there may be power to accumulate income (*IHTA 1984, s 89*), provided that the trusts ensure that not less than half of the fund which is applied during the beneficiary's lifetime is applied for his benefit. *FA 2006* has extended the definition of 'disabled trust', so that included within the meaning of 'disabled person's interest' are the cases where: (a) there is an express interest in possession for a disabled person; and (b) a person makes a settlement on himself (whether discretionary or interest in possession in form) in reasonable expectation of disability (new *ss 89A* and *89B* of the *IHTA 1984*).

Note that, rather unfairly, it is not possible to make a qualifying disabled trust in expectation of the disability of another person. The provisions for disabled trusts are, together with 'transitional serial interests' (see **6.58**), the exception to the principle that a non-charitable settlement made on or after 22 March 2006 will necessarily fall within the relevant property regime. To secure the favoured IHT treatment, one of the four sets of conditions must be satisfied at the outset; it is not sufficient if, not applying immediately, they come to be satisfied at some stage thereafter.

Protective trusts

2.11   This is an interest in possession trust, which will come to an end either if the life tenant (called the principal beneficiary) becomes bankrupt or if he takes any steps to sell or alienate his interest under the settlement. In that case the trust becomes discretionary (*Trustee Act 1925 s 33*).

Bare trusts

2.12 While there is legal ownership of the trust fund by the trustees, the beneficiaries are absolutely entitled or would be so entitled but for being under the age of majority of 18 (or some other incapacity). Here for all income tax, CGT and IHT purposes, there is a 'see through' analysis and the beneficiaries are treated as the taxpayers.

TRUSTS DISTINGUISHED FROM ESTATES

2.13 The main distinction is, obviously, that a trust is made by someone in their lifetime, whereas a deceased estate arises only on death. However, a trust can arise either under a will or indeed under an intestacy, if the beneficiaries are not entitled to both income and capital. (An intestacy happens where, or to the extent that, a person dies without having made a will, in which case there are statutory rules that determine who becomes entitled to what and when.) It, therefore, becomes important to be able to determine at what point the administration of a deceased estate comes to an end and the ensuing will trust begins. Very often the same individuals may be both personal representatives (PRs) of the estate and trustees of the will trust, though the tax rules can be different, as illustrated at **2.16**.

Deceased estates will vary considerably in their flexibility. A very simple case might be this: a husband dies owning all his property (comprising just say the family home, personal effects and bank accounts) jointly with his wife as 'joint tenants'. Here, there is a special rule whereby, on the death of a joint tenant, his interest passes automatically by operation of law to the surviving joint tenant(s). There would be no estate administration at all, nor indeed a continuing will trust. At the other end of the scale, the will itself might provide for quite complicated trusts.

Estate administration

2.14 Quite apart from the terms of the trust, the nature of the assets owned by the deceased may mean that quite a few years are taken in completing the administration of the estate. For example, where there are large numbers of assets, which it may be difficult to ascertain and to agree their value with HMRC.

The general rule is that once the PRs have paid out any legacies, have 'ascertained' the residue (ie what is left after paying the legacies and any liabilities of the estate) and have paid off or quantified all tax due, the administration is complete. In practice, this will happen when the estate accounts have been drawn up and signed by the beneficiaries. Before that the PRs may make interim distributions of capital to the beneficiaries entitled.

Rights of beneficiaries

2.15   In a deceased estate no beneficiary has a right to any particular asset (even if the asset is the subject of a specific gift in the will to the beneficiary), until such time as the PRs choose to release that asset from the estate. All that the beneficiary has meanwhile is what is called a 'chose in action', that is, a right to have the estate properly administered and in course of time his entitlement paid over. Therefore, for CGT, if the PRs sell a particular asset, which the will has 'earmarked' for one beneficiary, the disposal is that of the PRs.

Income tax

2.16   For trustees and personal representatives: rate of tax

2008/09

	Trusts	*Estates*
Discretionary and accumulation	32.5%/40%	10%/20%
Life interest	10%*/20%	10%/20%

2009/10

	Trusts	*Estates*
Discretionary and accumulation	32.5%/40%	10%/20%
Life interest	10%*/20%	10%/20%

* For all dividends and (within a very small limit) certain bank and building society interest

For beneficiaries: basis of tax

	Trusts	*Estates*
Discretionary and accumulation	Receipts basis	Receipts basis
Life interest	Arising (or 'see through') basis	Receipts basis

Capital gains tax 2008/09

2.17

	Trusts	*Estates*
Rate of tax	18%	18%
Annual exemption	£4,800 (subject to reduction: see **5.36–5.39**)	£9,600 in year of death and two following tax years

Capital gains tax 2009/10

2.18

	Trusts	*Estates*
Rate of tax	18%	18%
Annual exemption	£5,050 (subject to reduction: see **5.36–5.39**)	£10,100 in year of death and two following tax years

Inheritance tax

2.19

	Trusts	*Estates*
Discretionary – or 'relevant property'	Exit and ten-year charges	No implications. Will trust succeeding estate administration deemed to commence at date of death
Accumulation and maintenance regime (trusts made before 22 March 2006)	No implications, up to 6 April 2008: continues thereafter only if absolute right to capital at age 18	No implications. Will trust succeeding estate administration deemed to commence at date of death
Life interest	Where 'estate' life interest, charge on death of beneficiary (subject to quick succession relief). If made on or after 22 March 2006, relevant property treatment applies, unless a transitional serial interest or a disabled trust.	Where 'estate' life interest, charge on death of beneficiary (subject to quick succession relief). No charge on death if a non-estate' life interest (eg created by a life-time transfer made on or after 22 March 2006, other than for a disabled person)

11

Chapter 3

Starting a trust

CGT DISPOSAL

3.1   Setting up a trust will involve a settlor parting with property. Initially, this may be only a nominal sum such as £10 or £100 (as a trust cannot exist without some property). In that case the transfer of what might be called the 'substantive trust fund' will occur shortly thereafter. Alternatively, the substantive trust fund may be transferred at the outset. Subsequent transfers of property may be made by the settlor (or indeed anyone else).

A gift is a disposal

3.2   Any such transfers of property to the trust will be an occasion of gift and therefore disposal. Certain assets are exempt for CGT, eg sterling cash (though not cash in another currency). Alternatively, any transfer may be within the settlor's annual exemption, taking other disposals into account, viz £10,100 for tax year 2009/10. Otherwise, a chargeable gain may arise, if in the tax year 2009/10, tax at a rate of 18% will fall due on 31 January 2011. It may, however, be possible to defer any such tax payable through a relief called 'hold-over'. See **3.5–3.7**.

Losses

3.3   The act of settlement might give rise not to a gain, but rather to a loss for the settlor. Losses are generally deductible from gains in computing the total taxable gains for the year. However, there is a special anti-avoidance rule under *TCGA 1992, s 18(3)* where the transferor is 'connected' with the transferee. A settlor is connected with the trustees of the settlement. In such case the loss cannot be offset against the settlor's general gains, but must be carried forward and can be used only against a gain arising on a disposal from the settlor to that set of trustees.

Example 3.1—Life interest trust

Alistair's father is a farmer. Into the trust for his son on 1 January 2006 he put 200 acres of farmland which he had acquired in 1999 at £3,250 per acre, ie with a total base cost of £650,000. He also settled a farmhouse which he had acquired two years before, albeit carrying no gain on disposal. The land was on 1 January 2006 worth only £3,000 per acre, a total of £600,000. A loss of £50,000 arises to the settlor. However, this cannot be set against his general gains and can be used only to offset a gain arising on a disposal by the settlor to the same set of trustees.

On 1 March 2008 Alistair's father settled cash of £100,000, for the trustees to invest, and a cottage worth £90,000 subject to an assured tenancy. The gift of the cottage triggered a gain of £30,000: £9,200 of this is covered by the settlor's annual exemption for 2007/08 and the balance by the brought forward 'connected party' losses.

Statutory definitions for income tax and CGT

3.4

- Statutory rules with effect from 2006/07 define the expressions 'settled property' and 'settlor' in the same terms both for income tax (*ITA 2007, ss 466–473*) and for CGT purposes (*TCGA 1992, ss 68A, 68B* and *68C*).

- There is no general definition of 'settlement' (except for anti-avoidance purposes: see below). The CGT definition of 'settled property' (in *TCGA 1992, s 68*) is broadly any property held in trust other than assets held by someone as nominee or bare trustee for another person; as from 2006/07 it is applied also for income tax purposes (*ITA 2007, s 466*).

- The expression 'settlement' is defined for anti-avoidance income tax purposes to include 'any disposition, trust, covenant, agreement, arrangement or transfer of assets' and 'settlor' in relation to a settlement means 'any person by whom the settlement was made' (*ITTOIA 2005, s 620(1)*).

- The rules relating to anti-avoidance take (a) property comprised in a settlement as including any property originating from that settlor and (b) income arising under the settlement only as income originating from that settlor (*ITTOIA 2005, s 644(3)*).

- Interestingly, although for CGT purposes the expression 'settlement' is in *TCGA 1992* is given the income tax definition, this is only for certain offshore trusts purposes. Otherwise, there is no CGT definition of

13

settlement. The anti-avoidance settlor interest rule in *TCGA 1992, s 77* simply ensures, in the spirit of income tax, that gains are assessed on the settlor only in relation to property originating from that person (whether directly or indirectly): see **5.21–5.22**; however, this rule applies only up to and including 2007/08. It has been repealed from 2008/09, with the introduction of a uniform rate of CGT of 18%.

CGT HOLD-OVER RELIEF

Two categories

3.5   Hold-over defers the gain arising to the settlor, by passing it to the trustees so as to fall into charge on the trustees when they come to sell the asset. The relief falls into two categories:

- under *TCGA 1992, s 260* for (broadly) transfers that are treated as immediately chargeable for IHT purposes, typically transfers into a discretionary trust – even if within the nil rate of £325,000 for 2009/10, thus occasioning no positive charge to IHT; or

- under *TCGA 1992, s 165*, which is defined not in terms of the type of transfer but by reference to the type of asset concerned, viz a business asset: this will include, for example, an asset used in the settlor's profession or trade, shares in an unquoted trading company and property that qualifies as 'agricultural property' for purposes of agricultural property relief from IHT.

In a situation where both sections apply, eg a gift of shares in a private trading company to a discretionary trust, *s 260* relief takes priority (*TCGA 1992, s 165(3)(d)*). The significance of this is that *s 260* relief does not suffer from various restrictions that apply to *s 165* relief, eg where the asset has not been used for business purposes throughout the settlor's period of ownership.

Note that, from 10 December 2003, a hold-over claim may not be made for a transfer to a trust which is, or within (broadly) six years, becomes settlor-interested (*TCGA 1992, ss 169B* and *169C*). From 2006/07, this will include the case where under the terms of the trust a minor unmarried child of the settlor can benefit.

The claim

3.6   Hold-over relief must be expressly claimed on help sheet HS 295. The claim must be made before the expiry of five years and ten months from the end of the tax year in which the disposal was made (*TMA 1970, s 43(1)*). This period is to become four years from the end of the relevant tax year with effect from 1 April 2010, as specified by Treasury order (*FA 2008, s 118* and *Sch 29, para 12*; the *Finance Act 2008 Schedule 39 (Appointed Day, Transitional Provisions and Savings) Order 2009, SI 2009/403*). Help sheet HS 295 requires the settlor to specify under which section the hold-over claim is made. For a valid hold-over claim, the settlor need not compute the gain that is held over, nor indeed necessarily obtain a professional valuation of the asset. He must simply confirm on help sheet HS 295 that a gain would occur (Statement of Practice SP8/92).

The effect

3.7 The effect of hold-over relief is to treat the transferee, in this case the trustees, as acquiring the asset concerned at the acquisition cost of the settlor, plus, for a transfer prior to 6 April 2008, any indexation allowance accrued to April 1998 (when indexation allowance was repealed for individuals and trustees). The 'bad news' for the settlor on such a transfer was that any accrued taper relief that he had built up on the asset, whether a business or a non-business asset, would effectively be forfeited. For a gift into trust on or after 6 April 2008, neither indexation allowance nor taper relief applies and the transferor will simply be electing to hold over a gain which would otherwise be charged at 18% – subject to any applicable reliefs.

If a gain is held over into a trust that is, or becomes, interest in possession, the held-over gain is crystallised on the death of the life tenant. It may be possible further to hold over the gain at that point.

Example 3.2—Discretionary trust

On 31 August 2009, Albert transfers to the trustees listed shares that have a market value of £260,000. There are 15 individual holdings. The gain arising to Albert after taking account of indexation allowance is £100,000. He uses his annual exemption for 2009/10 of £10,100 covering two of the holdings to reduce the chargeable gain on the remaining 13 holdings to £89,900 which he elects to hold over under *s 260*. His self-assessment for the year notes the disposal and the relief is claimed on help sheet HS 295. The annual exemption accounts for the gain on one of the holdings, which the trustees are therefore treating as having acquired at market value. In respect of the other 14 holdings the trustees are treated as acquiring at Albert's indexed base cost.

Example 3.3—Accumulation and maintenance trust

Adrian transfers on 1 March 2006 to the trustees of the settlement made by his wife Belinda and him (pre-22 March 2006) shares in a private company for which he subscribed when the company was set up in 1994. He paid £1,000. The shares are now worth £100,000. The company is a qualifying unquoted trading company and therefore the gain is eligible for hold-over relief under *s 165*. Adrian has made use of his annual exemption for 2005/06 in various disposals on the stock market and wants to hold over the whole of the gain on making the settlement. He does this in his self-assessment for the year and duly makes the election on help sheet IR 295 (as was).

The trust was A&M in form, though the beneficiaries become entitled to an interest in possession on attaining the specified age. Should one of the beneficiaries die having a life interest, there will, so far as the trustees are concerned, be a capital gains tax free uplift to market value at that stage. However, the held-over gain that arose on settlement will come into charge at that point.

COMPLIANCE: FORM 41G (TRUST)

3.8   There are three specialist trust districts within HMRC: Edinburgh, Nottingham and Truro.

The 1990 change in practice

3.9   Until 1990, it was the accepted practice when creating a new trust to send a copy of the trust deed to the Inspector of Taxes who, following consultation with a trust specialist, would provide a ruling on the tax treatment of the trust. That practice was often useful in ensuring confirmation from the then Inland Revenue that the tax treatment desired by the draftsman had, in fact, been achieved, eg that the settlor and spouse had effectively been excluded from benefit so that the settlor-interested anti-avoidance rules would not apply (see **4.24–4.29** and **5.21–5.22**) and that, for IHT purposes, a valid accumulation and maintenance trust had been established. Now, however, possibly occasioned by pressure of work within HMRC and indeed the general thinking behind self-assessment to put the onus on the taxpayer to 'get it right', a similar principle applies here.

HMRC requirements

3.10   On the making of every trust, details should be submitted to HMRC who will then set up a tax reference, which will in particular prompt the despatch of annual self-assessment returns. The information required by HMRC is set out in form 41G (Trust).

It is good discipline for either the solicitor draftsman of the settlement, or perhaps the accountant who acts for the family, to submit form 41G (Trust) within a month or two after the settlement to ensure that notification to HMRC is not forgotten. Form 41G (Trust) is not required by statute and the information can be supplied in some other form, though it is most convenient to use the non-statutory form 41G (Trust) in all substantive trust cases (ie it is not required with a bare trust). The information required is as summarised in **3.11**. In particular, if CGT liabilities do arise on settlement, this will ensure that they are dealt with in a timely manner. The situation is different for IHT (see **3.12–3.20**).

See **3.11** for the text of Form 41G (Trust) (author's numbering)..

Form 41G (Trust)

3.11   *Part A—Complete in all cases.*

1.   Full title of the trust.

2.   Full names and addresses of the trustees. The 'first named' trustee will usually be the one who receives self-assessment returns etc.

3.   Name, address, telephone number and reference of any professional agent.

4.   Is the trust governed by the law of a country outside the UK? Is its general administration carried on outside the UK? Is the trust established under Scots law? Is the trust employment-related? Is this a trust for a vulnerable beneficiary?

Part B—Complete if the trust is established by a will or intestacy.

5.   Full name and last address of the deceased.

6.   Date of death and date of commencement of trust.

7.   HMRC office, and reference in that office or NI number of the deceased.

8.   Whether the administration period has ended and if so when.

9.   Whether the will or intestacy provisions have been altered by a deed of variation or family arrangement; if so, date of the deed. Details are

required of any person giving something up under the deed (which makes them a 'settlor' for income tax and CGT purposes) and whether the deed established a new trust in addition to the one under the will or intestacy provisions.

Part C—Complete if the trust was established by deed of variation or family arrangement.

10. Was the trust additional to the Will trust?

11. Was the trust a replacement for the Will trust?

Part D—Complete if the trust was established in the settlor's lifetime.

12. Date trust was established.

13. Name and address of settlor, HMRC office that deals with the settlor's tax affairs, and tax reference in that office or NI number of the settlor.

14. Details of the assets settled by each settlor including values (if land or buildings the address should be stated; and if shares, the number, class and company number).

Part E—Complete in all cases.

The form must be signed and dated, with a note of the capacity in which the form is signed, eg whether settlor, trustee, solicitor, etc.

INHERITANCE TAX

Potentially exempt transfers

3.12   Just as for CGT purposes the gift to the settlement involves a disposal, so there may also be IHT implications. IHT is both a gifts tax and an estate duty. That said, however, many lifetime gifts into trust made before 22 March 2006 will be exempt from IHT as 'potentially exempt transfers' (PETs), which become exempt by reason of the donor surviving the transfer by at least seven years.

A transfer of value is, broadly, a disposition which causes the value of the donor's estate to decline as a result (*IHTA 1984, s 3*). Since 22 March 2006 a PET is a transfer of value made by an individual either to another individual or to the trustees of a disabled trust, which is not an exempt transfer (*IHTA 1984, s 3A*). A PET is assumed to be exempt unless the donor dies within seven years. No notice for IHT needs to be given of exempt transfers or PETs.

A gift to a life interest trust or to an accumulation and maintenance (A&M trust) before 22 March 2006 was a PET. A gift to a life interest trust on or after 22 March 2006 (even where for the benefit of the settlor or his spouse) is an immediately chargeable transfer (see **3.17–3.20**), unless it is a qualifying trust for a disabled person. The favoured A&M regime cannot apply to any transfer made on or after 22 March 2006.

A chargeable transfer is a transfer of value which is not protected by an exemption, eg the spouse exemption or the £3,000 annual exemption (*IHTA 1984, s 2*). A PET should be contrasted with a chargeable transfer, which a PET will become if the donor fails to survive for seven years. Equally, a chargeable transfer will embrace any lifetime transfer of value that is not a PET.

Failed PETs

3.13   If the donor dies within seven years, the PET becomes chargeable (*IHTA 1984, s 3A(4)*) and there may be IHT implications, which will arise through the administration of the estate. Because, however, the failed PET will turn out to have been a chargeable transfer, it will be necessary for the form (Inheritance Tax Account IHT 100), described at **3.20**, to be completed and returned. If the amount of the transfer of value was within the nil rate band of the settlor, there will be no immediate implications of the gift (though it would have the effect of denying to that extent the nil rate band available to subsequent lifetime gifts and/or the deceased estate).

Who bears the tax?

3.14   One important point where a lifetime gift is chargeable is who bears the tax. The primary responsibility for bearing the tax on a failed PET is traditionally reckoned to fall on the transferee (if an outright gift) or the trustees in whom the property is vested (*IHTA 1984, s 199(1)(b) and (c)*): this is confirmed in HMRC's Inheritance Tax Manual at IHTM 30042. However, at IHTM 14593 HMRC say that it is only if the transferor is obliged to pay the tax on a failed PET (which would in practice be paid by the personal representatives of his estate) that he is treated as having made a further gift, which, therefore, needs to be grossed up in order to calculate the tax liability. The personal representatives of the transferor are secondarily liable subject to the limitations set out in *IHTA 1984, s 204(8)*, as confirmed by HMRC in their Inheritance Tax Manual at IHTM 30042. IHTM 30044 confirms that in practice personal representatives will be liable only in limited circumstances. By contrast, in the case of an immediately chargeable transfer HMRC regard the settlor/transferor as primarily liable (*IHTA 1984, s 199(1)(a)*), and grossing up will apply if he pays the tax. Subject to the limitation in *s 204(6)* the trustees can also be liable under *IHTA 1984, s 199(1)(c)*, as confirmed at

3.15 *Starting a trust*

IHTM 30062 (which contains a helpful table summarising HMRC's views on the order of liability).

A&M trust

3.15   The gift by Adrian to the trustees (see **3.7**, Example 3.3) was a PET, though it would not have been if made on or after 22 March 2006. If he survives the gift by at least seven years, the transfer would become exempt. However, even if he does not so survive, the subject matter of the gift viz shares in an unquoted trading company, attracted business property relief at 100% and therefore there was a chargeable transfer of nil, with no IHT implications. This assumes that Adrian had not 'reserved a benefit' in the gift (see **6.16–6.21**), though possibly academic in the event of 100% relief continuing until his death and that the negative 'clawback' conditions were satisfied (see **6.25**).

Life interest trust

3.16   Here, the property transferred by Alistair's father (see **3.3**, Example 3.1) was (a) farmland worth £600,000 and (b) the main farmhouse worth on the open market £400,000 but with an 'agricultural value' of only £300,000. It was accepted that the house is 'agricultural property' attracting relief. In the case of agricultural property relief (APR), as against business property relief (BPR), relief is given not on the market value but on the 'agricultural value': this requires the presumption that the property is subject to a perpetual covenant prohibiting non-agricultural use. See **11.62–11.65** for APR.

Suppose the settlor dies five years after the gift, having reserved no benefit in the gift, and assume the law stays the same. The farmland attracted APR at 100% reducing the chargeable transfer to nil. However, given the agricultural value restriction, the chargeable transfer of the house was £100,000. The settlor had made no chargeable transfers within seven years before the gift to the trust and therefore the £100,000 has first call on the settlor's nil rate band, with the effect, however, of denying the nil rate band to that extent to the death estate. The gift will be included in the Inheritance Tax Account submitted by the PRs. Indeed, following *FA 1999* the PRs have a statutory duty to record details of all lifetime gifts made within seven years before death (*IHTA 1984, s 216(3)(b)*).

Chargeable transfers

3.17   The distinction between PETs and chargeable transfers was explained at **3.12**. Apart from PETs, which become chargeable transfers because the settlor dies within seven years, the most common form of chargeable transfers before 22 March 2006 was gifts to a discretionary settlement. Since then, lifetime gifts to any form of settlement (called 'relevant property trusts' after the IHT regime which governs them), other than for a disabled person, will be chargeable transfers. Such transfers have an advantage in enabling any gain on non-business assets to be 'held over', thus deferring the gain until ultimate disposal by the trustees (see **3.5–3.7**).

The IHT implications of the transfer into a relevant property trust will depend upon the amount of the chargeable transfer and the cumulative amount of all chargeable transfers made by the settlor in the previous seven years. If the aggregate of the value going into the trust plus gifts made by him in the previous seven years does not exceed the upper limit of the nil rate band (£325,000 for 2009/10), the IHT charge is at 0%. To the extent that it exceeds the upper limit the IHT charge is at 20%; however, if the settlor dies within seven years there will be a further 20% charge for the trustees to pay at that stage.

The annual exemption

3.18   In computing the chargeable transfer, exemptions such as the £3,000 annual exemption may be taken into account. Note that any unused part of the annual exemption for the previous year may also be used. The annual exemption is, according to HMRC Inheritance Tax, granted to gifts in the order that they are made during the tax year, including PETs (though disputed by many, including the author). The moral is that if a person wishes to make both, say, a discretionary trust and a disabled trust at about the same time, he should make the discretionary trust at least a day before the disabled trust. This has two beneficial effects:

- maximising the use of the annual exemption, which might otherwise be wasted; and

- if he does die within seven years after making the disabled trust, its existence would not be taken into account in computing the IHT consequences attributable to the discretionary trust (see **6.30–6.36**).

Payment of tax and notification of transfer

3.19   IHT payable on a lifetime transfer must be paid at the end of six months following the end of the month of transfer, unless the transfer was made after 5 April but before 1 October; then the tax becomes due on the following 30 April (*IHTA 1984, s 226*). While the settlor is primarily liable for any tax due, it is better to have the tax paid by the trustees out of the transfer; payment by the settlor is treated as a further gift to the trust.

Notice of the transfer, even if tax is not payable, should be given within 12 months after the end of the month in which the gift was made. The *de minimis* provisions, absolving the settlor from having to give notice, have recently been updated, with effect from 6 April 2007 (*Inheritance Tax (Delivery of Accounts) (Excepted Transfers and Excepted Terminations) Regulations 2008, SI 2008/605*). If only cash or quoted shares or securities have been transferred, no account is required if their value together with the total of the transferor's chargeable transfers in the previous seven years does not exceed the IHT threshold for the year of transfer (ie £325,000 for 2009/10). Otherwise, the conditions are that (a) the value of the chargeable transfer plus the transferor's chargeable transfers in the previous seven years does not exceed 80% of the IHT threshold (ie £260,000 for 2009/10); and (b) the value of the transfer of value does not exceed the IHT threshold (£325,000) less the total of chargeable transfers made by him in the previous seven years. Note that the transferor cannot rely on the 100% reduction by agricultural or business property relief to avoid giving notice if the gross value of the transfer exceeds the threshold.

Form IHT 100

3.20 The following information is requested, to which notes in form IHT 100 refer:

- Name, address and reference of the person dealing with the account.

- Date and type of transfer, ie whether in particular a PET chargeable on the transferor's death within seven years or a gift to a discretionary trust.

- Details of the transferor.

- Details of the transferees.

- Details of the transfer including:
  - any associated transfers;
  - the date and value of the gift;
  - deductions, eg liabilities;
  - reliefs and exemptions, eg the annual exemption or agricultural or business property relief;
  - details relating to agricultural and business and property relief (the so called 'clawback' rules), which must be satisfied in the event of the transferor's death within seven years: see **6.25, 11.60** and **11.66**.

- Payment of tax: whether the tax is to be borne by the transferee, whether any tax is to be paid by instalments (see **11.92–11.95**) and whether any deductions are claimed.

- Whether the transferor has made any other transfers of value since 26 March 1974.

- Declaration by the transferor.

Example 3.4—Discretionary trust

The gift of listed shares worth £260,000 (see **3.7**, Example 3.2) is within Albert's nil rate band (having made no chargeable transfers in the seven preceding years), though he must still make a return on form IHT 100. The return will be relatively straightforward. The basis of valuation in a case of quoted shares will be the 'quarter-up' rule for CGT purposes and no deductions or exemptions will be available. However, Albert may deduct his annual exemptions for 2009/10 and (not having been used) for 2008/09, reducing the chargeable transfer to £254,000.

STAMP DUTIES

3.21   Stamp duties are the oldest form of taxation in the UK, going back to 1694. A major reform occurred in 2003, with the introduction of a new tax (stamp duty land tax or SDLT) on transfers of UK land and the repeal of stamp duties on all other types of property except shares and marketable securities. Prior to that, in 1996, stamp duty reserve tax (or SDRT) was introduced to impose a 0.5% charge (the same rate as stamp duty) on agreements to transfer marketable securities for a consideration: this applies largely to dealing through The Stock Exchange, being paperless and not otherwise caught by stamp duty insofar as it applies only to documents.

If trustees acquire shares or land, stamp duty (at 0.5%) and SDLT (at rates up to 4%) will apply as they do to purchasers in the ordinary course: see **7.1–7.5** for further details. It is more likely, however, that on starting a trust the settlor will give to the trustees, if not cash, either shares or land. In either case, there is no stamp duty or SDLT to pay.

Compliance

3.22   In the case of shares the transfer document will be 'self-certified' with Category L under *The Stamp Duties (Exempt Instruments) Regulations 1987, SI 1987/516*, avoiding the fixed duty of £5 that would otherwise be chargeable, at least before 13 March 2008. For gifts of shares and securities made on or after 13 March 2008 the fixed £5 duty has been abolished (*FA 2008, s 99* and *Sch 22, para 10*).

In the case of land, the trustees will self-certify the transfer document as exempt under *FA 2003, Sch 3, para 1* and will complete a self-certification form SDLT 60. Each of these documents is then used as appropriate to trigger re-registration, whether in the books of the company or at one of the UK land registries. There is now no need to complete form SDLT 60 for land transactions occurring on or after 12 March 2008 (*FA 2008, s 94* and *Sch 30*); now it is the Land Registry transfer form TR1 which is used to procure re-registration.

Only a 'pure' gift will attract the exemption. There is a trap where land is charged with a liability, typically a mortgage, and the transferee (in this case the trustees) accepts liability for the mortgage: the amount of the mortgage constitutes consideration paid by them. (The same principle applies to shares, though it would be extremely unusual for shares to be so charged.) If the amount of the mortgage does not exceed £175,000 for residential property (£125,000 before 2 September 2008 and after 31 December 2009) or £150,000 for non-residential property, there will still be no positive SDLT liability. However (assuming the mortgage is £1,000 or more, or, from 12 March 2008, £40,000 or more) the document cannot be self-certified and the trustees must, within 30 days of the gift, complete form SDLT 1 and send it to the Stamp Office at Netherton, from whom they will receive Revenue Certificate SDLT 5, which is sent to the Land Registry to procure registration.

Example 3.5—Shares

Adrian made a gift of unlisted shares to the trustees of his accumulation and maintenance trust on 1 March 2006 (see **3.7**, Example 3.3). The stock transfer forms will have been certified, typically by Adrian, as exempt from stamp duty under Category L of the *1987 Regulations*. The trustees will send these certified forms to the registrars of the respective companies to procure re-registration of the trustees as owners of the shares.

Example 3.6—Land

Suppose that the land given by Alistair's father to the life interest trust for Alistair on 1 January 2006 (see **3.3**, Example 3.1) had been burdened with a mortgage of £140,000 (which would have reduced the transfer of value for inheritance tax purposes). The trustees assume direct liability to the mortgage lender for payment of interest and repayment of capital. This £140,000 is treated as consideration paid by the trustees for the land. However, being within the nil rate threshold for non-residential property of £150,000, no SDLT is payable, though they must (to avoid a fixed penalty of £100, rising to £200 when more than three months late) get in to the Stamp Office at Netherton form SDLT 1 duly completed no more than 30 days after the transaction. Had the mortgage been £175,000, SDLT of £1,750 would have been payable and a cheque for this amount should accompany form SDLT 1.

ISSUES TO CONSIDER

Non-tax issues

3.23   Putting assets into trust should not be dictated primarily by tax, though it should be done in a tax-efficient manner. Consider the following advantages.

Protection

3.24   While the beneficiaries have the right to ensure that the trustees act properly in administering the trust, no beneficiary has a right to any asset in the trust, except to the extent that the trust deed so provides or the trustees so decide. That is, where the trust deed gives a right to income (but, while the trustees have a power to advance capital, no right to capital), there is no asset owned by the beneficiary that can be taken into account by a court in insolvency or matrimonial proceedings. Equally, there is no asset that a beneficiary who is inclined towards profligacy can sell. The beneficiary may have a right to income during his lifetime, although the trustees may be able to deprive him of that right at any time.

Control

3.25   It is generally, though not invariably, tax-inefficient if the settlor or spouse is a beneficiary (see **4.24–4.29** and **4.44–4.54** for income tax, **5.21–5.22** for capital gains tax (for 2007/08, but not for 2008/09 or 2009/10) and **6.16–6.21** for IHT). Note that the capital gains tax disadvantage of a trust being settlor-interested, that a hold-over relief election cannot be made (see **3.5**, last paragraph), persists for 2008/09 and 2009/10. However, there is nothing to prevent the settlor and spouse from being trustees, ie enabling them to maintain control over the trust asset, which may be useful where it is shares in a family company or a share in the family farm. That said, they must remember to administer the trust property for the beneficiaries.

Settlor and spouse trustees should be aware that conflicts of interest could arise, eg where shares in a family company are put into the trust and it might be in the interests of the beneficiaries that the trustees accept an offer for purchase, whereas in relation to a residual holding retained by the settlor he may wish for sentimental reasons to reject the offer. It is always sensible for there to be at least one other trustee apart from the settlor or the settlor and spouse, if only 'to see fair play' and indeed to provide a continuing trustee should the settlor and spouse die unexpectedly.

Flexibility

3.26 A person may wish for estate planning reasons to make an effective gift of an asset, ie to remove it from his estate but is not yet sure to whom, among a number of children, the asset should ultimately go. If the children are under the age of 25, an A&M trust could have been made up to 21 March 2006 or since then, if within the nil rate band or in excess of that and comprising business assets, a discretionary trust, without an immediate inheritance tax liability. Alternatively, there could be a trust divided into life interests among the siblings with the trustees having an overriding power of appointment. Now, since 22 March 2006, any such lifetime trust, whatever its terms, will be an immediately chargeable transfer. This means that to the extent that the value settled causes the settlor to exceed his nil rate band, inheritance tax at 20% will be payable (to rise to 40% should the settlor die within seven years).

Tax efficiency

3.27 It is always sensible for those advising on a trust to have in mind the way that it fits into the overall family tax planning and to ensure that it is tax efficient. The following are merely some 'pointers':

- Unless there are particular reasons for wanting to include the settlor or spouse, ensure that they are irrevocably excluded. This will mean that income and gains are not assessed on the settlor and that for IHT purposes the settlor is treated as effectively alienated from the assets from his estate. One reason for perhaps including the settlor and/or spouse as beneficiaries might be with a view to securing capital gains tax efficiency, while accepting the inheritance tax downside. For example, inclusion of the settlor or spouse may be desirable to secure main residence relief for a house held by the trustees (see **5.25**), while accepting the consequential disadvantage for any residential property owned directly by the settlor and/or spouse (except within the last three years of ownership of either property, during which it is possible to have main residence relief running on two properties concurrently, through use of the election procedure).

- Decide what type of trust is appropriate to the circumstances. If all the prospective beneficiaries are children of a common parent or grandchildren of a common grandparent (and if with agricultural or business property, the eldest has not attained the age of 18 – the 'clawback' rule: see **6.25**) an A&M trust would have been sensible before 22 March 2006: it will now have to be a discretionary trust. Where there are a large number of, perhaps, not closely related beneficiaries, you may like to consider a discretionary trust, bearing in mind, however, that if the act of settlement takes the settlor over his nil rate band, there will be IHT to pay at 20% (with a further 20% to pay if the settlor dies within seven years). If the property is earmarked for just one beneficiary, or a few beneficiaries, a life interest trust may be appropriate. However, where made since 22 March 2006, a gift to a life interest trust will be an immediately chargeable transfer and so, if an immediate inheritance tax liability at 20% is to be avoided, should not cause the settlor to exceed his nil rate threshold. There may be income tax advantages of having a life interest rather than a discretionary structure, where there is one or just a few principal beneficiaries.

- *Dividend income.* The reform of dividend taxation from 5 April 1999 means that, in trusts without a brought-forward tax pool, there can within a discretionary or accumulation trust be an effective tax rate of 46% where trustees receive dividend income and pay it out by way of discretion to a higher rate taxpayer (see **4.111**, Example 4.26). The rate for a life interest trust would be only 40%. Alternative forms of investment, eg in instruments paying interest or commercial property paying land, do not carry this disadvantage.

- *CGT.* There is no tax distinction between types of trust in the rate payable by the trustees, which, subject to the annual exemption, is 18% for 2008/09 and 2009/10 (having been 40% in 2007/08). Consider the CGT implications on settlement. Will it be possible to hold over the gains (see **3.5–3.7**)? Bear in mind that a gain held over will crystallise on the death of a life tenant.

- *Type of return.* Trustees have to consider what type of investment return is more appropriate, given (for 2009/10) income tax of 40% (or 32.5% if dividend income) for either a discretionary or accumulation trust or indeed a life interest trust with a higher rate beneficiary. Indeed, from 2010/11 these rates were proposed at Budget 2009 to rise to 50% and 42.5% respectively (see **4.32**). The only limitation is that the first £1,000 of income of a discretionary or accumulation trust is taxed at the standard 20% rate or the 10% dividend ordinary rate. By contrast capital gains over and above the annual exempt amount are taxed at just 18%.

- *Compliance.* Do not forget the need to register the trust with the relevant trust district ideally with form 41G (Trust) – see **3.8–3.11** – having identified the type of trust concerned. And for IHT purposes, if a discretionary trust or other 'relevant property' trust, report the trust to HMRC Inheritance Tax (see **3.17–3.20**).

- *Agricultural or business property.* If such property is transferred into trust, ensure that the reliefs anticipated are in fact available (and continue to be available if the settlor dies within seven years: the 'clawback' rules, summarised at **6.25**).

CHARITABLE TRUSTS

3.28   This book (and in particular Chapter 8) does not deal with public charitable trusts, but rather with private charitable trusts. These are registered under the *Charities Act 1993, s 3* – before *Charities Act 2006* took effect in 2008. A detailed form is available from the Charity Commissioners to be filled in and supplied, with a copy of the draft trust deed, to confirm whether the trust will be treated as charitable. To fall within the definition of charity, the objects of the trust should be (now, under *Charities Act 2006, s 2(2)*):

- the prevention or relief of poverty;

- the advancement of education;

- the advancement of religion;

- the advancement of health or the saving of lives;

- the advancement of citizenship or community development;

- the advancement of the arts, culture, heritage or science;

- the advancement of amateur sports;

- the advancement of human rights, conflict resolution or reconciliation or the promotion of religious or racial harmony or equality and diversity;

- the advancement of environmental protection or improvement;

- the relief of those in need by reason of youth, age, ill health, disability, financial hardship or other disadvantage;

- the advancement of animal welfare;

- the promotion of the efficiency of the armed forces of the Crown, or of the efficiency of the police, fire and rescue services or ambulance services; and

- any other purposes recognised as charitable purposes under existing charity law or analogous to or within the spirit of those purposes or the purposes listed above.

These 13 'charitable descriptions of purposes' constitute broadly the first three historic heads of charity set out below, plus those purposes within the fourth head which the courts have accepted as 'charitable':

- the relief of poverty;

- the advancement of religion;

- education; or

- other purposes beneficial to the community.

Family charitable trust versus CAF account

3.29   An individual can set up their own account within the Charities Aid Foundation (CAF) such that payments to the account will attract gift aid relief (see **8.1–8.5**) and through a personal chequebook, donations may be made by the individual from time to time as they wish. However, a small administrative charge will be made by the CAF and cheques may be written only in favour of registered charities or other recognised charitable bodies, eg churches. The advantage, therefore, of a personal trust, although involving some complexity in terms of establishment and perhaps administration, is that, provided that the trustees are satisfied that income and capital are applied for charitable purposes, they need not necessarily find their way to a registered charity.

Tax advantages summarised

3.30   The operation of gift aid relief and the detailed tax exemptions for charities are explained at **8.1–8.18**. The following tax exemptions are available on setting up a charity:

- *Income tax*: Gift aid is given to cash gifts. Relief is also available for listed shares and units in authorised unit trusts, as well as (by *FA 2002*) freehold or leasehold interests in UK land.

- *CGT*: A disposal of a chargeable asset to a charity is exempt (*TCGA 1992, s 257*).

- *IHT*: Gifts and legacies to charities are exempt transfers (*IHTA 1984, s 23*). Similarly, there is an exemption for transfers out of a discretionary trust to charities. Note, however, that where there is a possibility of a benefit to the settlor, there are anti-avoidance provisions for IHT.

- *Stamp duties*: Transfers of shares to a charity are exempt from stamp duty subject to 'adjudication' by HMRC Stamp Taxes. Despite that exemption, however, most transfers to any type of trust (including charitable trusts) will be gifts, which may simply be self-certified as exempt (under Category L of *The Stamp Duty (Exempt Instruments) Regulations 1987*). Following the introduction of the present regime for land on 1 December 2003, gifts of real property can be self-certified as exempt from stamp duty land tax (*FA 2003, Sch 3, para 1*), although there is no longer the requirement for self-certification on form SDLT 60 for transfers on or after 12 March 2008. There is a specific exemption from stamp duty land tax for gifts of land to charities (*FA 2003, Sch 8*) and (by *FA 2004*) to charitable trusts.

Example 3.7—Starting a charitable trust

Zebedee has a personal interest in certain orphanages being run in Russia. As well as committing himself to those orphanages in terms of time, he wishes to provide for them financially out of a substantial share portfolio, which he has recently inherited from his father. He therefore decides to set up the Russian Orphanage Trust with £100,000.

A draft of the trust deed will have to be supplied for prior approval by the Charity Commission, which may take two to three months, under cover of their standard form, which will ask detailed questions about the charity, its proposed method of operation, the trustees etc.

Out of his share portfolio it would be sensible for Zebedee to select shares that carry the greater gain, since there will be no CGT on transferring the shares to the charity. Nor will there be any IHT implications. The gift may be certified category L for stamp duty.

Being listed shares, income tax relief will be available on the gift. That is, Zebedee's taxable income will be reduced by the market value of the shares given to the Trust. He will also benefit from the CGT relief.

Chapter 4

Running a trust: income tax

RESIDENCE

Residence and domicile explained

4.1   The general liability to UK income tax (and capital gains tax) is determined by residence. Residence is determined by physical presence in the UK during a tax year (6 April to the following 5 April). Residence should be distinguished from domicile, which is broadly the country in which a person intends to make his personal home. Domicile is not relevant to trustees, though residence is. A person can be resident (though not domiciled) in more than one country during a tax year (though non-UK countries will tend to use the calendar year as the measure of liability). In that case, a double tax treaty may apply to determine in which country a person should be treated as resident for a particular period.

Personal residence

4.2   Generally, for UK purposes, a person is treated as UK resident in a tax year if:

- he is physically present in the UK for more than 183 days during that tax year; or

- he spends 91 days or more on average per tax year in the UK over a four-year period; the latter is also called 'ordinary residence', which has the meaning of habitual residence (although he may also be UK resident in certain circumstances if he spends less than 91 days in the UK during a tax year).

Note that while the rule in the first bullet point is a statutory rule, that in the second is a matter of HMRC practice (based on case law), as described in their explanatory booklet HMRC6 (which has replaced IR20 with effect from 6 April 2009). *FA 2008, s 24* has introduced, for purposes of the statutory rule, a provision that (except for qualifying transit passengers), it is physical presence in the UK at midnight which will constitute as a day's presence in the UK. HMRC have said that they will apply this rule also to the non-statutory test.

UK residence means a liability to income tax on worldwide income (subject to a limitation where not UK domiciled). Non-UK residence limits that liability to income arising from within the UK.

HMRC and Treasury review of individual residence and domicile

4.3   A background paper was published in April 2003 to consider the possibility of modernising the present rules, which have been developed over the past 200 years. Specific statutory changes made by *FA 2008* are noted at **4.2**. While there were official indications in 2008 that an overall statutory test of residence might be introduced in future, the test for the present remains rather unsatisfactorily a mixed one of statute, case law and HMRC practice. *FA 2008* also introduced a new code of taxation for UK resident but non-UK domiciliaries, which is outside the scope of this book.

Trustee residence

4.4   As has been explained at **2.1–2.4**, both general and tax liabilities of a person as trustee are quite distinct from liabilities which he may have in his own capacity. The residence of trustees is determined as a body, though any individual trustee will be personally liable for the tax. If all the trustees are personally resident in the UK, they are treated as UK resident. If they are all personally resident outside the UK, the trustees are non-UK resident. If the trustees do not all have the same personal residence, the trustees' residence depends upon the residence, ordinary residence and domicile of the settlor until 'he ceases to be a settlor'. If he was resident, ordinarily resident or domiciled in the UK and at least one trustee is UK resident, at any point from the date of the settlement until that time, they are all treated as resident. If the settlor was not resident, ordinarily resident or domiciled in the UK, from the date of the settlement until that time, they are all treated as non-UK resident. A person ceases to be a settlor when no property of which he is the settlor is comprised in the settlement (and that might occur after his death), provided that there is no undertaking to provide property to the settlement in future and there is no reciprocal arrangement with another person to give property to the settlement. (*ITA 2007, ss 467–476*).

Note that the rules for residence for capital gains tax purposes have been revised from 2007/08: see **5.8–5.10**.

Example 4.1—The Albert Discretionary Trust

The trustees are Albert, Betty and their family solicitor. They are all personally resident in the UK. The trustees as a body are, therefore, UK resident.

Example 4.2—The Harry/Hector Discretionary Trusts

Grant is a wealthy Texan. He has two sons, Harry and Hector. Harry has married an English woman and has made his family home in London. Hector, on the other hand, lives in Texas and works in the family businesses.

Harry and Hector have each made a discretionary trust. The trustees of Harry's trust are Grant, Harry and a friend of the family now living and working in France. The trustees of Hector's trust are Grant, Hector and his brother Harry.

Each trust has 'mixed resident' trustees, in containing at least one who is, and at least one who is not, personally resident in the UK.

Harry's trust is treated as UK resident, because Harry the settlor is UK resident and ordinarily resident (even if he may not have acquired a UK domicile).

Hector's trust on the other hand is non-UK resident because the settlor Hector is not resident, ordinarily resident or domiciled in the UK: therefore the one UK resident trustee is treated for this purpose as being a non-UK resident.

THE BASIS OF INCOME TAXATION

4.5   Income tax is, generally, chargeable on income. 'Generally' because certain types of capital are treated for tax purposes as if they were income. For example; see below.

Some capital receipts treated as income

4.6

● Where a shareholder in a company sells his shares back to the company, the proceeds of sale in his hands may be treated either as income or as capital according to defined statutory rules. Where it is trustees who sell the shares, the proceeds are treated as income (even though capital treatment might be applied). Since 2004/05 the effective tax rate is 25%:

assume a cash dividend of 90 grossed up to 100 by the non-repayable tax credit. The trust rate for qualifying distributions is 32.5% which, less the tax credit, gives a residual liability of 22.5%. Expressed as a percentage of the cash dividend this is 25%.

- Capital receipts from the sale of land can, in certain circumstances, be subject to income tax if the land was acquired or developed with a view to realising a gain (*ITA 2007, Pt 13, Ch 3*).

- Where a person grants for a premium a lease of no more than 50 years, part of the premium (calculated on a formula basis) is assessed to income tax (*ITTOIA 2005, s 277*).

- More generally, there is a body of statutory rules designed to prevent a taxpayer from turning income into capital for tax purposes – 'the transactions in securities' regime now found in *ITA 2007, Pt 13, Ch 1*.

Oddly enough, the Acts themselves do not define income, other than stating that it is charged under specific provisions of *ITEPA 2003* or *ITTOIA 2005*.

Different types of income

4.7   In identifying the income of a trust for a particular tax year, it is essential to be clear under which charging provision the income falls, especially because there are different rules for losses. For the purposes of this book, the charging provisions may be found in the following parts of *ITTOIA 2005*:

Part 2 – Trading income

Part 3 – Property income

Part 4 – Savings and investment income

Part 5 – Chapter 5, dealing with amounts treated as the income of the settlor of a settlement

Part 8 – Foreign income: special rules

Part 9 – Partnerships

Part 9 of ITA 2007 contains special rules about settlements and trustees and in particular the provisions for discretionary and accumulation settlements.

COMPLIANCE IN SUMMARY

4.8   Trustees, like an individual, must return to HMRC their liabilities for income tax and CGT for each tax year. The system changed from 1996/97 to one of 'self-assessment', which has effectively transferred from HMRC to the taxpayer the responsibility for calculating the correct amount of tax.

Notifying the liability to tax

4.9   Trustees who first become liable to income tax or capital gains tax must normally notify HMRC no later than the 5 October following the end of the relevant tax year, unless they have already received a notice from HMRC requiring them to do so (*TMA 1970, s 7(1)*). See **4.11**.

Generally speaking, each first-named trustee will receive from HMRC, within a week or two after the end of the tax year, the self-assessment form SA 900 (see **4.55–4.63**). It will be the responsibility of the trustee or their adviser to request any necessary supplementary pages (see **4.67–4.87**) in respect of income that is not covered on the main SA 900. There are two options for calculating the tax. If the return is completed and submitted to HMRC on or before 31 October, HMRC will calculate the tax due. Otherwise, and the taxpayer always has the option, the tax must be calculated by the trustees. The self-assessment form must be submitted either, if in paper form, on or before the 31 October or, if electronically, on or before the 31 January following the end of the tax year, if penalties are to be avoided. That said, if a paper return for 2008/09 is delivered after 31 October 2009 but on or before 31 January 2010 and all tax due is paid on or before 31 January 2010, the late filing penalty will be mitigated to nil.

Paying the tax

4.10   Income tax is normally collected by two equal annual instalments, one on 31 January during the tax year, and the other on 31 July following the end of the tax year. To the extent that these two 'payments on account' are insufficient, a 'balancing payment' is due on 31 January after the end of the tax year, ie together with the first payment on account for the following year.

If for any tax year the payments on account exceed the total tax due, a repayment is due from HMRC. Interest on the tax payment will be paid by HMRC if repayment is made after 31 January following the tax year.

The first tax year

4.11   The advantage of following the form 41G (Trust) procedure (see **3.8–3.11**) when a trust is first set up is that this will generate the annual returns. A trust will typically be established during the tax year. The payment on account system does not operate until one year's liability has been paid. Therefore, for the first tax year, the liability will fall due on 31 January following the end of the tax year. If for any reason HMRC Trusts have not been notified of the existence of the trust and there is a tax liability for the year that is not notified to HMRC before 5 October after the end of the tax year, a penalty will be due.

Example 4.3—Existing trust: the Adrian and Belinda A&M (now 'relevant property') Trust

The A&M settlement was made on 1 January 1999 and form 41G (Trust) was submitted at that time. Income was received in tax year 2008/09 and Adrian as the first-named trustee has received a self-assessment. The two payments on account have been made on 31 January and 31 July 2009, each based on 50% of the tax liability for 2007/08. A balancing payment of any additional tax due for 2008/09 should be made on or before 31 January 2010 (together with any CGT for 2008/09). Assuming that Adrian decides to complete the trustees' self-assessment himself and to work out the tax, the self-assessment also must be delivered on or before 31 January 2010, if submitted online, or 31 October 2009 if in paper form.

Example 4.4—New settlement: the Tom Trust

Tom established a new family trust on 31 December 2008. As at 31 August 2009, however, he had omitted to inform HMRC of that new trust. Income arose to the trustees between 1 January and 5 April 2009. To avoid a penalty, they need to give notice to HMRC by 5 October 2009 of the liability to income tax. That liability will be due on 31 January 2010. The trustees should also have submitted the trustees' self-assessment by that date (assuming that the form is issued by HMRC before 1 November 2009).The trustees will not be liable to a penalty for notifying HMRC after 5 October 2009, so long as any tax liability is paid by 31 January 2010 (*TMA 1970, s 7(8)*), if they file their return in paper form on or before 31 October 2009 or electronically on or before 31 January 2010 – or, if later, within three months after the form is issued by HMRC (*TMA 1970, s 8A(1D), (1E)*). But see also the last sentence of **4.9** above.

Appeals, enquiries and discoveries

4.12   Appeals may be made against various HMRC notices or assessments. There is a strict time limit of 30 days following the issue of HMRC's notice or assessment.

The self-assessment regime enables HMRC to 'enquire' into a tax return. An enquiry must be begun within 12 months after the actual date of submission of the return (unless the return was submitted late, when the 'enquiry window' closes 12 months after the end of the calendar quarter in which the return was actually submitted). If the enquiry results in HMRC considering that the trustees have under-declared their tax, HMRC will amend the self-assessment, giving rise to the additional tax liability that the trustees must pay.

For a 'discovery assessment', there must have been fraud or negligence by the trustees or an agent (or at the end of the enquiry window HMRC cannot have been reasonably expected to be aware that too little tax has been charged, on the basis of the information supplied to HMRC). Apart from the 'discovery' mechanism, HMRC cannot challenge a return if they do not raise an enquiry within the specified time limit.

THE INTEREST AND PENALTY REGIME

4.13   It has always been important, and all the more so under the self-assessment regime, for a taxpayer to make timely payment to HMRC of any tax due. Any unpaid tax will carry interest from the due date until payment. If tax has been overpaid, a (non-taxable) repayment supplement is due. The rates of interest on unpaid and overpaid tax vary from time to time, with changes in the bank base rate and are published by press release; see **4.17–4.18**.

Interest will therefore be due (*inter alia*) on:

● late paid payments on account due on 31 January and 31 July;

● late payments of balancing payments of income tax and CGT on 31 January after the end of the tax year;

● tax payable on HMRC's amendment to a self-assessment; and

● surcharges or penalties (after 30 days have passed).

Surcharges

4.14   Where the trustees fail to pay income tax or CGT due 28 days or more after the due date, a surcharge of 5% of the unpaid tax becomes payable.

If the liability remains unpaid six months after the due date, the surcharge is doubled to 10% *(TMA 1970, s 59C)*.

Penalties

4.15   A comprehensive new penalty regime was introduced by *FA 2007, Sch 24*, as extended by *FA 2008, Sch 40* to apply across all the taxes including inheritance tax. For income tax (and capital gains tax) the new regime first applies to self-assessment returns for 2008/09. The new regime leaves in place the system of fixed penalties, which include;

- failure to make a return by the due date: £100;

- continuing failure to make a return: £60 per day;

- failure to produce documents: £50;

- fraudulently or negligently making an incorrect return: £3,000.

(TMA 1970, ss 93, 97AA and 98)

The new regime applies where: (a) the taxpayer gives inaccurate information to HMRC, whether carelessly or deliberately; or (b) the taxpayer fails to inform HMRC within 30 days of an assessment that the assessment is too low. A failure within (b) carries a maximum penalty of 30% of the 'potential lost revenue'. The maximum penalties for (a) are: 30% for a careless inaccuracy; 70% for a deliberate but not concealed inaccuracy; and 100% for a deliberate and concealed inaccuracy. The previous system of mitigation of penalties has been replaced by a statutory regime for a reduction for disclosure, depending on whether a disclosure is prompted by HMRC or is unprompted (viz made at a time when the taxpayer has no reason to believe that HMRC have discovered or are about to discover the inaccuracy). A 30% penalty can be reduced to zero if disclosure is unprompted or 15% if prompted. A 30% penalty can be reduced to 20% if disclosure is unprompted or 35% if prompted; and a 100% penalty can be reduced to 30% if disclosure is unprompted or 50% if prompted. HMRC can also reduce a penalty if they think it right to do so because of special circumstances.

A new penalty introduced in 2008 applies where a taxpayer gives inaccurate information to HMRC and that inaccuracy is attributable to a third party deliberately supplying false information to the taxpayer or to the third party deliberately withholding information from the taxpayer, with the intention that the relevant document contains the inaccuracy *(FA 2008, Sch 40, para 3)*. This penalty is chargeable on the third party (whether or not the taxpayer is liable to a penalty) with a maximum of 100% of the potential lost revenue.

Additional penalty regimes have been introduced by *FA 2009*: under *Sch 55* for failure to make returns etc and under *Sch 56* for failure to make payments on time. These provisions are expected to take effect on 1 April 2010.

The taxpayer account

4.16   Each taxpayer has an 'account' with HMRC, which will have a running balance of tax due together with interest (or perhaps repayments due with repayment supplement).

Interest rates: recent changes

Underpaid tax

4.17

From	6 September 2006	to	5 August 2007	7.5%
From	6 August 2007	to	5 January 2008	8.5%
From	6 January 2008	to	5 November 2008	7.5%
From	6 November 2008	to	5 December 2008	6.5%
From	6 December 2008	to	5 January 2009	5.5%
From	6 January 2009	to	26 January 2009	4.5%
From	27 January 2009	to	23 March 2009	3.5%
From	24 March 2009			2.5%

Overpaid tax

4.18

From	6 September 2006	to	5 August 2007	3.0%
From	6 August 2007	to	5 January 2008	4.0%
From	6 January 2008	to	5 November 2008	3.0%
From	6 November 2008	to	5 December 2008	2.25%
From	6 December 2008	to	5 January 2009	1.5%
From	6 January 2009	to	26 January 2009	0.75%
From	27 January 2009			0% *

* Subject to a minimum of 0.5% on tax repayments announced by HMRC on 29 July 2009 (to take effect from a date in September 2009).

Example 4.5—The Albert Discretionary Trust

The total income tax liability of the trustees for 2007/08 was £5,000. This means that for 2008/09 they should make payments on account of £2,500 on each of 31 January and 31 July 2009. On each of those dates they paid only £2,000 and plan to pay on 31 January 2010 the outstanding £1,000, together with any balancing payment due. (The total liability for 2008/09 turns out to be £7,375 (see **4.34**, Example 4.9). The remaining £2,375 will also fall due on 31 January 2010.)

Interest will be calculated as follows (assuming no further changes in rates):

	Tax underpaid	*Period*	*Rate*	*Interest*
From 1.2.09 to 23.3.10	£500	51 days	3.5%	£2.44
From 24.3.09 to 31.1.10	£500	314 days	2.5%	£10.75
From 1.8.09 to 31.1.10	£500	184 days	2.5%	£6.30
Total interest due				£19.49

ABSOLUTE ENTITLEMENT TO INCOME

4.19   A settlement in which the beneficiary has an interest in possession means that the beneficiary is entitled to the income as it arises. The trustees may deduct proper income expenses (see **4.118–4.120**), but otherwise the income is his. Distinguish this from a situation where the trustees have a discretionary power over income or power to withhold income: this is not an interest in possession settlement (see **4.32–4.34**). There may be some receipts of the trustees that are capital as a matter of trust law but income for tax purposes, eg premiums received under leases granted for less than 50 years – such receipts do not become income of the life tenant (*ITTOIA 2005, Pt 3, Ch 4*).

The life tenant's income

4.20   Although the life tenant may not physically receive the income until after the end of a tax year, it is his income for that tax year and it is the rates of tax in force for that year which determine both how much tax the trustees should withhold on account of lower rate or basic rate tax and the liability of the beneficiary to higher rate tax, if any. After making a payment to the beneficiary, the trustees must also complete a tax voucher (R 185) showing the gross income, tax at the 10%, lower or basic rate and the net sum to which the beneficiary is entitled. For 2008/09 the 10% starting rate is restricted to bank or building society interest within the band of £2,320 (but subject to the level of earnings) and the basic rate is 20% (the same as the previous lower rate applicable to non-dividend savings income).

From June 2003, a new form R 185 (Trust Income) replaced the previous versions, which were different depending on the type of trust.

Exempt income

4.21   This transparent (or 'see through') analysis will apply also to income that is exempt in the hands of the beneficiary, eg free of tax to residents abroad (FOTRA) government securities with a non-UK resident life tenant. In such cases, the trustees will arrange to receive interest gross, and they will pay this to the non-UK resident beneficiary without paying or deducting tax.

Annuity income

4.22   A trust might give a right to an annuity, eg £1,000 per annum. For the trustees this will be a 'charge on income', or if income is insufficient, on capital. The trustees must deduct tax to the extent that the annuity is paid out of income. For 2008/09 and 2009/10, where the income is paid out of non-dividend income there is no problem, since they are chargeable to 20% on the income and will deduct tax at 20% on paying the annuity. However, in either year, with dividend income the trustees are given credit only for the 10% non-repayable tax credit, so there will be a further 10% liability for the trustees, which again will be deducted from the gross annuity.

Rights to occupy property

4.23   A trust might give to a life tenant the right to occupy a property. With UK trusts there is no assessment of a notional income.

Example 4.6—Interest in possession settlement

The income of the trust for 2008/09 was £2,700 of dividends carrying a non-repayable tax credit of £300 plus rental income of £5,000. (The farm broke even.) The trustees have trust management expenses for the year of £500.

The dividends are mandated directly to Alistair and the rental income is paid into a trustee account from which all expenses, including the management expenses, are paid. Net payments of rental income are made to Alistair after the end of each tax year.

Accordingly, through 2008/09 Alistair has received dividends totalling £2,700 and on 1 June 2009 the trustees paid him a cheque for £3,455 together with form R 185. This showed trust income for 2008/09 as follows:

- Gross dividends: £3,000 less 10% tax credit £300, net income £2,700.

- Property business income: £5,000 gross, tax deducted @ 20% £1,000, trustee expenses £250.

Of the trustee expenses, half are deductible as managing the property and the other half are non-deductible, being general trust expenses.

The trustees will have to complete the Land and Property Supplementary Pages SA 903 (see **4.75–4.78**), because it is they and not Alistair who manage the property, and will account for basic rate tax on the net income.

Because no part of the trust income is subject to the trustees' discretion, question 13 on page 7 of form SA 900 does not apply.

SETTLOR-INTERESTED TRUSTS

4.24   All of income tax, CGT (prior to 2008/09) and IHT contain rules to ensure that tax cannot be avoided by putting assets into a trust from which the settlor or (apart from IHT) his spouse can benefit. The rules for income tax go back over many years and were significantly simplified in 1995.

Income taxed on the settlor

4.25   The general principle is that, if the anti-avoidance rules apply, the income (or gain) is treated as that of the settlor for tax purposes. There is one principal rule, in *ITTOIA 2005, s 624*: income of a trust is treated as belonging to the settlor, unless it derived from property in which he has no interest. A settlor is treated as having an interest in property if that property (or any property derived from it) could be applied for his benefit or for the benefit of his spouse or civil partner – see the examples below. Note that 'spouse' does not include widow or widower; similarly, if a civil partner can benefit only after the death of the settlor there is no liability on the settlor during his lifetime if the settlor is excluded from benefit. Note also that a settlement by one spouse or civil partner on the other is caught if the gift does not carry the right to the whole of the income or if the gift is a property, which really amounts to a right to income (*ITTOIA 2005, s 625*).

Any tax that a settlor pays on income which he does not receive, he can recover from the trustees, ie he is not left 'out of pocket'. Of course, if the income is actually paid to the settlor it will be treated as his anyway and he cannot recover from the trustees the tax on that income.

Where there is a settlor-interested discretionary trust and the settlor is only a basic rate taxpayer, that is in 2008/09, taxable income after allowances does not exceed £34,800, it will be beneficial (in the long run) for the trust to be settlor-interested. This is because although the additional rate bringing the trustees' liability up to 40% or 32.5% will apply, the settlor will be able to recover the tax and there will be a saving of some 20% in tax or, if dividend income, 22.5% (see **4.32**).

Capital sums

4.26   There is a further anti-avoidance rule to deal with capital sums (*ITTOIA 2005, ss 633–643*). These rules are aimed at settlements from which the settlor or spouse receives a capital sum from the settlement having been funded from trust income. This is unlikely, though it could arise in a situation where the trustees borrow money from the settlor or spouse and subsequently repay the loan. If there is undistributed income in the trust, the repayment is assessed on the settlor to the extent that it falls within the income available up to the end of that tax year or the following ten years. *Section 640* in effect gives the settlor credit for the tax paid by the trustees, which is likely to remove much if not all of the sting of this rule. However, there might seem to be a problem to the extent that the income concerned is dividend income, where the trustees will have paid tax at 32.5% but the settlor's liability is at 40%. The author understands that certainly in one case in practice HMRC have chosen not to take the point, though it does remain a problem on the drafting of the statute.

Treatment of income

Two examples from the courts

4.27   A case illustrating the rule was *Young v Pearce; Young v Scrutton* [1996] STC 743. Two husbands ran a profitable company owning all the shares. There was a reorganisation of the share capital as a result of which new preference shares were issued to the two wives, which entitled them to 30% of the profits of the company though virtually nothing else. The court held that this was a statutory settlement and that the husbands remained liable on the income from the preference shares. Interestingly, had the shares given to the wives been say a separate class of non-voting ordinary shares with rights to capital on a winding up, the appeals of the taxpayers should have succeeded.

4.28   More recently, in *Jones v Garnett* [2007] STC 1536, Geoff Jones was the sole director of a company in which each of he and his wife, Diana, owned one of two issued shares (having subscribed for cash). Diana Jones performs secretarial and administrative duties for a wage, but the fee earning work is all done by Geoff. Geoff draws a salary of much less than would be commanded by an independent director performing the same duties. Overturning both the Special Commissioners and the High Court, the Court of Appeal held that there was no 'arrangement' to be caught as a statutory settlement. While there might have been an expectation that surplus income would arise in the company, which could be distributed both to Geoff and to Diana Jones, there was no guarantee that that would be so. The unanimous decision of the House of Lords dismissing HMRC's appeal was issued on 25 July 2007. Agreeing with HMRC, the House of Lords held that there had been a statutory settlement (within what is now *ITTOIA 2005, s 625*) in Geoff giving the opportunity to his wife Diana to subscribe for a share at par, with the expectation of future profit. Geoff Jones' appeal, therefore, from the Court of Appeal on that point failed. However, the House of Lords went on to find, dismissing the appeal by HMRC, that the 'outright gift' exception for transfers between spouses (now *ITTOIA 2005, s 626*) would apply in this case. Although Diana had subscribed for her share herself, the element of 'bounty' contributed by her husband meant that there had been a gift. In the words of Lord Hope of Craighead:

'an arrangement by which one spouse uses a private company as a tax-efficient vehicle for distributing to the other's income which its business generates is likely to constitute a "settlement" on the other spouse ¼ but so long as the shares from which that income arises are ordinary shares, and not shares carrying contractual rights which are restricted wholly or substantial to a right to income, the settlement will fall within the exception'.

4.29 A day after the judgment was delivered, a Ministerial Statement was issued by the Exchequer Secretary to say that legislation would be introduced in due course to ensure that there is greater clarity in the law on the tax treatment of 'income splitting'. The Government took the view that individuals involved in such arrangements should pay tax on what is in substance their own income. Of course such legislation would apply only for the future and not for the past. Although, following the Pre-Budget Report on 9 October 2007, a consultative document and draft legislation was issued, the Chancellor of the Exchequer announced at Budget 2008 on 12 March 2008 that the proposed 'income shifting' legislation would be deferred until 2009. The draft legislation had been roundly criticised by the professional bodies and it is not known to what extent these will be taken into account by HMRC before any new regime is introduced. Happily, in his Pre-Budget Report on 24 November 2008, the Chancellor said that 'given the current economic challenges' income-shifting legislation would not be brought forward at *FA 2009*. However, the issue would be kept under review.

Example 4.7—Settlor-interested discretionary trust

Suppose that Albert's brother Algernon had also made a discretionary trust on 1 January 1998. While the trust deed excluded Algernon from benefit under the settlement, it did not exclude his wife while he was alive. Had the trust deed excluded his wife from benefit during Algernon's lifetime, the rules would not operate. Consequently, this is a settlor-interested trust and therefore the income is treated as that of Algernon, whatever happens to it.

Algernon is a higher rate taxpayer. The income for 2008/09 was £10,000 of which £9,500 is dividends and £500 is interest. On page 7 of form SA 900, question 13 will be completed as follows:

Amount of income charged at the 10% rate:

13.1 £9,500

Amount of income chargeable at the lower rate treated as that of the settlor:

13.3 £500

(with no reference to trust management expenses).

TRUSTS FOR SETTLOR'S MINOR CHILDREN

The general principle

4.30   A person cannot escape an income tax liability by having income from a settlement he has made paid to his minor unmarried children. Any such income is assessed on the settlor, subject to a *de minimis* limit of £100 per child, per parent, per annum (*ITTOIA 2005, ss 629–632*). Note that once the threshold has been exceeded, the whole of the income is taxable on the parent.

Income is assessed up to the amount of the available income for the year. In other words, the rules cannot be avoided by purporting to pay out capital and retaining income.

Retained income

4.31   The regime was tightened up by *FA 1999*. Before that the rules could be avoided by retaining income within the trust until the child became 18, in other words the settlor was assessed only to the extent that income was paid out. The old rules continue to apply to income from capital transferred to settlements made before 9 March 1999.

To avoid the tax charge on the parent settlor it remains essential that the income concerned is not subject to the discretionary or accumulation regime, ie it is the income of the child. However, income would not be paid out to the child, as the child could not give a good 'receipt' for the income until reaching the age of 18. The income would thus be retained by the trustees in a separate account, but for income tax purposes it would be that of the child and, therefore, could benefit from the child's personal allowance, lower and basic rates of income tax.

However, for settlements made on or after 9 March 1999 and for income from capital added on or after that date to existing settlements, the anti-avoidance rules apply whether or not the income is paid out or is retained by the trustees.

Example 4.8—The Adrian and Belinda A&M (now, 'relevant property') Trust

Of the trust fund Adrian contributed £125,000 on 1 January 1999 and Belinda £125,000. Adrian is a higher rate taxpayer. Belinda has taxable income of £10,000; rental income of £3,000 was applied by the trustees in 2008/09 for the benefit of Caroline, who had her 11th birthday on 1 January 2009.

£1,500 is treated as Adrian's income and £1,500 treated as Belinda's income for 2008/09. Each settlor has a right of recovery from the settlement for tax paid. The trustees will pay the 40% rate. Adrian will have no further personal liability. Being a basic rate taxpayer only, Belinda may seek a repayment of tax from HMRC of 20% (40% less 20%) of £1,500, viz £300 (which she must remit to the trustees – see **4.32**).

POWER TO ACCUMULATE OR A DISCRETION OVER INCOME: TAX RATES

4.32   The rate of tax payable by trustees of a settlement, where the income can be accumulated or the income is subject to the discretionary trust regime is 40% or in the case of dividend income called 'the special rates' (see **4.34**). As from 2006/07 the rate applicable to trusts or the special rates are payable even on the income of settlor-interested trusts (see **4.26–4.29**); the settlor will be credited with the tax paid by the trustees, though he must account to the trustees for the benefit (*ITTOIA 2005, s 646(5)*).

As from 2010/11 the special rate for dividend income was proposed at Budget 2009 to be increased to 42.5% and for non-dividend income 50%, subject only to the £1,000 standard rate band (see **4.35**).

This mechanism arises under *ITA 2007, Pt 9, Ch 3*. (There is a quite separate procedure under *ITA 2007, Pt 9, Ch 3*, which arises where payments are made by trustees to the beneficiary; see **4.41–4.43**.)

Permitted accumulation periods

4.33   A settlement where there is a power to accumulate income is treated for income tax purposes in the same way as a discretionary trust. Very often a discretionary trust will itself contain a power to accumulate. A power to accumulate in an otherwise interest in possession trust would prevent it from being interest in possession and would bring it within the discretionary and accumulation regime. Apart from a charitable trust, the trustees can accumulate income only over periods laid down in law, these include:

● 21 years from the date of the settlement;

● during the infancy of a beneficiary; or

● during the lifetime of a person in being at the date of the settlement, eg the settlor or spouse.

Following enactment of the *Perpetuities and Accumulations Bill 2009* there will be no statutory restriction on trustees' power to accumulate income (subject always to the provisions of the trust deed): see **9.1** for the impact on existing trusts.

Different types of income

4.34   Trustees may receive income falling into different categories:

● Dividend income from UK companies, which they will receive with a non-repayable tax credit of 10%. That is, a dividend of £90 will carry a non-repayable tax credit of £10 producing gross income of £100. This is dividend income, which in the hands of discretionary or accumulation trustees is subject to tax at the trust dividend rate of 32.5%, of which 10% is met by the tax credit, leaving a further 22.5% of the gross to be paid by the trustees. From 2008/09 this tax credit is extended to dividends from non-UK companies provided that the shareholding is less than 10% (which limit has been removed from 2009/10 by *Sch 19* to *FA 2009*, subject to conditions).

- Interest income received subject to deduction of tax at 20% (the basic rate). Here, out of gross income of £100 the trustees receive £80 and must pay to HMRC a further £20 to produce a total tax liability of 40%.

- Income received gross, eg rental income. Here the trustees must pay 40%.

Example 4.9—Discretionary trust

The Albert trustees received the following income for 2008/09:

Dividend income	£15,000
Less tax credit	(£1,500)
Net	£13,500
Interest income	£1,000
Less tax deducted at source	(£200)
Net	£800
Rental income	£10,000

The tax liability will be as follows:

	Rate computation	Credit	Trustees' tax liability
Dividend income £15,000	Dividend trust rate @ 32.5%	£4,875 less 10% tax credit £1,500	£3,375
Interest income £1,000	20% (see **4.35**)	£200 less tax deducted at source £200	£0
Rental income £10,000	40%		£4,000
Total			£7,375

THE STANDARD RATE BAND

4.35 A new *de minimis* rule applying from 2005/06 was one of only two changes to the trust regime to be enacted by *FA 2005* (the other being a special regime for trusts with vulnerable beneficiaries – see **4.37–4.40**). This *de minimis* rule applies where a trust is subject to the special rates, ie is discretionary or accumulation in character (see **4.32–4.34**). These are 32.5% for dividend income and otherwise 40%. In 2005/06 the first £500 of taxable income for the year is charged at the basic rate (22%), the lower rate (20%) or the dividend ordinary rate (10%) as is appropriate to the type of income concerned. From 2006/07 the standard rate band has been increased to £1,000. This £1,000 is divided between all the settlements made by the same settlor, up to a maximum of five, that is the standard rate band cannot be less than £200. The standard rate band is allocated first to basic rate income before dividend income. Deductible trust management expenses (see **4.118–4.120**) are obviously deducted before arriving at the amount falling within the lower rate band. It is possible also that, if ever a 'streamed income' regime is introduced, income taxed on the beneficiary as 'streamed income' will also be deducted: see the Appendix.

Distributions of income

4.36   Where trustees exercise a discretion to distribute income (see **4.41**) the amount treated as deducted at the 'special rates' may be taxable on the trustees, although tax payable on certain types of income can be set against this liability. Added to those types is tax payable at the lower rates under this new rule. Amendments have been made to the existing legislation to ensure that this benefit cannot be obtained twice, ie under the new rules as well as under the previous regime.

Example 4.10—Effect of trust management expenses

A discretionary trust receives interest income of £2,000 in tax year 2009/10. The trustees incur qualifying management expenses of £150, leaving them with £1,850. Tax at the basic rate of 20% is deducted from the interest. The computation is as follows:

Interest income (gross)	£2,000
Less management expenses	(£150)
	£1,850
Charged at the basic rate	(£1,000)
Charged at the special rates	£850
Tax liability at 20% on £1,000	£200
Tax liability at 40% on £850	£340
Less tax paid at source on £2,000 interest	(£400)
Further tax payable by the trustees	£140

TRUSTS FOR VULNERABLE BENEFICIARIES

4.37 These rules, introduced by *FA 2005*, apply from 2004/05. They enable a discretionary or accumulation trust which would otherwise be taxed at the special rates, to be taxed according to the personal financial circumstances of one or more beneficiaries, so long as they are qualifying 'vulnerable persons'.

'Vulnerable persons' include 'disabled persons' and 'relevant minors'. Disabled persons are defined broadly in relation to the inheritance tax definition in *IHTA 1984, s 74(4)*. A 'relevant minor' is simply a person under 18 with at least one parent having died. The trust must be a 'qualifying trust' as defined. In the case of a disabled person that means that where any trust property is applied for the benefit of a beneficiary it must be applied for the benefit of that disabled person. In the case of a relevant minor, a qualifying trust may be either a trust arising by statute on intestacy or a will trust (or one established under the Criminal Injuries Compensation Scheme), which ensures that the minor receives capital and income and accumulations absolutely at age 18.

Electing for special treatment

4.38 The election must be made on or before the 31 January in the tax year following that where the regime is to apply. It can most easily be made at Box 10B of the self-assessment return. Therefore, to adopt the regime for 2008/09 the election must be made on or before 31 January 2010. The election must have been made both by the trustees and the vulnerable person – or someone on his behalf. HMRC will specify what must be contained in the election, which is irrevocable. The election will cease to have effect when the person ceases to be vulnerable or the trust is no longer qualifying or comes to an end, in which event the trustees must inform HMRC within 90 days.

Special treatments

4.39 The rule is intended to make the vulnerable person's personal allowances and savings and basic rate available to the trustees. This treatment must be claimed each tax year and does not apply where the trust income is taxed on the settlor as a settlor-interested trust (see **4.26–4.29**). *FA 2005* provides a series of steps to calculate what is known as the 'vulnerable person's liability' and then to ascertain the reduction in the income tax liability of the trustees (*FA 2005, ss 23–45* and *Sch 1*). For CGT purposes, the relief must be claimed and the applicable provisions vary as to whether the vulnerable person is UK resident or non-UK resident. Note that, if the election is made for this special treatment, and income is distributed to the beneficiary by the trustees, the regime for discretionary payments under *ITA 2007, Pt 9, Ch 7* still applies (see **4.41–4.43**). From 2008/09, with the introduction of a flat rate of 18% capital gains tax, consequential changes to the vulnerable person's regime have been made by *FA 2008, Sch 2, paras 11–22*.

Administration

4.40 HMRC are empowered to confirm that the beneficiary is, indeed, vulnerable and that the settlement is a qualifying trust, subject to giving a minimum of 60 days' notice. If HMRC find that the statutory requirements are not met (or that since the effective date of the election there has been an event that terminates the validity of the election), they can give notice that the election never had or has ceased to have effect.

Example 4.11—Vulnerable beneficiary illustration

Both William's parents were killed in a car crash in 2004, neither having made a will. Under the intestacy rules, a trust has been established for William, aged 14, which for 2008/09 produces gross dividend income of £20,000 and gross interest income of £10,000 and makes gains of £10,000. William has no other income.

Assuming that the trustees and William (or rather his guardian) make the necessary election on or before 31 January 2010, the effect of the new regime is as follows:

Income tax

TLV1 (see below) = (£1,367)
TLV2 (see below) = £0 (William's other income)
TQTI (see below) = £7,236
VQTI (see below) = £8,603

VQT1: Reduction in the trustees' tax liability on a claim is £8,603 (£7,236 + 1,367). A reduction for the dividend tax credits of £2,000 and the tax of £2,000 deducted at source from the interest income is given in the ordinary way.

4.40 *Running a trust: income tax*

	William's assumed tax liability £	Trustees' actual tax Liability £
Dividend income	20,000	20,000
(with tax credits £2,000)		
Interest income	10,000	10,000
(before tax deducted £2,000)		–
	30,000	30,000
Personal allowance	(6,035)	–
Taxable	23,965	30,000
£2,320 @ 10%	232	
Next £1,645 (interest at 20%)	329	
£20,000 (dividends at 10%)	2,000	
	2,561	
Trust, first slice (£1,000 @ 20%)		200
Next £9,000 (interest at 40%)		3,600
Dividends at 32.5%		6,500
	–	10,300
Less:		
Dividend tax credits	(2,000)	(2,000)
Tax deducted from interest	(2,000)	(2,000)
Income tax repayable/payable	(1,439)	6,300

Capital gains tax

	William's assumed tax tax liability £	Trustees' actual tax liability £
Gains arising	10,000	10,000
Less annual exemption	(9,600)	(4,800)
	400	5,200
Gains charged at 18%		
Tax payable	72	936

Summary

	William's assumed tax liability £	Trustees' actual tax liability £
Income tax repayable/payable	1,439	6,300
Plus capital gains tax	72	936
	(1,367)	7,236
	(TLV1)	(TQT1)

DISCRETIONARY PAYMENTS

4.41   A special charging regime operates under *ITA 2007, Pt 9, Ch 7* where trustees make payments of income in exercise of a discretion. By definition, the regime cannot apply to accumulations of income, which are generally added to capital net of the 40% (or 32.5%) charge. That said, however, a trust deed may empower trustees to make payments out of accumulated income as if they were income of the current year. In that case the distribution regime will apply.

Liability of the beneficiary

4.42   The thinking behind the regime is that, for any payment made to a discretionary beneficiary, it must be clear that tax has been borne by the trustees and paid over to HMRC at the rate of 40%. Except to the extent that tax relates to the 10% non-repayable credit on dividends, the beneficiary may then recover all or part of the tax (unless he is a higher rate taxpayer).

The tax pool

4.43   However, this does not simply mean that the trustees must pay over 40%, because it can be covered by tax that they have already paid (known as the 'tax pool'). At the beginning of each tax year a discretionary settlement will typically have a tax pool (except in the circumstance where it was set up since 6 April 1999 and has only ever had dividend income, or where it simply pays out all its income each year). The change of dividend taxation from 6 April 1999 has made a significant difference in so far as the notional tax credit on dividends does not enter the tax pool, although the additional 22.5% making it up to the dividend trust rate does go into the pool.

Note that tax pools in hand at the end of 1998/99 can never be augmented (except in relation to non-dividend income) and will simply be run down through distributions of income over the years.

The tax pool system may be repealed from some future date: see the Appendix.

Example 4.12—Restriction on trustees' ability to distribute income

Assume Example 4.9. In 2008/09 the trustees have a net dividend income of £13,500 and have had to pay out an additional £3,375 under *ITA 2007, s 479* leaving them with net income of £10,125. However, disregarding the interest and rental income, they cannot simply distribute that amount to the beneficiaries. The reason for this is explained by the following table.

Net income of trust		£10,125
Liability @ 40% under *ITA 2007, s 494* on gross payment of £13,500 to beneficiaries	£5,400	
Met by trustees' payment above	(£3,375)	
Remaining liability of trustees		(£2,025)
Available for distribution to beneficiaries		£8,100
Grossed up under *s 494* @ 40%, ie add		£5,400
Gross income of beneficiaries		£13,500
Tax thereon @ 40%		(£5,400)
Net income of (higher rate) beneficiaries		£8,100

THE PRE-OWNED ASSETS REGIME

Summary

4.44   This charge to income tax applies from 2005/06 (*FA 2004, Sch 15*). The charge is applied to the value of the benefit of enjoying 'pre-owned assets' at any time from 2005/06 onwards. These generally are assets that were previously owned by the taxpayer and that have been disposed of in whole or in part since 18 March 1986. According to the *Finance Bill 2004* Standing Committee Report, the declared target of this new charge is: '¼ the range of schemes that allow wealthy taxpayers to give their assets away, or achieve the appearance of doing so, and so benefit from the inheritance tax exemption for lifetime gifts, while in reality retaining continuing enjoyment of and access to those assets, much as before.'

In broad terms, the aim of the pre-owned assets regime is to create an adverse income tax consequence for arrangements which have, according to the courts, successfully evaded the reservation of benefit regime for inheritance tax (see **6.16–6.21**) while enabling the taxpayer to continue to enjoy some benefit for the asset which he has given away. This is the point of the transitional provisions described at **4.52**: HMRC intend that a person should 'pay' for the continuing enjoyment of an asset which has been given away, whether in the form of the reservation of benefit code, under which he is treated as continuing to be beneficially entitled, or, if not, under the pre-owned assets regime.

Separate rules apply to:

• land;

• chattels; and

• intangible property comprised in a settlement where the settlor retains an interest.

Land

4.45   There is an income tax charge where a taxpayer occupies any land, whether alone or with others, and the disposal condition or the contribution condition is met (*FA 2004, Sch 15, paras 3–5*). The disposal condition is that the taxpayer has, since 17 March 1986, disposed of all or part of his interest in the land other than by an excluded transaction. The contribution condition is that at any time since 17 March 1986 he has directly or indirectly provided (other than by an excluded transaction) any of the consideration given by someone else for the acquisition of an interest in the land.

Where the regime applies, it is the 'appropriate rental value' that is charged to income tax, less any payments made in pursuance of a legal obligation. That rental value equates broadly to the rent payable on a landlord's repairing lease.

Chattels

4.46   Principles similar to the above apply for chattels (*FA 2004, Sch 15, paras 6–7*) except that:

• instead of occupation the test is possession or use of a chattel; and

• instead of the appropriate rental value the charge is on the appropriate amount, which is the official rate of interest, at the beginning of the relevant tax year (6.25% for 2008/09 and 4.75% for 2009/10).

Intangible property comprised in a settlement where the settlor retains an interest

4.47   Here the charge is based not on the enjoyment of benefits but rather on the satisfaction of a set of circumstances (with no let-out for any payments made by the chargeable person): *FA 2004, Sch 15, para 8*. The set of circumstances is:

- under the settlement any of the income arising would be taxed on the settlor (see **4.26–4.29**);

- any such income would be treated as so taxable disregarding benefits received by his spouse; and

- that property includes any 'relevant property', viz intangible property, which is or represents a property settled by or added to the settlement by the chargeable person after 17 March 2006.

Intangible property would include cash and investments (though not land or chattels). The purpose of this charge is to catch certain (though by no means all) inheritance tax avoidance schemes based on the use of trusts. The tax is charged at the official rate of interest (see **4.46**) at the beginning of the relevant tax year.

Exclusions

4.48   These are defined separately for the disposal and contribution conditions respectively (and in any case apply only to land or chattels). Broadly speaking, these embrace the following (*FA 2004, Sch 15, para 10*):

- there was a disposal of the individual's whole interest in the property except for any right expressly reserved by him, whether by an arm's-length transaction with an unconnected person or by a transaction that might be expected to be made at arm's length between unconnected persons;

- regulations made in March 2005 added an exemption for certain part disposals; significantly, where made 'inter family' after 6 March 2005, the exemption will not apply if the consideration takes the form of cash or marketable securities;

- the transfer of a property to his spouse (or former spouse under a court order);

- a disposal to a life interest trust in which his spouse or (under a court order) former spouse continues to have an interest in possession (except on the death of the beneficiary);

- the disposal was one within the exemption from inheritance tax for dispositions for the maintenance of the family;

- the disposal is an outright gift to an individual, which is wholly exempt from inheritance tax under either the annual exemption or the small gifts exemption.

An important additional exclusion in the case of the contribution condition is where the contribution consisted of an outright gift of money made at least seven years before the occupation of the 'relevant property' begins.

The exemptions

4.49   Again, the drafting is complex, but the exemptions (which apply to all three categories within the regime) are (*FA 2004, Sch 15, para 11*):

- the taxpayer's estate for inheritance tax purposes includes the relevant property (or property which derives its value from the relevant property);

- the property would be treated as part of the taxpayer's estate as property subject to a reservation of benefit (see **6.16–6.21**);

- the property would be subject to a reservation of benefit apart from certain prescribed exemptions, eg gifts to charities;

- the relevant property would be treated as a gift with reservation but for the exception for co-ownership arrangements under inheritance tax, ie insofar as the chargeable person has given part of their interest to someone with whom they share occupation;

- the relevant property would fall to be a gift with reservation of benefit but for an exemption which either (a) requires payment of full consideration in either money or money's worth or (b) allows occupation as a result of a change in circumstances, which was unforeseen when the gift was made, the donor cannot maintain himself through old age, infirmity or otherwise and the occupation represents a reasonable provision by the relative donee for the donor's care and maintenance.

De minimis exemption

4.50   There is a very small *de minimis* exemption where the aggregate of the amounts otherwise chargeable under the regime do not exceed £5,000 (*FA 2004, Sch 15, para 13*). If they do exceed that sum the whole amount is taxable.

Post-death variations

4.51   A person who disposed of property received under a will or intestacy by an inheritance tax protected variation (see **13.1–13.4**) is not caught by the new regime (*FA 2004, Sch 15, para 17*).

Transitional provisions

4.52   A person who is caught by the new regime can make an irrevocable election to opt (back) into the reservation of benefit regime (*FA 2004, Sch 15, paras 20–22*). This means that the property concerned is treated as part of his estate on death with a liability for inheritance tax on the donee. The election must be made before the 31 January following the end of the tax year in which the new regime first applies. This is likely to be 31 January 2007. Although in autumn 2006 HMRC issued form IHT 500 for making the election, regulations authorising the form, were not made until 19 October 2007, to have effect from 14 November 2007. Despite the late appearance of the enabling regulations, HMRC do not agree that new forms IHT 500 submitted before 14 November 2007 were invalid (and so should arguably be treated as never having been made). That said, however, *FA 2007, s 66* gives HMRC discretion to accept a late election, whether for 2005/06 or subsequently.

Scope

4.53   Although the regime is specifically targeted at schemes made with a view to avoiding the reservation of benefit regime, whether in relation to houses, land, chattels or insurance policies, the breadth of the rules will mean that many 'innocent' arrangements will also be caught. Ideally, a careful review will have been made before 6 April 2005 of all action taken since 18 March 1986 that might produce an income tax charge under the new regime, to decide what should be done in vulnerable cases viz whether:

● to pay the income tax charge;

● to pay to the donee such an amount each year as will escape the charge;

● to bring the benefit to an end (most probably as a deemed potentially exempt transfer for IHT purposes: see **6.16–6.22**); or

● to opt into the reservation of benefit regime, with an IHT liability for the donee following the donor's death.

Application

4.54   The pre-owned assets regime is far from straightforward, despite publication by HMRC in March 2005 of Guidance Notes, which have been updated. In cases that might be caught by the new rules, there is no alternative to careful professional analysis of whether the arrangements adopted are in fact caught and, if so, what action should now be taken.

Example 4.13—Land

On 1 July 1999, on advice from his solicitors, Richard entered into a 'home loan' or 'double trust' scheme with his family home, which he owned himself. He sold the house to a new life interest trust for himself, of which the trustees were Richard, his wife Marion and his solicitor. The purchase price of £750,000 was satisfied by an IOU from the trustees to Richard on commercial terms, though not secured on the house. Richard then gave the IOU to a second trust, on life interests for their three children, from which he and Marion are irrevocably excluded. The idea was that, once seven years have expired from the gift of the IOU, that falls out of his estate for inheritance tax purposes and that, on his death, only the excess in value of the house at that time over £750,000 would attract inheritance tax. The house is now worth £1 million.

Assume that the arrangement is and has since 2005/06 been caught by the pre-owned assets regime. Richard has had a choice between, broadly, paying income tax year by year, so long as he continues to occupy the house, on the appropriate rental value of £750,000 worth of the house or unscrambling the scheme (whether by virtue of powers in the settlements or by opting into the reservation of benefit regime). There are plenty of i's to be dotted and t's to be crossed with either of these routes. At all events, Richard should have been taking professional advice long before 6 April 2005.

Example 4.14—Chattels

Rosemary, a widow, gave to her two children outright on 1 April 1987 £300,000 worth of chattels. None of the chattels was worth more than £6,000 and so no capital gains tax was payable. Rosemary made an agreement with each of her children that she would continue to keep the chattels at her home and pay the insurance, together with an arm's-length fee (negotiated independently by valuers acting for each side) of, it turns out around 1% of capital value. This fee is renegotiated every three years. The children pay income tax on the fee, but the potentially exempt transfer is now exempt.

The argument is that there is no reservation of benefit for inheritance tax purposes (see **6.16–6.21**) because full consideration is paid by Rosemary for her continuing enjoyment. Equally, it is now argued, and accepted in principle by HMRC, that if the amount paid by Rosemary does constitute full consideration, there will be no pre-owned assets issues. Although HMRC were tending to contest such an argument as it was being raised in the course of 2006, it appears that at some stage in 2007 HMRC relaxed their stance and indeed are known to have accepted the argument following death in a few specific cases. The above said, note that HMRC do not take this view in their pre-owned assets guidance at http://www.hmrc.gov.uk/poa/poa_guidance2. htm#21, saying: 'Note that the charge is computed differently from land and while any rental payments made to the owner will reduce the amount on which he is chargeable [viz based on the official rate], the fact that he pays a market rent for their use does not prevent an income tax charge arising.'

Example 4.15—Settled intangible property

On 1 June 2001 Rodney entered into an *'Eversden'* IHT planning arrangement (see *IRC v Eversden* [2003] STC 822, CA) for his grandchildren based on an insurance policy issued by a major life company. This arrangement (no longer possible, under *FA 2003*) involved Rodney's making a settlement of the policy on a life interest trust for his wife, Tania, with power for the trustees to bring Tania's interest to an end in favour of trusts for a variety of family beneficiaries (including Rodney). That action the trustees duly took after six months and the policy is now held in trust for Rodney's eight grandchildren. But there is always the possibility of the trustees exercising their powers to pay all or part of the capital back to Rodney.

The arrangement is caught by the pre-owned assets rule. And, if Rodney does or has done nothing more, the 'official rate' (see **4.46**) applied to the value of the policy at the beginning of each tax year (£1 million as at 6 April 2008) will be assessed on him for income tax purposes. That is, as a higher rate taxpayer, he will suffer £25,000 income tax (40% of £62,500) for 2008/09. For 2009/10 the charge falls to 47,500 (assuming the same value of the policy) on which he will pay income tax at 40% of £19,000. It would be possible to avoid the charge for the future, if Rodney were irrevocably to give up his interest under the trust, perhaps keeping his wife Tania as a beneficiary. That would put paid to the pre-owned assets charge.

SELF-ASSESSMENT FORM SA 900 (FOR 2008/09)

4.55 Since the introduction of self-assessment in 1996/97, the self-assessment compliance returns and related literature have been subject to continuous revision, based in no small part upon comments made by practitioners. The basic trust and estate form SA 900, contains 12 pages for

2007/08. The significant revisions to the self-assessment return forms from 2008/09 touch rather on those for individuals than for trustees, who will notice little change from 2007/08.

Basic details

4.56   Page 1 gives at the top a tax reference, a date (typically 6 April 2009), the addressee, viz the first named trustee or personal representative, the name of the trust and the trust district and telephone number. Page 2 carries 2 steps.

Step 1: What type of trust

4.57   Step 1 enables the trustee to go directly to question 19 on page 11, that is to confirm details of the trustee, if:

- the trust is a bare trust and the beneficiary has an immediate and absolute right to both capital and income; or

- the addressee is a PR and (broadly) no gross income has been received (see **12.1–12.5**); or

- the trust is interest in possession and no tax liability arises to the trust, eg because it has all been received net, or because all the income has been mandated to the beneficiaries.

Step 2: Supplementary pages

4.58   Step 2 directs the taxpayer to questions 1 to 7 to confirm whether any of the following supplementary pages need to be completed and returned:

- trade;
- partnership;
- land and property;
- foreign;
- capital gains;
- non-residence;
- charities.

In the case of estates there is an additional form (estate pension charges etc), though not relevant to trusts.

On page 3, step 3 confirms that blue or black ink must be used to complete the return and that pence should not be included. Income and gains are rounded down to the nearest pound and tax credits and tax deductions are rounded up.

Any supplementary pages should be completed before going to questions 9 to 21.

Rate of tax

4.59   Question 8 asks for the capacity in which the return is being completed, eg if a trustee, whether the trust is liable to income tax, at either/both the trust rate (40%) or the dividend trust rate (32.5%) on any part of the income.

Details of other income

4.60   Question 9 on pages 4 to 5 asks for details of any other income not already included on the supplementary pages, eg interest, dividends, gains on UK life insurance policies, life annuities and other income.

On page 6, question 10A asks whether the trustees wish to claim any reliefs. Question 10B asks whether the trustees want to claim special income tax treatment where a valid vulnerable beneficiary election has effect (see **4.37–4.40**). Question 11 asks whether any annual payments were made out of capital or out of income not brought into charge to income tax (in which case the trustees must account to HMRC for the tax deducted). Question 12 asks whether any assets or funds have been put into the settlement: this covers initial trust property, as well as subsequent additions.

Types and rates of income, trustee expenses

4.61   On page 7, question 13 is appropriate only to discretionary or accumulation trusts. Question 13 asks whether any part of the trust income is not liable to tax at the rate applicable to trusts or the dividend trust rate. The function of this page is to separate out income that is treated as that of the settlor, income that belongs to a life tenant, and income that is subject to the trustees' discretion and in each case to identify the trust management expenses.

Payments of income or capital

4.62   On page 8, question 14 asks discretionary trustees whether discretionary payments of income have been made to beneficiaries and question

15 asks whether any capital payments have been made to or for minor unmarried children of the settlor during his lifetime. Question 15A asks whether there were any capital transactions between the trustees and the settlors.

Final questions

4.63   Question 16 on page 9 addresses trusts that are, or have ever been, non-UK resident, or have received any capital from another, non-UK resident, trust. If the answer is yes, HMRC want to know whether the trustees have made any capital payments to, or provided any benefits for, the beneficiaries. This question is designed to apply some special anti-avoidance tax rules which are beyond the scope of this book.

On page 10, question 17 asks the trustees whether they want to calculate the tax and question 18 whether they want to claim a repayment of tax.

On page 11, question 19 requests details of trustees' representatives and question 20 asks whether there are any changes to the names and addresses of the trustees or PRs.

Question 21 on page 12 is for other information: for example, has the trust or the administration period of an estate come to an end when the date is requested (Box 21.2)? Or has the administration period come to an end and there is a continuing trust (Box 21.3)? Box 21.5 admits the possibility of provisional figures only being available. Boxes 21.27 and 21.8 refer (for the first time) to disclosure of tax avoidance schemes specified by statute (especially under *FA 2006* for direct taxes), in which case a scheme reference number must be given and the tax year in which the expected advantage arises specified. Box 21.11 is the famous 'white space' for the provision of additional information. Question 22 is the declaration that the information given is correct and complete to the best of the trustee's knowledge and belief.

REVENUE GUIDES

Trust and Estate Tax Return Guide: SA 950

4.64   Form SA 950 is 'essential reading' for trustees. As stated on page 1 this guide has step-by-step instructions to help you fill in the trusts and estates tax return. The notes are numbered to match the boxes in the tax return. Further help is offered by telephoning either the relevant HMRC office or the helpline.

Successive tax years have seen improvements to the drafting of the tax return guide, which for 2008/09 runs to 30 pages.

The guide starts with a step-by-step explanation of the tax return, including a helpful flow chart on pages 6 to 7. Each of the supplementary pages is summarised on pages 8 to 9 and the balance of the guide contains a detailed commentary on the relevant boxes, including a summary of the relevant law. For 2008/09 there are nine supplementary pages, seven of which are discussed below from **4.67** to **4.87**. Form SA 908 on pensions and form SA 909 on estate pension charges etc are not considered in this book.

Discretionary payments: income or capital?

4.65 For example, question 14 asks whether discretionary payments of income have been made to beneficiaries. The general rule (though not necessarily so) is that what is capital in the hands of the trustees will be capital for the beneficiary and similarly with income. The guidance notes state helpfully on page 25 (Boxes 14.1 to 14.14) that:

- 'Payments out of trust capital or accumulated income are not to be regarded as the income of a beneficiary irrespective of the purposes for which they are made and should not therefore be included.

- If, exceptionally, the terms of the trust empower the trustees to release monies in order to bring up a beneficiary's income to a certain defined level, the total amount of the monies released should be included even if part of it represents capital or accumulated income.

- Payment is regarded as taking place when a beneficiary is legally entitled to require money to be paid over, for example, when it becomes irrevocably their property following the trustees' resolution to allocate or appropriate it to them.'

Example 4.16

If therefore, the trustees make regular payments from the trust capital to fund part of the school fees of a child (an income purpose) this will not make the payments income for the beneficiary. The only exception in the school fee trust type case noted by the guide is where, let us say, the trustees are to pay a beneficiary income of £5,000 per annum, they only have £3,000 of income to this end and have to resort to capital for the remaining £2,000. In that case, the £2,000 will be income for the beneficiary.

Trust and Estate Tax Calculation Guide: SA 951

4.66 Form SA 951 is obviously for use only where the trustees (or personal representatives) or their advisers compute the tax and not where the tax return is submitted to HMRC on or before 31 October, in which case they will calculate the tax. Incidentally, if the return is delivered after that date, HMRC will calculate the tax but they do not guarantee to have done so by 31 January; if any tax due is not paid by that date, there would be interest implications.

The calculation is split into eight stages, of which stages 3 and 8 will apply only to discretionary and accumulation trusts:

- Stage 1 applies to all the income and deductions the trustees have included in their tax return and sorts them into the trust and estate tax return categories which will be taxed later in the process. All trustees and personal representatives should complete stage 1.

- Stage 2 is for personal representatives only.

- Stage 3 is for trustees who are taxable at the trust rate or the dividend trust rate. Certain types of income and deemed income are chargeable at the trust rate or the dividend trust rate whether or not the trustees are normally taxable at the basic/savings/dividend ordinary rate. These types of income include accrued income charges, income from deeply discounted securities, gilt strips, offshore income gains, income from companies purchasing their own shares and gains on life insurance policies, life annuities and capital redemption policies. If, apart from these types of income, the trustees are taxable at the basic/savings/ dividend ordinary rate only, or the trustees are the trustee of an unauthorised unit trust, which is generally taxable at the basic rate only, the trustees should complete stage 4. These stages will charge the income listed above at the correct rates. Stage 3 is to be completed by the trustees who are chargeable to the trust rate or dividend trust rate, on any income other than that listed above.

- Stage 4 is for trustees of an unauthorised unit trust.

- Stage 5 is for other trustees, not taxable at the trust rate or the dividend trust rate.

- Stage 6 brings in all the tax the trustees have already deducted from income (so the trustees will need the tax return and any supplementary pages again), and works out any non-payable tax credits.

- Stage 7 makes adjustments to the tax calculated in earlier sections and adds in capital gains tax. The final box of stage 6, box T6.26 gives the figure for box 17.1 in the trust and estate tax return.

- Stage 8 works out what the trustees have to pay HMRC by 31 January 2010, or what HMRC have to pay the trustees, and checks if the trustees will have to make 2009/10 payments on account.

- Stage 9 is for trustees who make discretionary payments to beneficiaries.

SUPPLEMENTARY PAGES

Trade

Form SA 901

4.67   Like all supplementary pages, form SA 901 carries its own set of notes, SA 901 (Notes). The main tax return consists of pages TT1 to TT4 and Notes TTN1 to TTN8. Trustees who carry on a trade, whether as sole traders or in partnership, are like any other taxpayer. They will need either the accounts for the business covering the basis period for tax year 2008/09, eg the year ended March 2009 or, if no accounts, the relevant books and records.

How long must I keep records?

4.68   Page TTN1 warns that records of all business transactions must be kept until at least 31 January 2015, in case they have to be produced for HMRC.

Profit and loss

4.69   Page TT1 asks for details of the business, capital allowances and balancing charges and income and expenses. Only if the annual turnover is £30,000 or more, should the more detailed description of income, expenses and necessary tax adjustments on page TT2 be completed. When the annual turnover is less than £30,000, Boxes 1.24, 1.25 and 1.26 on page TT1 should be completed with turnover, expenses and net profit. In all cases, page TT3 requests the adjustments required to arrive at the taxable profit or loss.

Having said that, it seems to be the current experience that small businesses with an annual turnover of less than £30,000 are more likely to be targeted for an enquiry. That likelihood could perhaps be reduced by including full figures in the SA 901.

Balance sheet

4.70   Page TT4 asks for a summary of the balance sheet. These details do not have to be completed if there is no balance sheet (or if the turnover was less than £30,000, though see the warning in the preceding paragraph). Box 1.116 is the 'white space' for additional information.

None of the supplementary pages need in themselves to be signed. However, as they form part of the main tax return, the information in them is therefore covered by the declaration on the tax return.

Example 4.17—Trading trust

The Graham Discretionary Trust owns a small garage in the village. For the year ended 31 March 2009, accounts profits, after paying a manager, were £30,000. Form SA 901 must be completed in full. The business details will give the business name and description, its address and the dates of the accounting period.

Capital allowances are shown as follows:

- £2,000 as a writing-down allowance on a truck not used for private motoring; and

- £2,000 on other plant and machinery.

The turnover exceeds £30,000 and therefore page TTT2 must be completed. The business being registered for VAT, it must be stated that the figures exclude VAT as well as stating the turnover.

Summary details of income and expenses produce gross income of £50,000 and total expenses of £35,000, a net profit of £15,000. This is reduced for tax purposes by the capital allowances to £11,000. No adjustments are required on page TTT3 (eg brought forward losses) and the total taxable profits are shown as Box 1.92.

A summary balance sheet is included on page TT4.

Partnership

Form SA 902

4.71   Again, form SA 902 comes with SA 902 (Notes). It is more common to find trustees trading in partnership than as sole traders.

The partnership tax return

4.72   The main partnership tax return will be made by the 'representative partner'. This will include a summary of the share of profits, losses or income allocated to each of the partners during the relevant period. This summary is called the 'partnership statement' and the information on it will be used to complete the trust and estate partnership page. Most partnerships will issue a short or abridged version of the partnership statement, which will show trading income (or loss) and interest received less tax deducted. The 'full' version covers all the possible types of partnership income. If the trustees belong to more than one partnership, they will receive separate partnership statements and should complete a set of the relevant trust and estate partnership pages for each business.

Form SA 902 asks for the partnership reference number, the partnership trade and whether commencement or cessation of the partnership happened during 2008/09. Under the share of the partnership's trading or professional income the basis period is given, together with the partner's share of the profit or loss for tax purposes. Adjustments are made for 'overlap profit' (which occurs when there is an overlapping of basis periods, so that the same profits are taxable in two different tax years). Overlap relief exists to relieve the profits in a later tax year, so that over the life of the business, tax is paid by the trust or estate on no more profits than are earned. There is then in the case of farm or market gardening trades an adjustment for farmer's averaging and, where a loss arises, the treatment of the loss. Total taxable profits are mentioned at Box 2.22 for entry in the main return.

Trading trustees

4.73   A partner or a sole trader is personally responsible for the debts and liabilities of the business, even to the extent of his own personal assets. While no protection is available for a sole trader, it may be possible within a partnership to get limited liability under the *Limited Partnerships Act 1907* (or even, more recently, under the *Limited Liability Partnerships Act 2000*, when the whole partnership has limited liability).

The *1907 Act* assumes there is at least one 'general partner' who will have unlimited liability. The partnership needs to be registered. A limited partner may not participate in the management of the firm but will have his, its or their liability limited to the capital subscribed. All the capital tax reliefs available to traders may be enjoyed by members of a limited liability partnership, eg agricultural or business property relief from IHT and roll-over relief from CGT.

Record keeping

4.74   As with sole traders, record keeping must be taken seriously, with records used to make the partnership tax return 2008/09 kept until at least 31 January 2015. In the absence of fraud or negligence and assuming the return was submitted on or before 31 October 2009, if in paper form or 31 January 2010 if submitted electronically, HMRC will have up to 12 months from the date on which the return was delivered to decide whether to make an enquiry.

Land and property (UK property)

Form SA 903

4.75 The relative notes, SA 903 (Notes), consist of eight pages. The form should be completed if the trust (or estate) has:

- rental income or other receipts from UK land and property;

- premiums arising from UK leases of less than 50 years;

- furnished holiday lettings in the UK; or

- a 'reverse premium' (viz where the trustees enter into a lease with a landlord and receive a payment as an inducement from the landlord to take up the lease. That payment will be taxable on the trustees as income of a property business).

Form SA 903 itself runs to only two pages. Page TL1 deals with furnished holiday lettings in the UK (see **4.77**). That is, if the trust has rental income, which does not derive from furnished holiday lets, the trustees need complete only page TL2. If the trust does have income from furnished holiday lets, then having completed page TL1, the total is carried forward to the top of page TL2 at Box 3.19 to which are added rents and other income, chargeable premiums and reverse premiums. There follow summary details of expenses to give net profit and then the tax adjustment.

In terms of the details on page TL2, the notes at TLN5 confirm that if the gross property income is less than £15,000 per annum, the expenses do not have to be listed separately and the total figure can be entered at Box 3.29. Of course, it may be that trust accounts have been prepared which show the expenses.

Deductible expenses

4.76 The notes are helpful in summarising the types of expenditure that are allowable for tax purposes and those that are not.

On tax adjustments, there has traditionally been, and remains, a 10% allowance of gross rents for 'wear and tear' as an alternative to capital allowances (which are not available to the landlord of furnished UK property which is not furnished holiday accommodation). The allowance is intended to cover the cost of renewing furniture in the normal way.

Furnished holiday lettings

4.77 Income from furnished holiday lets is generally treated as trading income, with more favourable treatment given for income tax and CGT. To qualify, the property must be (*ITTOIA 2005, ss 323–326*):

- furnished and let on a commercial basis with a view to profits;

- available for holiday lettings to the public on a commercial basis for 140 days or more during the year;

- actually let commercially as holiday accommodation for at least 70 days during the year; and

- not occupied continuously for more than 31 days by the same person for at least seven months during the year.

For 2009/10 this deemed trading treatment is applied to property anywhere in the European Economic Area. However, as from 2010/11 this treatment will come to an end as announced at Budget 2009).

'Whose property business?'

4.78   Trustees might own property, but have delegated its management to a beneficiary under the *Law of Property Act 1925, s 29(1)*. In such a case, it will usually be the beneficiary rather than the trustees who is regarded as carrying on the rental business and all the income and expenses should be included in the beneficiary's return. This could be helpful if the beneficiary owns other property beneficially, which he lets, as all the income will be added together as a single property business. If one property gives rise to a loss, and the other to a profit, the loss can be offset against the profit in computing the total tax position.

Example 4.18 – Trust with property income

Alistair's trust owns a cottage, which is let furnished. The rent is £5,000 per annum and the total expenses amount to £1,500. Box 3.20 shows gross income of £5,000. Because this is less than £15,000, the expenses do not have to be detailed (though the receipts etc should be kept to answer any HMRC enquiry), and the total of the expenses should be put at Box 3.29. A 10% allowance of £500 can be claimed at Box 3.36 with the adjusted profit at Box 3.39 of £3,000.

Foreign

Form SA 904

4.79   Form SA 904 (Notes) accompanies the five-page SA 904.

Basis of taxation

4.80 Given that the trustees are UK resident, any income from abroad is taxed as it arises, regardless of whether the trustees bring that income to the UK. The only exception is in a case of 'unremittable' income, for example on account of exchange controls, in which case a claim can be made that it should not be taxed in the current year, ie until such year as it is remitted to the UK (*ITTOIA 2005, s 842*).

To calculate the UK tax liability, the conversion rate of foreign currency is that in force when the income arose, ie not necessarily the rate at the end of the tax year.

Treatment of foreign tax

4.81 Foreign income will typically be subject to tax in the country where it arises. The trustees have a choice between setting the foreign tax paid against the UK tax liability, (which will generally be more favourable) and simply deducting the foreign tax from the income received in the UK. The former is called 'tax credit relief'.

The UK has negotiated double tax agreements with large numbers of foreign countries, which seek to restrict the possibility of double taxation in both the UK and other relevant countries. Under such agreements, there will be a restriction of the amount of foreign tax that can be relieved against UK tax. Pages TFN 20 to 24 show, in each case, the rate of withholding tax deducted by the foreign country in the case of dividend interest, royalty and management/technical fees. The treaty will provide a maximum of tax credit relief. If more than that maximum has been paid in foreign tax, a refund of that excess might be claimed direct from the overseas tax authorities.

Pages TFN 16 to 19 constitute a working sheet for calculating tax credit relief where the UK trust or estate is *not* liable to pay tax at the rate applicable to trusts. Special instructions are given for calculating tax credit relief where the trust is liable to pay tax at the rate applicable to trusts.

Different types of income

4.82 The types of foreign income that might arise are:

- foreign savings;

- income from land and property abroad; and

- other overseas income, eg income from foreign trusts.

Of these the first, foreign savings, is the most likely. Where, as in the usual case, the income is taxed on the arising basis, the details are given on page TF1.

Example 4.19—given on page TFN14 of SA 904 (Notes)

A discretionary trust's income comprises overseas interest of £3,000 from which foreign tax of £450 has been withheld, and rental income from a foreign property of £10,000 on which foreign tax at a rate of 45% (£45,000) has been paid. No deductions are due and the whole of the income is liable to UK tax at 40%.

The property income has been subjected to foreign tax at a rate in excess of 40% and so tax credit relief is restricted as follows:

	UK tax at 40%	*Tax credit relief*
Interest £3,000	£1,200	£450
Property £10,000	£4,000	(Max) £4,000
	£5,200	£4,450

The balance of the foreign tax paid on the property income (£4,500 – £4,000 = £500) is not available to credit against the UK tax on the interest income, nor can it be repaid or carried forward or back.

Non-residence, etc

Form SA 906

4.83   The general assumption in this book is that the trust or deceased estate is UK resident. If this is so, there is no need for supplemental page SA 906. There may, however, be cases where the page is relevant.

The preliminary questions on form SA 906 request confirmation as to:

* whether the trustees or personal representatives are as a whole resident or non-resident in the UK for income tax and separately for CGT purposes;

* whether they are resident in a country other than the UK under a double taxation agreement at the same time as being UK resident; and

* in the case of a deceased estate, whether the deceased was non-UK domiciled at the date of death.

Information is then requested if the trustees or PRs claim to be non-resident in the UK for income tax and, separately, CGT purposes, in particular as to whether, when claiming to be non-UK resident for 2008/09, they were UK resident for 2007/08.

An annual status

4.84   Generally speaking, residence or non-UK residence is a state that exists throughout the year. Although there are concessions for both income tax and CGT, which apply to periods of residence and non-UK residence respectively during the same tax year, the general rule is that a person is UK resident if resident in the UK for any part of the tax year.

Page TNR2 of SA 906 requests certain information if the trustees or personal representatives claim to be dual resident.

A non-UK resident trust: income tax consequences

4.85   The trustees will be liable to income tax on UK source income, for example:

- dividends from UK companies, which will carry the 10% non-repayable tax credit;

- interest on income from bank deposits, etc, which may have suffered a 20% withholding at source; and

- gross income received from rents as a property business.

Discretionary or accumulation trusts will be subject to income tax at 40% (or the dividend trust rate at 32.5% on dividends), notwithstanding that they are non-UK resident. It would obviously be advisable for such trusts not to own UK property.

Anti-avoidance regime for settlors and beneficiaries

4.86   There is a complex set of provisions in *ITA 2007, Pt 13, Ch 2* comprising the separate transferor and benefits charges. The first of these generally catches the settlor of the trust (as the 'transferor') and the second the beneficiary (as the recipient of a 'benefit' from a trust). The regime applies where a transfer of assets has been made and as a consequence of which income becomes payable to persons resident or domiciled outside the UK and:

- in the case of the transferor charge the settlor who is ordinarily resident in the UK has 'power to enjoy' the income of the non-UK resident person, in this case trustees, or receives a capital sum from the trustees. Where this applies, the income is treated as that of the settlor;

- under the benefits charge a beneficiary ordinarily resident in the UK receives a benefit from the trustees and there is in the trust either for that or preceding tax years 'relevant income', viz income out of which a benefit can be paid.

Both charging regimes have a limitation in that, where the settlor or beneficiary is domiciled outside the UK and the income arises and remains outside the UK or the benefit is enjoyed outside the UK, the remittance basis applies (subject to a claim) to relieve any charge to tax.

Both regimes have also historically had the benefit of a 'purpose test' (before 2007/08, in *ICTA 1988, s 741*), ie they will not apply if it can be shown that:

- tax avoidance was not a purpose of the transfer in the first place; or

- the transfer was a *bona fide* commercial transaction and was not designed to avoid a tax liability.

With effect from 5 December 2005, the 'purpose test' has been tightened up through what is now to be found in *ITA 2007, ss 736–742*. A person will escape liability under either regime only if he satisfies HMRC that either Condition A or Condition B is met:

- Condition A is that it would not be reasonable to draw the conclusion, from all the circumstances of the case, that the purpose of avoiding liability to taxation was the purpose, or one of the purposes, for which the relevant transactions or any of them were effected;

- Condition B is that:

    - all the relevant transactions were genuine commercial transactions, and

    - it would not be reasonable to draw the conclusion, from all the circumstances of the case, that any one or more of those transactions was more than incidentally designed for the purpose of avoiding liability to taxation.

- Further provisions fill out this new exemption and, in particular, deal with cases where there are transactions both before and on or after 5 December 2005.

Charities

Form SA 907

4.87   Supplemental form SA 907 is different from the other forms in so far as it constitutes a claim to exemption from tax and requires signature.

Separate references must be stated for HMRC charity repayment reference and the Charity Commission registration number (or if in Scotland the Scottish charity number).

Form SA 907 envisages that the claim to exemption may be for part rather than all of the charity's income and gains, though usually it would be for all. It must be confirmed that all income and gains claimed to be exempt have been, or will be applied, for charitable purposes.

Information must be returned either for the year ended 5 April 2009 or for a period ending in that tax year. Accounts should be enclosed.

Repayments may have already been claimed on form R68 though further repayments may be due.

The form asks for a summary of the heads of income on which exemption is claimed, for expenses as included in the charity accounts and summary of assets.

Example 4.20—Charity income and gains

The Russian Orphanage Trust established by Zebedee (see Example 3.7 at **3.30**) should submit each year:

- form SA 900; and
- supplementary page SA 907.

The income of the trust comprises principally of dividends but also of a small amount of interest.

As for the dividends, charities like other taxpayers, suffer from the present regime of dividend taxation, applying from 6 April 1999. Interest income can be paid gross.

Any gains made by the trustees on selling shares will be free from CGT.

The trustees are well able to certify that all income and gains have been, or will be applied for charitable purposes.

INTEREST

Different types of income

4.88   Question 9 on pages 4 and 5 of the trust and estate tax return, asks 'Did the trust or estate receive any other income not already included on the supplementary pages?'. A look at pages 5 to 8 of the trust and estate tax calculation guide will show a distinction between:

● income other than savings or dividend type income (carried through from the supplementary pages, viz, trade, partnership, land and property, foreign income and other income);

● savings type income; 20%; and

● dividend type income; 10%.

Deemed income will include proceeds of a company purchase of own shares (with a 10% non-payable tax credit).

Income carried over from any of the supplementary pages will feature in the first column. The next four columns respond to question 9 of the main tax return.

Savings type income

4.89   The heading 'savings type income' responds to the main subheading, interest, on page 3 of the tax return. The interest may have been received gross, or net, ie subject to deduction of tax. Interest received gross from UK banks, building societies and deposit takers is entered in Box 9.1. At Boxes 9.2 to 9.4, the trustees should enter:

● the net amount received;

● the amount of tax deducted; and

● the gross amount of interest before deduction of tax.

Gross or net receipt

4.90   Most interest will be received net, that is after deduction of tax at 20% (the 'lower' savings rate). Interest from the National Savings Bank will be received gross (recognised at Box 9.8). Otherwise, in a situation where there are no resident UK beneficiaries, it is possible to achieve gross payment by either a bank or a building society. Gross payment is not possible if the trustees are non-UK resident, but there are UK resident beneficiaries.

Types of interest

4.91

● Interest from UK banks, building societies and deposit takers:

  – paid gross; or

  – paid net after deduction of tax.

- Interest on certificates of tax deposits where applied in payment of a tax liability.

- Interest on government stocks.

- Interest on other loan stocks.

- The interest element within purchased life annuities.

- Interest distributions from UK authorised unit trusts and open-ended investment companies (note, not dividends).

- National Savings (other than First Option and Fixed Rate Savings Bonds) – paid gross.

- National Savings First Option and Fixed Rate Savings Bonds.

- Other income from UK savings and investments (except dividends).

Tax vouchers

4.92   A payment of interest will usually be accompanied by a tax voucher, issued by the borrowing institution. Note the position with accumulation units or shares in UK authorised unit trusts and open-ended investment companies, when the interest distribution is automatically reinvested in the unit trust or open-ended investment company. The gross interest, tax deducted and net interest distribution invested must still be returned and income tax paid.

By contrast, any amount shown on the tax voucher as 'equalisation' is not subject to income tax being a repayment of capital. When CGT is calculated, the amount of equalisation should be deducted from the cost of the units or shares purchased during the year.

Calculation of tax deduction where not shown on the voucher

4.93   Suppose the statement reveals interest paid of £80 after tax:

Tax deducted after tax amount 25%: £8,025% £20.

Suppose the statement shows interest of £100 before tax:

Tax deducted before tax amount 20%: £8,025% £20.

ACCRUED INCOME SCHEME

4.94   Interest-bearing securities such as government loan stock (or gilts) will be acquired (or sold) either 'ex-dividend' (or 'ex-div') or 'cum-dividend' (or 'cum-div'). A purchase ex-div means that the next interest payment belongs to the seller; whereas a purchase cum-div will be entitled to the next interest payment. The fact that a security may be ex-div or cum-div will be reflected in the price.

The aim behind this scheme is to ensure that each person pays income tax on the interest on securities, which accrues during his period of legal ownership. Tax is, therefore, charged on an accruals basis and by reference to legal rather than beneficial ownership (*ITA 2007, Pt 12*).

Trust law/tax law difference

4.95 For trust law the purchase price of a security cum-div is paid out of capital and the proceeds of sale will be a capital receipt. For tax law, the accrued income scheme seeks to identify the element of income arising in a purchase or sale and to subject that income to income tax.

Scope of the scheme

4.96 The accrued income scheme includes all interest-bearing securities including permanent interest-bearing shares in a building society, government loan stock and company loan stock, though not including shares in a company or National Savings Certificates (*ITA 2007, s 619*).

There is a *de minimis* exemption from the scheme if the nominal value of all the accrued income securities held by an individual, or by trustees of a disabled trust, or by personal representatives, did not exceed £5,000 throughout that year and the preceding year (*ITA 2007, s 639*). However, there is no such general exemption for trustees.

How the scheme works

4.97 When trustees purchase interest-bearing securities cum-interest, they are treated as purchasing the interest that had accrued by the settlement date of the transfer. The accrued interest is called the 'rebate' amount. Note that a gift to trustees carries the same consequence. Similarly, when the trustees sell cum-interest, they are treated as having received the accrued interest as income, known as the 'accrued amount', which is assessable on the trustees and is shown on the stockbroker's contract note (*ITA 2007, ss 628–635*).

Relief is given for the rebate amount either against the next interest received from that security or against the accrued interest on sale, whichever comes first. The relief can be given in a different year of assessment from that in which the purchase is made.

Each security must be dealt with separately. The total of all the chargeable amounts should be entered by personal representatives in Box 9.14, but by trustees in Box 9.38.

Example 4.21—Accrued income scheme: purchase of stock

24 May 2008: Trustees buy £10,000 of 5% Treasury Stock 2018

Accrued interest therein is £106.85 (7 March to 24 May)

7 September 2008: Interest payment

Interest paid gross	£250.00
Relief for accrued interest in the purchase	(£106.85)
Income for tax purposes	£143.15

Example 4.22—Accrued income scheme: sale of stock

24 May 2008: Trustees buy as in Example 4.21

24 June 2008: Sale of stock

Accrued interest:		
On sale	106 days	£145.20
On purchase	178 days	£106.85
Assessable (as miscellaneous income)		£38.35

Example 4.23—Life tenant entitled to income

The whole of the interest received belongs to the beneficiary. There are two views:

● Method 1: In Example 4.21, the beneficiary receives the income plus the tax recovery;

● Method 2: Alternatively, if the trustees must pay tax on the accrued income out of capital, which is the case for trust law, they should retain the recovery on a rebate amount.

HMRC do not mind which method is used, as in either case the statutory income is £143.15 gross.

The trustees receive:

Gross interest	£250
Less tax	(£50)
Net	£200

Recovery of tax on rebate amount:

$$£ 143.15 @ 20\% = £28.63$$

- Method 1: If the beneficiary receives the tax recovery as well as the interest, he has £228.63.

- Method 2: If the trustees withhold the recovery, the beneficiary has £200.

DIVIDENDS

4.98 The system of dividend taxation changed with effect from 6 April 1999 (tax year 1999/2000). This book does not deal with the 'old system'.

The non-repayable tax credit

4.99 A dividend from a UK company carries a 10% tax credit, which is generally non-repayable, but is set against the taxpayer's liability to tax (*ITTOIA 2005, s 397*). The same principle applies to 'other qualifying distributions' from UK companies, which are not dividends. Similarly, with dividend distributions from UK-authorised unit trusts and open-ended investment companies, shown separately on page 4 of the tax return.

The dividend voucher from the UK company (or authorised unit trust or open-ended investment company) will show separately the net amount received, the tax credit and the gross dividend or distribution.

Dividends received from non-UK companies will be foreign income dealt with on supplementary page SA 904.

Example 4.24—Trustees self assessing dividend income

In 2008/09 the trustees receive dividends from UK companies totalling £4,500 carrying a tax credit of £500, representing gross income of £5,000. They also receive a distribution from an authorised UK unit trust of £900, carrying a tax credit of £100.

The amounts are entered as follows:

Box					
9.15	£4,500	9.16	£500	9.17	£5,000
9.18	£900	9.19	£100	9.20	£1,000

SCRIP (OR STOCK) DIVIDENDS

4.100 A company may choose to pay a dividend, not in cash but in the form of shares in itself. This assumes that the company has the power to do so in its articles of association. A company was more likely to pay a scrip dividend before the dividend regime changed on 6 April 1999. This was because, before then, a cash dividend carried an obligation for the company to make a payment of 'advance corporation tax' (ACT) to HMRC, which did not apply to scrip dividends. There was, therefore, a possible cash flow advantage to the company, especially in circumstances where it did not have a liability to mainstream corporation tax against which the ACT could be offset. Now, however, the old disadvantage for the company continues, that is in watering down its equity, and therefore such a dividend might be expected to be relatively uncommon. That said, however, as illustrated by Example 4.25, the use of pre-sale stock dividends could before 2008/09 significantly reduce the liability of the shareholders to CGT.

Trustees

4.101 Trustees of discretionary or accumulation trusts are treated as having received the 'cash equivalent of the share capital', which is either the amount of a cash alternative or the market value of the shares received (*ITTOIA 2005, ss 410(3), 411(2)* and *412*). The trustees are treated as if the dividend had been chargeable to the dividend ordinary rate tax: the trustees will have a further 22.5% income tax liability (ie the difference between the dividend trust rate of 32.5% and the 10% tax credit).

Trustees of life interest trusts are treated as though the appropriate amount in cash was received by the individual life tenant (*ITTOIA 2005, s 410(2)*). The beneficiary will have an additional tax liability only if he is a higher rate taxpayer. There is a further problem, however, in that as a matter of trust law, the stock dividend may be received by the trustees as capital, although of course the life tenant is entitled to income. This is a problem that arises especially with 'enhanced' stock dividends where the value of the stock may be say, 50% higher than a cash alternative: the problem is illustrated in Example 4.30 at **4.117**. The easiest solution with an ordinary stock dividend would, no doubt, be for the trustees simply to treat the life tenant as receiving the stock with no further tax liability for the trustees and any additional tax depending upon the personal circumstances of the beneficiary.

Personal representatives

4.102   A stock dividend received by the PRs is treated as forming part of the aggregate estate income (*ITTOIA 2005, s 413(4)(a)*). They will have no further tax liability. The stock dividend will be a 'non-qualifying distribution' and a payment to a beneficiary funded out of it will be taxed as made under the deduction of non-repayable dividend ordinary rate tax. Therefore, a beneficiary will be taxed on a payment from the estate as if he had received the distribution direct.

Example 4.25—Pre-sale dividends

Pre-sale dividends have been used for some time to extract value from a company in a tax efficient way in order to reduce the shareholder's liability to CGT. To do so, however, the company must have sufficient distributable profit or reserves: if not, a stock dividend can provide a useful solution.

Sarah had acquired for £100,000 all the shares in a trading company, for which she had received an offer of £500,000 in 2007/08. She is a higher rate taxpayer and, apart from the annual exemption, her liability to CGT would be £160,000. The company had no distributable reserves. The company decided, instead of a dividend, to issue new shares on the basis of four for one.

For CGT purposes, the original shares must be treated separately from the new shares. 20% of the proceeds of sale, that is £100,000, are attributed to the original shares, with no chargeable gain.

The remaining £400,000 is treated as given for the new shares. This attracts income tax rather than CGT. Because the sale of the company followed immediately after the issue of the stock dividend, the stock dividend is valued on the basis of the sale consideration, ie £400,000. Income tax on this amount is charged at 22.5% (ie the dividend upper rate after the tax credit) viz £90,000.

The saving to Sarah was thus £70,000 (£160,000 – £90,000).

Had this happened in 2008/09, with the reduction in the CGT rate to 18%, the comparison would be rather different, as the CGT payable, in the absence of a stock dividend, would be £72,000 – or even £40,000 if Sarah was entitled to the entrepreneurs' relief. And so the CGT analysis is more favourable than an income tax liability.

LIFE INSURANCE POLICIES ETC

Non-qualifying policies and chargeable events

4.103   There is a general exemption from CGT on qualifying life insurance policies (*TCGA 1992, s 210(2)*). However, there is a very complex set of provisions in the income tax legislation, which charge to income tax certain gains on non-qualifying policies (*ITTOIA 2005, Pt 4, Ch 9*). Details here are requested on page 5 of form SA 900. Where the gain is paid gross, the amount is entered in Box 9.29; where net, the gain is put in 9.31 with the tax deducted in Box 9.30.

Cases where income tax arises are called 'chargeable events' and the relevant insurance company will be able to advise whether the particular policy is exempt from tax or whether the gain triggers income tax. Very often the insurance company will already have informed HMRC of the event and the gain.

Where the chargeable event is the death of the policyholder, the income will usually be that of the individual for the year in which he died, and therefore is properly entered in form SA 900. In very rare circumstances, a gain will be taxed on the personal representatives, but only to the extent that tax at the basic rate has *not* been deducted.

If the person who made the policy wrote the benefits in trust, any gain will usually be treated as his income *unless* he was non-UK resident or dead when the chargeable event occurred (*ITTOIA 2005, ss 465, 467*). If, therefore, he had died by the time of the chargeable event, the gain will be taxed on the trustees at 40%.

Other income

4.104   Specifically mentioned at the foot of page 5 is proceeds received from a company when it purchases its own shares. The general tax rule is that the cash received by the shareholder is treated as income, unless (in prescribed circumstances) the shareholder qualifies for capital investment. The company will usually get confirmation from HMRC in advance whether income or capital investment applies.

However, in 2008/09 (and indeed since 1997), where the shareholders are trustees, they will be taxed at the dividend trust rate of 32.5% less the 10% tax credit (except in a case where the trust is settlor-interested and the proceeds will be taxed on the settlor, whether as capital or as income). Such distributions are treated as dividends and, like dividends, the associated tax credit is not repayable.

Qualifying policies

4.105

- Whole of life policies (whether single life or joint lives and survivor).

- Term assurance.

- Endowment policies for at least ten years (or the earlier death of the life assured). No capital payment must be made other than on whole or partial surrender of the policy. Premiums must be payable at least annually.

Non-qualifying policies

4.106

- Single premium bonds.

- Term assurance of less than ten years unless the surrender value does not exceed the premiums paid.

- Certain unit-linked whole of life policies.

Chargeable events on non-qualifying policies

4.107   These include (under *ITTOIA 2005, s 484*):

- Death of the life assured.

- Maturity of the policy.

- Surrender in whole of the policy rights.

- Assignment for money or money's worth of the rights under the policy.

DISCRETIONARY PAYMENTS OF INCOME

4.108 Question 14 on page 8 of the tax return asks, 'Have discretionary payments of income been made to beneficiaries?' Seven boxes are provided to give the names of the beneficiaries and the amount of the payment (which will be a net payment). Further, a box is to be ticked if the beneficiary was a minor and unmarried child of the settlor who was alive when the payment was made; this is because the income will be taxed on the settlor (see **4.30–4.31**).

The purpose of this question is to ensure that payments of income are made subject to the deduction of tax at 40% (see **4.41–4.43**). This is a requirement of *ITA 2007, Pt 9, Ch 7*. If the trustees have paid income tax in the past, which has not already been used to 'frank' income payments to beneficiaries, this will constitute the 'tax pool' which can be used to pay over the tax due on distributions. Hence, Box 14.15 asks for details of any amount of an unused tax pool brought forward from 2007/08.

The tax pool

4.109 The tax pool is of use only insofar as the trust continues within the discretionary or accumulation regime: see **4.112** for an example. Hence, it is very important to ensure that the tax pool is 'stripped' in the years before (for example) an accumulation and maintenance settlement ceases to be such, whether before 6 April 2008 or after 5 April 2008. Interestingly, if there are several beneficiaries of an A&M trust, and one of them attains 25, this does not in itself reduce the tax pool. The regime will apply if:

● a payment is made by the trustees in an exercise of discretion; and

● the sum is income of the beneficiary for tax purposes.

Note that it is possible that the tax pool may disappear from some future year (subject to a transitional period of say three years), following the present consultation on the taxation of trusts: see the Appendix.

Income or capital

4.110 Decided cases have addressed the situation (and possible argument by HMRC) that a payment of capital by the trustees might constitute income in the hands of the beneficiary. Now, however, HMRC apply a relatively relaxed practice – see **4.65**.

The tax voucher

4.111   After making a payment to the beneficiary, the trustees must also complete a tax voucher (R185 (Trust Income)), showing the gross income, the amount of tax deducted and paid to HMRC and the net sum to which the beneficiary is entitled.

Example 4.26—Trustees' tax liability on distributing income (for 2008/09)

Assume the trustees have post-tax dividend income of £67.50, having paid the 32.5% dividend trust rate of £22.50 with £10 met by the tax credit. The tax paid by the trustees, though not the tax credit, can be used to 'frank' the tax under *ITA 2007, s 466* which they must deduct on making the distribution.

Net income of trust		(£67.50)
S 496 liability on gross payment of £90 to beneficiary	£36.00	
Met by trustees' payment above	(£22.50)	
Remaining liability of trustees	(£13.50)	(£13.50)
Available for distribution to beneficiary		£54.00
Grossed up under *s 494* @ 40%		£36.00
Gross income of beneficiary		£90.00
Tax thereon @ 40% (met by trustees)		(£36.00)
		–
Net income of beneficiary		£54.00

The point therefore is that, in the absence of a brought forward tax pool to pay the £13.50 above, a higher rate taxpayer will receive only £54 cash out of an original gross dividend received by the trustees of £100, an effective rate of tax for the beneficiary of 46%.

Operation of the tax pool

4.112

Example 4.27—Tax pool illustration

Imagine that the trustees have brought forward to 2008/09 cash of £5,500 and a tax pool of £4,500. If in 2008/09 they distribute to a beneficiary the net cash as income, form R185 (Trust Income) given to the beneficiary would show:

Gross	£9,167
Tax @ 40%	(£3,667)
Net	£5,500

In the absence of any other transactions the tax pool would be:

Brought forward	£4,500
Used 2008/09	(£3,667)
Balance carried forward	£883

LOSSES

4.113 A trading loss will arise in a particular year where the allowable expenses exceed the taxable income. The loss may be set against general income of that or the preceding tax year and, to the extent unused, may be carried forward against future profits from that trade (*ITA 2007, s 64*).

FA 2009, Sch 6 has extended the periods of carry back loss relief for trades incurred in 2008/09 and 2009/10. Losses remaining after carry back to the preceding year can be carried back, up to a maximum of £50,000, against income of the two preceding years, with losses carried back against later years first.

A property business loss can be carried forward for use only against future property business profits (*ITA 2007, s 118*).

Trust management expenses may exceed the income in that year and this will trigger a loss. Some, though not all, of the losses may be set against certain types of income from other transactions in the category of 'other income' of which the gross amount is shown in Box 9.34. In the absence of such income, losses can be carried forward to be set against similar income in future years. Losses cannot be set against annual payments.

4.114 Trading losses in 2008/09 may be:

* offset against other income for 2008/09;

* carried back to 2007/08; or

* carried back (not exceeding £50,000) to 2006/07 and then 2005/06; or

* carried forward against future profits from that trade.

There are provisions that restrict losses from farming or market gardening where more than five years of consecutive loss have occurred (subject to concessionary relief such as in the circumstances of foot and mouth).

Page TT2 asks for details of any share of investment income arising for the partnership and share of losses on partnership investments. Box 2.25 is the 'white space'.

Example 4.28—Partnership losses

Adam has transferred a one-third share in his family farm into a new discretionary settlement. The partnership capital is £330,000. The partnership is a limited partnership under the *Limited Partnerships Act 1907*. Adam is the general partner with a two-thirds share of the income and capital and the trustees, a limited partner, with one-third. For the year ended 31 March 2008 there is a loss of £15,000. A similar loss accrued in the previous year.

Form SA 902 is completed showing the trustees' share of the loss of £5,000 in Box 2.7. The whole of the loss is shown in Box 2.15 as offset against other income for 2008/09.

INTEREST PAYMENTS BY TRUSTEES

Deductible interest

4.115   The tax system gives relief for interest paid by trustees in certain circumstances, eg:

- interest on money borrowed for use as capital in a trade (*ITTOIA 2005, ss 29* and *52*); and

- interest on a loan to purchase property let within a property business (*ITTOIA 2005, s 272(1)*).

All the above will be recognised as deductions in computing the profits of the trade, partnership or property business as the case may be.

There are other statutory reliefs for payments of interest, given generally to 'a person' under *ITA 2007, s 383*, which of course includes trustees as well as an individual. However, most of the specific provisions in that part of *ITA 2007* are, perhaps somewhat curiously, restricted to individuals, for example the relief under *ss 398* and *399* on interest paid on a loan to invest in a partnership. That said, it is possible that HMRC have not challenged some claims to interest relief by trustees which are not allowed by the legislation. HMRC have confirmed that the statutory distinction in treatment as between individuals and trustees is correct.

Non-deductible interest

4.116 Certain types of interest are not allowable, eg interest on overdue tax.

Question 10A on page 6 of the trust and estate return is phrased 'do you want to claim any reliefs or have you made any annual payments?' These might be:

- Interest (or alternative finance payments) eligible for relief on qualifying loans, of which the only one mentioned is a loan to pay IHT. This relief is given *only* to personal representatives to pay IHT before a grant of probate, but only in respect of personal property, ie not including tax on land. Relief is given solely on interest paid for one year. If the interest cannot be relieved in the year of payment it can be carried back to the previous year and then forward to subsequent years of assessment (*ITA 2007, ss 403–405*).

- Other charges, viz annuities and other annual payments. Here the trustees must deduct basic rate tax and account to the beneficiary for the net amount as recorded on a tax deduction certificate. The assumption is that the trustees have, in the relevant tax year, taxable income equal at least to the amount of the gross annuity. If not, and there is a shortfall, the trustees are taxable on it, ie they will find themselves out of pocket, which they may have to make good by resorting to capital.

Example 4.29—Annuity (2008/09)

The trustees have income of £10,000 made up as follows:

		Tax	Gross
Dividend income	£900	£100	£1,000
Interest	£3,200	£800	£4,000
Rental income	£4,000	£1,000	£5,000

The trust deed requires the trustees to pay a gross annuity of £3,600. Tax on this is £720. They have sufficient income to pay the annuity out of income and thus fill in the return as follows:

Box
10A.2   £2,880   10A.3   £720   10A.4   £3,600

ANNUAL PAYMENTS OUT OF CAPITAL

Duty to withhold tax

4.117 Question 11 also embraces annual payments out of income not brought into charge to income tax. On making the annual payment the trustees must withhold tax at the basic rate for 2008/09 (20%) which they hand to HMRC paying over to the beneficiary the balance only. The beneficiary also receives a tax deduction certificate and may be able to reclaim the tax or, if a higher rate tax payer, will have to pay a further 20% on the gross amount.

If the trustees do not have income, or sufficient income, to make the payment, it will be made out of capital and the trustees must account for the tax due to HMRC.

Examples might be:

- an annuity paid out of capital; or

- as mentioned in the return guide notes, enhanced scrip dividends received by the trustees against which they have made compensatory payments out of capital to beneficiaries. As explained in **4.100–4.102**, the trustees must determine, as a matter of trust law, whether the enhanced scrip dividend is received as trust income or as trust capital. Here they face a conundrum as illustrated below.

Example 4.30—Enhanced stock dividend

Trustees receive an enhanced stock dividend worth £150, which has a 'cash alternative' of £100. This belongs to the capital of the trust. The trustees decide to compensate the life tenant for loss of the income and, following the case of *Re Malam, Malam v Hitchens* [1894] 3 Ch 578, they pay the life tenant the value of the cash alternative, namely £100 gross or, after deduction of basic rate tax, £80.

According to HMRC, the trustees make an annual payment from which they must deduct basic rate tax. As a matter of trust law they must balance the interests of income and capital beneficiaries. With a net amount of £100 and grossing up at 20%, the gross income becomes £125. However, that might prejudice the capital beneficiaries and/or require the trustees to sell some of the shares.

Therefore, they might deduct the basic rate tax from the cash equivalent and distribute the balance. However, no tax credit is due and a life tenant who is a higher rate taxpayer, would therefore be worse off as a result. That is, the beneficiary is much worse on the stock dividend alternative than receiving a cash dividend.

	Cash dividend	*Re Malam analysis*
Beneficiary's gross income	£111.11	
Less tax credit	(£11.11)	
Beneficiary's cash receipt	£100	£80
Less higher rate tax: 32.5% of £111.11 less tax credit of £11.11	(25.00)	
Less 20% higher rate tax on £100 gross		(£20)
Beneficiary's net cash receipt	£75	£60

Given also the professional costs of dealing with usually relatively small amounts plus the CGT implications of selling the stock, etc it is likely, as explained in **4.100–4.102**, to be better to take the cash alternative. Happily, such situations are comparatively rare.

TRUST MANAGEMENT EXPENSES

Trust and tax law

4.118   While the distinction between income and capital will generally be the same for tax law as it is for trust law, this will not always be the case; for example, some capital receipts for trust law purposes are subject to income tax (generally for anti-avoidance reasons). This parallel is true with expenses, in that while a particular expense may be properly deductible against trust income, it will not necessarily be deductible for tax purposes.

An expense may be deducted from trust income if:

● it is under trust law properly chargeable against income, eg management expenses of a property within a property business; and

● it is actually paid out of income for the year.

In *Bosanquet v Allan; Carver v Duncan* [1985] AC 1082, the House of Lords held that, in the absence of special provisions in the trust deed, premiums on life assurance policies were chargeable to capital not to income. A well-drawn trust deed will allow trustees to set such premiums, however, either against income or against capital. Legal expenses or fees paid to other professional advisers, which are not directly referable to the income, should be charged to capital.

Following a review of the tax implications of management expenses, HMRC issued on 2 February 2006 a final version of their guidance paper first released in draft in September 2004. Detailed attention should be given to these expressed principles, with any deviation clearly noted in the 'white space' in the self-assessment return. Following the House of Lords decision in *Carver v Duncan*, HMRC expressed the view that an expense, even if recurrent, which is incurred for the benefit of the whole trust fund, should be charged to capital. There is only limited scope for apportionment, in the case of some accountancy and audit fees. The main disagreement with the professional bodies is the trustees' annual management fee, which HMRC claim is to be charged wholly to capital.

4.119   The test case on trust management expenses was finally decided by the Court of Appeal on 19 December 2008. There were five categories of disputed fees: the accountancy fees, the custodian fees, the trustee management fees, the bank charges and the investment managers' fees. Following the decisions of the Special Commissioner and the High Court (largely in favour of the taxpayers and HMRC, respectively), it had been agreed between the parties and the Court of Appeal held that a proper apportionment between income and capital was permitted for all of the bank charges, custodian fees and the professional fees for accountancy and administration.

4.120   That left the substantive issue of the deductibility of the fees paid to both the executive and the non-executive trustees. Here the Court of Appeal ruled in favour in principle of the taxpayer trustees (*RCC v Trustees of the Peter Clay Discretionary Trust* [2008] EWCA Civ 1441). The Special Commissioners had erred in law in ruling in favour of an attribution between income and capital in respect of the trust management fees on 'the general principle of fairness'. This approach was not permissible in the light of the House of Lords decision in *Carver v Duncan*. However, in finding for an apportionment for the fees charged by the executive trustee, the Court of Appeal went on to say that, if professional fees incurred by the trustees for accountancy services could properly be apportioned on a time basis between income and capital, it was impossible to see why the fees charged by the executive trustee should not also be capable of apportionment. Indeed, there was no reason in principle why the, much smaller, fixed, fees of the non-executive trustees could not also be apportioned insofar as it could be estimated, if not ascertained, what part of their time was devoted to income matters. Finally, as to the investment management fees, those were chargeable against capital as determined by the Special Commissioners; only (which was not the case here) could expenses incurred before the trustees had made the decision to accumulate income be charged against income. The decision is now final. HMRC will no doubt have to amend their guidance paper on management expenses.

Trust management expenses

Life interest trusts

4.121 Subject to specific deductions in calculating taxable income, eg for trade or property business purposes, trust management expenses are deducted from the life tenant's net share of income, which is then grossed up to produce the statutory taxable income.

Discretionary or accumulation trusts

4.122 Trust management expenses may be deducted from the income taxed at the rate applicable to trusts or at the dividend trust rate. However, such expenses cannot be deducted in calculating the income taxed only at the 10% dividend rate or the 20% basic rate (for 2008/09 and 2009/10).

Expenses are deducted in the order that is most useful to the beneficiary:

● UK dividend or scrip dividends, which carry a non-repayable 10% tax credit;

● foreign dividends for which a claim is made for the non-repayable tax credit under *ITTOIA 2005, s 397A*;

● foreign dividends not carrying such a tax credit; and

● 20% rate income,

Two useful examples are given on pages 22 and 23 of the Trust and Estate Tax Return Guide; see Examples 4.31 and 4.32.

Example 4.31—Allowable expenses: HMRC's Example A

The total trust income is £5,000, comprising rental income of £4,000 and interest of £800 (lower rate tax of £200 has been deducted). £500 is allocated for specific purposes. You pay allowable expenses of £500. One-half of the income is taxable at the rate applicable to trusts. You can calculate the amount of income taxable at the rate applicable to trusts as follows:

	Rent	Interest
Income	4,000	1,000
minus		
income allocated for specific purposes (apportioned at a ratio of 4:1)	(400)	(100)
	3,600	900
minus		
income not taxable at the rate applicable to trusts	(1,800)	(450)
	1,800	450

		Rent	Interest
Expenses	500		
minus apportioned to income allocated for specific purposes $500 \times \dfrac{500}{5,000}$	(50)		
minus	450		
apportioned to income not taxable at the special trust rates $450 \times \dfrac{2,250}{4,450}$	(225)		
Allowable against income taxable at the special trust rates			(281)
Amount taxable at special trust rates		**1,800**	**169**

Example 4.32—Allowable expenses: HMRC's Example B

You are trustee of a trust in which the beneficiary has a life interest. (The beneficiary is called a 'life tenant'.) In 2008/09 you receive rental income of £1,000 and bank interest of £800 (basic rate tax of £200 has been deducted) and pay allowable expenses of £250.

	Rent	Interest
Your gross income is	1,000	1,000
Tax due from you	200	200
Net income	800	800

You will receive credit for the tax deducted at source from the bank interest (£200) so you will have to pay £200 in tax.

The life tenant's income for tax purposes will be:

	Rent	*Interest*
Net income (as above)	800	800
minus		
Management expenses	–	(250)
	800	550
Grossed (@ 20%)	£1,000	£687

CAPITAL PAYMENTS

4.123   Questions 15 and 15A require details of two types of capital payment made by the trustees.

Payments to settlor's children

4.124   These are capital payments to, or for the benefit of, minor unmarried children of the settlor during the settlor's lifetime.

Such payments will include the transfer of assets as well as cash. This is relevant in the context of *ITTOIA 2005, ss 629* to *632* (see **4.30–4.31**). The rule cannot be avoided by the trustees purporting to distribute capital when there remains within the trust a balance of undistributed income, which might otherwise escape assessment on the settlor. Of course, if all the income has been distributed and assessed on the settlor, there will be no further income tax implications for the trustees making such capital payments.

Example 4.33—Parental income

The trustees of a pre-9 March 1999 parental settlement have undistributed income from 2007/08 of £2,500 and from 2008/09 of £5,000. On 31 March 2009, they advance to a child £10,000 of capital. £7,500 is assessed on the settlor for 2007/08 under *ITTOIA 2005, s 629*.

Capital transactions between the trustees and the settlors

4.125   This refers to the anti-avoidance provision in *ITTOIA 2005, ss 633– 642*. The anti-avoidance rules for settlements have traditionally attacked situations where the trustees have retained undistributed income in the trust that HMRC perceive is being used for the benefit of the settlor. The particular mischief in question is where the trustees lend money to the settlor, or repay money to the settlor that the settlor has previously lent. Payments to the settlor's spouse are caught, as are payments to a third party at the direction of the settlor, or payments that may be applied for the settlor's benefit. The capital sum might be paid directly or through a company connected with the settlor.

Answers to this question might trigger situations where these rules might be in point. This could have the result that, for up to a period of ten years, any undistributed income would be assessed on the settlor up to the amount of the capital payment.

Example 4.34—Repayment of loan to settlor

(Based on a 1964 House of Lords decision *De Vigier v IRC* [1964] 1 WLR 1073.)

The trustees wanted to take up a rights issue on shares that they owned. To do so they borrowed money from the wife of the settlor. They repaid the money within the year. However, the trustees had undistributed income and the settlor was assessed up to the amount of the loan. The amount of the repayment is assessed on the settlor to the extent that it falls within the income available up to the end of that tax year or the following ten years.

The tax is charged on the relevant amount, grossed up at 40% (with the 40% tax credit). Accordingly, £10,000 is grossed up to £16,667, producing a tax liability of £6,667 for a higher rate taxpayer. Interestingly, the settlor has no right of reimbursement for the tax from the trustees (as he has elsewhere in the settlement code). However, set against the tax chargeable on the settlor is 'the deductible amount' computed under *ITTOIA 2005, s 640*. This is expressed as the lowest of three amounts and has the effect (in particular) that tax paid by the trustees on the grossed up income available during the tax year in question such as corresponds to the sum assessed on the settlor constitutes the deductible amount. This effectively avoids double taxation and so in circumstances where as at present the special rates for trustees and the marginal rate for individuals are the same, the settlor effectively suffers no penalty.

CALCULATION OF TAX

4.126   The trustee who has managed to wade through the tax return to question 17, and is then faced with the question 'Do you want to calculate the tax?' may be forgiven for answering, 'No' with no little gusto.

If he wants HMRC to calculate the tax for 2008/09, he must ensure that the completed form is with HMRC on or before 31 October 2009. This will give HMRC time to calculate the income tax and CGT due, after taking into account the instalments paid on 1 January and 31 July 2009, and to tell the trustees before 31 January 2010 how much they have to pay.

If the trustees want HMRC to calculate the tax, but get the form in after 31 October, HMRC will still do so, but with no guarantee that they will meet the 31 January deadline. In this case the trustees have satisfied their statutory obligation to make the return, though if they wish to avoid paying interest on tax, they should estimate the amount due and pay it on or before 31 January 2010. That said, see **4.9** and **4.128**.

If on the other hand the trustees do want to calculate the tax, they should make use of form SA 951, the 2008/09 Trust and Estate Tax Calculation Guide (see **4.66**), in which event HMRC will have the opportunity to amend the trustees' self assessment.

Repayments due

4.127   If it turns out (or there is a possibility) that the trust has paid too much tax, the 'Yes' box, question 18 must be ticked. If not, any amount owed will be set against the next tax bill (which will normally happen if the amount is small, eg below £10). A repayment made on or before 31 January 2009, will not carry interest from HMRC. If paid thereafter, repayment supplement (which is non-taxable) will be due; see **4.18** for the rates (currently nil).

Tax year 2008/09: relevant dates and time limits

4.128

First payment on account	31 January 2009
Second payment on account	31 July 2009
Deadline for submission of tax return if HMRC are to calculate the tax liability	31 October 2009
Notification of liability to tax, if no return received	5 October 2009
Tax return to be submitted by and tax paid by*	31 January 2010
Tax enquiry window (return submitted on 31 January 2010)**	31 January 2011
Discovery assessments (fraud or neglect)	
Business records to be retained until	31 January 2015

*   31 October 2009 is the due date for submission of paper returns (and 31 January 2010 for online returns). But no penalty will be levied for late submission of a paper return if it is filed, and all tax due is paid, on or before 31 January 2010.

**   If a return is submitted before 31 January 2010, the enquiry window closes 12 months following submission of the return. If later than 31 January 2010, the window closes 12 months after the end of the quarter in which the return was submitted.

Chapter 5

Running a trust: capital gains tax

THE REGIME IN SUMMARY

Actual and deemed disposals

5.1   CGT is payable on actual disposals, which include a gift (*TCGA 1992, s 1*). CGT is charged also on deemed disposals, eg where within a life interest trust (which does not fall within the relevant property regime, as made on or after 22 March 2006), the life tenant dies or where, within any type of trust, one or more beneficiaries becomes absolutely entitled to the property against the trustees. This situation is discussed in more detail in **9.5–9.11**.

Disposal proceeds

5.2   The gain has to be calculated. In simple terms the gain is the sale proceeds less the cost of acquisition. In the case of a gift, the market value at the date of the gift is used. The same 'market value' rule applies where the trustees make a disposal, even by way of sale, to a 'connected person', eg the settlor or anyone related to him.

Deductions

5.3   Base cost: if the asset was acquired before 31 March 1982, the value at 31 March 1982 is, generally speaking, the 'base date'.

Also allowed as a deduction from the gain are the professional and other incidental costs of acquiring and disposing of the asset.

Until April 1998 an allowance was given for the effect of inflation, namely the 'indexation allowance'. However, the indexation allowance was 'frozen' at that date from when the relief was in general terms replaced by taper relief. No indexation allowance or indeed taper relief is given for disposals on or after 6 April 2008.

There are various other reliefs that are dealt with in the course of this book and these are listed below.

Finally, after the application of any reliefs and losses (see **5.13–5.15**), a deduction is allowed for the annual exemption (see **5.36–5.39**) which, for 2008/09, will vary in amount between £5,050 and (because of the rules described at **5.37–5.38**) £1,010.

The rate of CGT payable by trustees for both 2008/09 and 2009/10 is 18% (reduced from 40% in 2007/08).

Various reliefs

5.4

- Main residence relief (see **5.25–5.27**). In parallel to the relief given to individuals, trustees making a gain on disposing of a house that has been used as the only or main residence of a beneficiary, may have the gain wholly or partly relieved. Legislation in *FA 2004* with effect from 10 December 2003 prevents the combination of deferral by hold-over of the gain arising on the gift of a residence into a discretionary trust and main residence relief for the trustees on ultimate sale by them (see **5.27** and Example 5.9).

- Entrepreneurs' relief (see **5.32–5.34**) which was introduced from 2008/09, to mitigate the effect of the withdrawal of business assets taper relief. To a large extent this represents a return to the old retirement relief which came to an end on 6 April 2003 (not considered in this book, though for a description see **5.34–5.36** of the 2007/08 edition).

- Taper relief was introduced in 1998, but has been withdrawn from 2008/09. It is designed to relieve the impact of CGT according to the length of time the particular asset has been owned, with very significant favour being given to business assets.

- Roll-over relief (see **5.28–5.31**) – this is a relief given to trustees who trade, whether by themselves or in partnership, in giving a deferral of a gain realised on the sale of one business asset into the acquisition cost of another.

- Enterprise investment schemes (EIS) allow trustees to defer a gain realised on any asset by making an investment in a qualifying EIS company, see **5.23–5.24**.

- Hold-over relief. The trustees may defer CGT, which accrues on a gain, when they advance certain assets to a beneficiary. The in-built gain becomes charged to tax when the beneficiary comes to sell the asset (or when the beneficiary becomes non-UK resident within (broadly) the following six years).

DEFERRED CONSIDERATION

5.5   CGT is triggered by a disposal. The date of the disposal for CGT purposes is the date on which a binding contract is made (even if the sale is 'completed' in a subsequent tax year) (*TCGA 1992, s 28(1)*). A disposal requires the passing of beneficial interest and will not occur if the contract is not completed (*Underwood v HMRC* [2008] EWCA Civ 1423).

If the contract is conditional, the date of disposal occurs on the date the contract becomes unconditional (*TCGA 1992, s 28(2)*).

Instalment reliefs

5.6   Any tax falls due on 31 January following the end of the tax year in which the disposal takes place. The fact that the sale proceeds might not be paid for some time makes no difference. That said, however, there is a relief (historically called 'hardship' relief) where the whole or part of the proceeds is receivable by instalments over a period exceeding 18 months, beginning no earlier than the date of the disposal (*TCGA 1992, s 280*). In such a case, the taxpayer can ask for instalment relief and may agree with HMRC a plan for payment of the tax over a period not exceeding eight years and ending not later than the date of the last instalment. There is no longer any need to satisfy HMRC that payment in one sum would cause undue hardship. In practice, HMRC will agree a payment plan that ensures that the taxpayer does not have to pay in tax more than 50% of what he has received.

Tax may also be paid by instalments over a ten year period where the disposal was a gift (*TCGA 1992, s 281*): see **5.52** for details.

Contingent consideration

5.7   The seller of a business may agree with the buyer that the price paid is, in part, determined by the results of the business over say, the next three years. This is colloquially known as an 'earn out'. While part of the price may be paid shortly after the contract, it will not be known for another three years or so whether any further element will become known and payable. This is a so-called *Marren v Ingles* [1980] 1 WLR 983, situation, named after the House of Lords case in 1980. Some valuation has to be placed on the future right. That valuation is part of the price received on sale. In three years' time, when that right becomes quantified, there is a further disposal, which may itself give rise to a gain or a loss.

Example 5.1—Completion in a later tax year

The trustees agree to sell Blackacre on 31 March 2009, with the contract being completed on 30 April 2009. For CGT purposes the disposal falls into tax year 2008/09.

Example 5.2—Instalment payment

The trustees have agreed to sell Blackacre for £100,000, payable in four equal annual instalments. The first instalment is due 30 days after the contract and the next three instalments on each anniversary of the contract. It would be open to the trustee taxpayer to apply for instalment relief.

Example 5.3—Earn-out provision

Trustees sell a business for £500,000 plus 10% of the profits shown by audited accounts over the next three years, payable nine months after the year-end in three years' time. The right to receive the further profits is quantified at £50,000. The immediate sale proceeds are therefore £550,000. In three years and nine months' time, the amount actually payable is £75,000. Therefore, a further gain of £25,000 arises at that time.

If, for disposals on or after 10 April 2003, a loss arises on realising the further right, that loss can (subject to conditions) be set off against the original gain (*TCGA 1992, s 279A*).

RESIDENCE

5.8   The CGT test for residence was before 2007/08 different from the income tax test (see **4.1–4.4**). Up to and including 2006/07, the CGT test did not look at the individual trustees, but rather presumed trustees (as a body of persons) to be resident and ordinarily resident in the UK unless:

- the general administration of trusts was ordinarily carried on outside the UK; and

- the trustees, or a majority of them, were not resident or ordinarily resident in the UK (*TCGA 1992, s 69(1)*).

There was a further provision which used to help the UK professional trustee (before 2007/08). This allowed a professional trustee even though resident in the UK, eg a London solicitor, to be treated as non-UK resident *if* the settlor was not domiciled, resident or ordinarily resident in the UK. In such a case, all or the majority of the trustees were treated as non-UK resident and the general administration of the trust was treated as carried on outside the UK (even if, as a matter of fact it was carried on in London).

The rules for residence have been revised from 2007/08 (*TCGA 1992, s 69*). The income tax test now described in **4.1–4.4** applies also for capital gains tax purposes. And the favourable rule for UK professional trustees described above has been repealed.

Anti-avoidance

The settlor and capital payments charges

5.9   The advantage of a trust being resident outside the UK is that, apart from anti-avoidance rules (see **5.58–5.60**), and assuming the trustees do not realise gains from UK assets used in a UK business, the trustees do not have a liability to CGT. This is the case even in relation to the disposal of assets situated in the UK. This ostensibly favourable position led to a considerable number of UK resident domiciliaries establishing offshore trusts, in particular, throughout the 1980s. The ideal asset to put into such a trust would be one showing no current gain but with a significant prospect of a substantial future gain, eg subscription shares in a private trading company. The idea would be that the trustees would sell the asset in due course, realise a significant gain and then use it in such a way as to benefit the beneficiary and his family but without advancing capital to him. It was in response to such situations that substantive anti-avoidance legislation was enacted in 1991, 1998 and 2000. The capital payments charge has been further refined in 2008/09, following the changes to taxation made for UK resident non-UK domiciled beneficiaries generally by *FA 2008*: see **5.59–5.60** for more detail.

The use of double tax treaties

5.10   Most recently, in the light of attempts to exploit the application of specific double tax treaties to procure a UK CGT advantage, *F(No 2)A 2005, s 33* prevents the use of a double tax treaty to argue that trustees are not UK resident in a particular year of disposal, with effect from 16 March 2005. It appears from the High Court decision in *Smallwood v HMRC* [2009] STC 1222 in favour of the taxpayer that such legislation was indeed necessary.

Example 5.4—Trust residence

The Harry Trust is UK resident, and is therefore taxed on its gains as they arise on a worldwide basis.

The Hector Trust is non-UK resident. It was made by a person resident and domiciled outside the UK, who continues to be so, and therefore, the settlor charge does not apply and no-one is taxed on the trustees' gains in the UK as they arise.

However, the capital payments charge (see **5.59–5.60**) will apply to the Hector Trust even though the trust was made by a non-UK domiciliary. As and when payments of capital are received by a beneficiary resident in the UK, the 'trust gains' (or, from 2008/09, the so-called 'section 2(2) amounts') (*TCGA 1992, s 87A*) of the settlement will be attributed to these payments in so far as they have not been earlier attributed to other capital payments (including payments outside the capital payments charge made to a non-UK domiciled beneficiary). For capital payments received up to 2007/08, the charge applies only where the beneficiary is domiciled in the UK. From 2008/09 it matters not where the beneficiary is domiciled, though if outside the UK and the payment is received outside the UK a remittance basis may apply. (See further **5.60**.)

EXPORTING THE RESIDENCE

5.11   It is unlikely, in the context of the present legislative climate, that trustees of a UK trust or indeed the family behind the trust will consider making the trust non-UK resident. If they do, however:

- there must be power in the trust for a successor body of non-UK resident trustees to be appointed;

- that new body would be appointed as trustees and the existing UK trustees would retire in the normal way. It is essential that the new trustees are properly appointed, viz under *Trustee Act 1925, s 37,* that they comprise at least two persons or a trust corporation. In a recent case, *Jasmine Trustees Ltd v Wells & Hind* [2007] WTLR 489, only one individual and a non-trust corporation company were appointed (at a time when two individuals were required), so the new (non-UK) trustees were not validly appointed and the former undischarged trustees remained liable for CGT on disposals in the interim;

- that act of appointment of non-UK resident trustees would cause a deemed disposal and re-acquisition by the UK resident trustees of the assets in the trust at that time (*TCGA 1992, s 80*). Any resulting CGT would be a liability of the retiring UK trustees (and they should therefore retain sufficient funds to pay the tax as well as to satisfy any other liabilities, eg professional costs); and

- any gains held over by a settlor on putting assets into a trust within (broadly) the previous six years will become immediately assessable on the UK trustees and, if not paid within 12 months, on the settlor (*TCGA 1992, s 168*).

The fact that the trustees would become non-UK resident would open up the possibility of the settlor charge and/or the capital payments charge. However:

- the settlor charge would apply only in relation to any tax year if the settlor was during that tax year alive and resident and domiciled in the UK;
- the capital payments charge would apply only if capital payments were made to a beneficiary resident and domiciled in the UK or (from 2008/09) to a UK resident beneficiary wherever domiciled. (See **5.59– 5.60** for further detail.)

Considerations of changing the governing law and also issues of future administration (including cost) should also be borne in mind.

Exporting the residence of a UK resident trust is not a step to be taken lightly. Probably, since 1998, rather more non-UK resident trusts have been brought back to the UK than UK resident trusts exported. However, depending on the nature of the assets and indeed the circumstances of the principal family, eg if one or a number of beneficiaries were to become non-UK resident and domiciled, it might be a step worth taking.

Example 5.5—Exporting a trust

The Harry Trust has been UK resident for many years. Harry, having married an English girl and brought up his children in the UK, has now reached retirement age. All his children have left home and are living in various parts of the world, none of them in the UK. He and his wife decide to retire to Switzerland.

The trust has not made huge gains over the years, though if certain investments recently made do 'come good', it might become quite valuable. Harry wishes to move the residence of the trust to a tax haven jurisdiction and his co-trustees are happy to do so. He is prepared to 'bite the bullet' by accepting an 18% tax charge on in-built gains on exporting the trust.

The settlor charge will give no concerns for the future as Harry, the settlor, will become resident and domiciled outside the UK. Nor indeed will the capital payments charge, as all the beneficiaries have long since abandoned their English domiciles of origin and have made their permanent homes, and tax residence, elsewhere.

TAXABLE GAINS AND ALLOWABLE LOSSES

5.12   In principle, a gain realised on the disposal of any asset (see Example 5.13 at **5.55** for the method of calculation) is chargeable. That said, there are certain exempt assets such as sterling cash and indeed certain exemptions, such as main residence relief (see **5.25–5.27**).

Losses

5.13   A loss will be allowable if the disposal of that asset at a gain would have been taxable (*TCGA 1992, s 16*). Allowable losses realised in the same year as a taxable gain *must* be deducted from those gains in computing the taxable amount for the year (even if the effect is to 'waste' the annual exemption). By contrast, losses in a given year, which are not used, for example, because there are no gains against which to offset them, may be carried forward. Such brought forward losses need not 'waste' the annual exemption and the taxpayer trustees can choose to utilise only so much of the losses as are necessary to bring the gains down to the annual exemption threshold. Any losses remaining can then be carried forward further.

A loss must be claimed within five years and ten months after the year in which it arose, in principle by recording it in the capital gains self-assessment pages (see **5.54**). The time limit is to be reduced to four years, following *FA 2008, Sch 39* from 1 April 2010 (*The Finance Act 2008 Schedule 39 (Appointed Day, Transitional Provisions and Savings) Order 2009, SI 2009/403*).

5.14   Trustees, as also individuals and personal representatives, are potentially affected by an anti-avoidance rule with effect from 6 December 2006 (*TCGA 1992, s 16A* inserted by *FA 2007, s 27(3)*). A loss is not an allowable loss if it accrues 'directly or indirectly in consequence of, or otherwise in connection with, any arrangements [which includes any agreement, understanding, scheme, transaction or series of transactions (whether or not legally enforceable)], and the main purpose, or one of the main purposes, of the arrangements is to secure a tax advantage'.

The expression 'tax advantage' is defined to mean: relief or increased relief from tax, repayment or increased repayment of tax, the avoidance or reduction of a charge to tax or an assessment to tax, or the avoidance of a possible assessment tax; and 'tax' means CGT, corporation tax or income tax.

HMRC have published revised guidance on the new rules on 19 July 2007, but it is not always easy to see why one type of transaction is said to be unaffected whereas another not dissimilar one will be caught. Careful study should be made of the various examples supplied. Extreme caution is required in both effecting and reporting any transaction which may be affected by the new rule.

Connected party losses

5.15   If the trustees realise a loss by making a disposal to a 'connected person', eg the settlor, or a relative of the settlor, they cannot offset that loss generally against their gains (*TCGA 1992, s 18(3)*). The loss must be carried forward for use only against a gain that arises from the trustees disposing of another asset to that same connected person.

Shares: identification rules

Background

5.16   Generally speaking, each asset must be treated separately for CGT purposes. Up to April 1998, however, there was a 'pooling' system for shares. Under this, each block of shares of the same class in the same company, held in the same capacity (viz as trustees as opposed to personal ownership) was regarded as a single asset, which would increase with purchases and decrease with sales. Immediately before each transaction the appropriate amount of indexation allowance (for inflation) was added to the pool.

This system changed with the introduction of taper relief in 1998, since this required the identification of each asset to which the appropriate taper percentage could be applied. At the same time, the 'anti bed-and-breakfast' rule was introduced, whereby (broadly) share acquisitions are identified with shares in the same company disposed of within the previous 30 days. (This 30-day rule is disapplied where the person acquiring the shares is not UK resident: this is a measure introduced by *FA 2006, s 74* from 22 March 2006, following an avoidance technique successfully applied by taxpayer trustees in 2005 in a case called *Hicks v Davies* [2005] STC 850.) The identification rule may therefore be stated as follows. Shares disposed of are identified with acquisitions in the following order:

(i)   shares acquired on the same day;

(ii)   shares acquired within the following 30 days;

(iii)   shares acquired since 5 April 1998;

(iv)   the pool of shares held at 6 April 1998; and

(v)   the pool of shares held at 31 March 1982.

Example 5.6—Share identification

The trustees own 1,000 shares in XYZ plc, which have been acquired at various times. They disposed of 500 shares on 1 February 2008 (and acquired 50 shares nine days later). These shares are identified in order with:

- 50 shares acquired on 10 February 2008 (point ii above);

- 300 shares acquired on 1 September 2004 (point iii above);

- 150 shares held in the pool at 6 April 1998 (point iv above).

Note: The balance of 500 pooled shares may in fact have a greater base cost using indexation and re-basing at 31 March 1982 than in comparison with those that are now being sold, but the trustees will not at this stage be able to utilise this.

2008/09 and 2009/10

5.17   With the reform of CGT from 2008/09, the rules for share identification return broadly to the pooling system which prevailed up to 6 April 1998 (as described in the first paragraph at **5.16**). In addition, the rules described at (i) and (ii) at **5.16** continue to apply.

BASE COSTS

5.18   To compute the gain, the base (or acquisition) cost of the asset is required. This will be the original cost of the asset or, if the asset was acquired by the trustees by way of a gift, the market value when the asset entered the settlement. If, however, the trustees have owned the relevant asset since before 31 March 1982, it is likely to be the market value on that date (to which generally, costs were re-based in 1988), for a disposal before 6 April 2008. For disposals since that date, it will be the 31 March 1982 value.

Fixing the base cost

5.19   It may happen, however, typically with trusts, that the base cost has not been formally agreed with HMRC. Property may have been put into a settlement, especially if a life interest or an accumulation and maintenance settlement, which is a potentially exempt transfer for IHT and therefore is assumed to be exempt, and any gain was held over for CGT. The hold over of a gain does not require the formal agreement of valuation with HMRC. All the relevant election (on help sheet HS 295) requires is a statement that a gain does arise on disposal; see **3.5–3.7**.

Post-transaction valuation check

5.20   Let's suppose the asset is now sold, perhaps relatively early in the tax year, say, on 1 May. On the face of it, it will not be until after the following 5 April that in completing their self-assessment return the trustees can record the gain and put some estimate on the base cost and therefore the gain on which they must pay tax on the following 31 January. The agreement of a gain with HMRC may take some time. To assist this conundrum, HMRC have introduced a process called a post-transaction valuation check explained in leaflet CG 34. What CG 34 does, once the asset concerned has been sold, is to start the valuation process running with, in the case of land, the district valuer, or with shares, the shares valuation division. The form requires the applicant trustees to supply a CGT computation based on the valuation figure that the trustees offer. They should provide any comparables and itemise any release due or to be claimed. HMRC warn that any inaccuracy in the responses on form CG 34 may invalidate a valuation agreed on the basis of it. It is therefore a procedure to be adopted with care.

Interestingly, HMRC Trusts have advised generally that, under self-assessment, CG 34 should be submitted in all cases where the base cost is uncertain, with the appropriate reference made on the self-assessment return. The intention behind this is to avoid or mitigate the possibility of a subsequent liability to interest or to penalties.

Example 5.7—Illustrative computation

Trustees sold on 1 August 2009 for £500,000 land that was transferred to the settlement just under four years ago and which throughout their period of ownership they have used for farming. The value has recently been much enhanced by a change in planning policy by the local authority and by the trustees having obtained planning permission for residential development with the benefit of which the land was sold. What, however, is the gain?

The trust is a discretionary trust and when four years ago the land was transferred, it was so transferred under a hold-over election. The settlor himself had acquired the land on the death of his late wife (spouse exempt for IHT) six years ago. In his view the land was then worth £10,000 and when put into settlement, say £25,000. The value on settlement is, of course irrelevant for CGT purposes, although it is material for IHT as having been a chargeable transfer, albeit within the nil rate band. It was in fact that value of £25,000, less the current and previous year's annual exemptions of £3,000, which the settlor returned on form IHT 100.

What matters now is an agreement of value on the death of the late wife. The trustees would, of course like this value to be as much as possible, in order to mitigate the gain. There does not seem to be much prospect of that. They have, however, found a valuer who is prepared to value the land at £20,000 which, if accepted, would save CGT of £1,800 (18% of the additional £10,000).

The trustees proceed with the CG 34 procedure and compute the gain as follows:

Sale proceeds		£500,000
Market value on acquisition, say	£25,000	
Less settlor's base cost, say	(£20,000)	
Gain held over	£5,000	
Acquisition cost	£25,000	
Less	(£5,000)	
		£20,000
Chargeable gain		£480,000

Submission of form CG 34 invites the district valuer to agree.

SETTLOR-INTERESTED TRUSTS

5.21   These anti-avoidance rules follow the income tax regime discussed in **4.24–4.25**. The CGT rules were introduced in 1988, and while originally there was a separate code, this has now been generally aligned with the income tax provisions, although the legislation is not exactly the same. Both sets of rules apply whenever the settlement was made.

For disposals before 6 April 2008, the settlor will be treated by *TCGA 1992, s 77* as if the gains of the trustees were his gains in any situation where:

● trust property or 'derived property' will or may benefit the settlor or his spouse. The expression 'derived property' means income from the property or any other property directly or indirectly representing the proceeds of the sale of that property; or

- there is a benefit for the settlor or his spouse that is derived directly or indirectly from the settlement property or derived property.

The rules do not apply if the spouse can benefit only after the settlor has died.

Note that, while, from 2008/09, the gains of a settlor-interested trust are assessed on the trustees and not on the settlor, the concept of a 'settlor-interested trust' remains. It is material for purposes of hold-over relief: a gain arising on a transfer into a settlor-interested trust cannot be held over (see **3.5**)

The old rules (prior to 2008/09)

5.22　The effect of the rules up to and including 2007/08 was as follows:

- The net trust gains of the year, after deducting trustees' losses for that and earlier years, are treated as gains of the settlor.

- The annual exemption applicable will, of course, be that of the settlor and not of the trustees.

- The relevant rate of tax will depend upon the settlor's other income and gains and could therefore be as high as 40%, or as low as 10% – as against the trustees' rate of 40%.

- Before *FA 2002* the settlor could not reduce trust gains assessed on him by use of personal losses. However, as from 2003/04, a settlor's personal losses in excess of personal gains can be offset against trust gains assessed on him. (Further, he had the right to elect for this treatment in any of tax years 2000/01, 2001/02 and 2002/03.)

- If a settlor-interested trust has losses for a particular year, these cannot be transferred to the settlor for use against his personal gains, but must be carried forward to offset subsequent gains made by the trustees.

- The settlor can recover from the trustees the tax assessed on him, though not in compensation of the use of his annual exemption or losses.

- If a settlement has sub-settlements or separate funds, and the settlor or spouse can benefit under one but not under others, the whole of the trust gains will be assessed on him and not only those gains that are funds that are 'settlor-interested'. However, see **5.40–5.43** for the 'sub-fund' election from 2006/07.

- From 2006/07 a settlement will also be 'settlor-interested' if during the tax year any of the settlor's minor unmarried children, not in a civil partnership, can benefit (*TCGA 1992, s 77(2A)* added by *FA 2006*).

ENTERPRISE INVESTMENT SCHEME (EIS)

5.23   In the context of 'sheltering' or deferring gains from CGT, other than on business assets, almost the only opportunity for individuals, trustees and PRs is presented by EIS. The present regime dates from 1998 and derives from the old reinvestment relief regime.

EIS effectively contains two separate codes:

- Deferral of CGT; thus the gain that would otherwise trigger CGT is effectively 'rolled into' a qualifying subscription in EIS shares and 'comes home to roost' only when those new shares are sold.

- An exemption from both income tax and CGT, for which the rules are far more stringent, but which in any case is not available for trustees.

The regime for both deferral and exemption is extremely complex. The relevant company must carry on a qualifying trade and the shares subscribed should be newly issued. From 2006/07, the assets of the company must not exceed £7m before the issue of shares, and £8m immediately afterwards (*ICTA 1988, s 293(6A)* amended by *FA 2006*). The company must carry on a 'qualifying trade'; from which certain 'low-risk' activities are excluded, eg farming and market gardening, operating or managing hotels and nursing homes, among others.

For deferral there is no limit on the proportion of the company owned (whereas in the case of exemption for individuals it must not exceed 30% taking other associated shareholdings into account).

To defer a gain on EIS, subscription must be made within 12 months before, or three years after, the disposal.

An EIS claim is made by completing and submitting to HMRC form EIS 3 issued by the company. The claim must be made before 31 January following five years after the end of the tax year in which the gain arose.

Deferral relief into venture capital trusts is not available for trustees.

EIS for trustees

5.24   The relief is extended to trusts:

- With a discretionary trust: all the beneficiaries must be individuals.

- With an interest in possession trust: relief is given if any of the beneficiaries are individuals, although if there are non-individual beneficiaries, *pro rata* relief is obtained according to the proportion of the individual interests in possession borne to all the interests in possession. While individuals include charities, interests in possession do not include interests for a fixed term.

Assuming the trustees have realised the gain it is the trustees who must make the qualifying EIS investment.

Example 5.8—EIS relief

The trustees sold some shares realising a taxable gain of £10,000 on 1 January 2009. They have available to them the annual exemption of £4,800 leaving a gain of £5,200 in charge to tax. It is open to them to make a qualifying reinvestment under EIS of £5,200 at any time before 1 January 2012. The shares must be new shares in a qualifying trading company and the trustees must ensure that the anti-avoidance rules do not claw back the relief.

The CGT on the disposal would normally have to be paid on 31 January 2010. The trustees can pay the tax, subsequently make the investment and claim a refund of tax plus repayment supplement. Alternatively, the trustees can claim in their self-assessment that they will make the EIS investment and only if the investment is not made will they have to pay the CGT due plus interest from 31 January 2010.

MAIN RESIDENCE RELIEF

5.25   The legislation extends to trustees the familiar main residence relief given to individuals. Although contained in just eight sections of the Act (*TCGA 1992, ss 222–226B*) the relief is extremely complex and, to be understood, must be read in the context of a number of decided cases and HMRC statements and concessions. The general principle for trustees under *s 225* is that:

- the trustees sell a dwelling-house (viz a house or flat);

- during all or part of their period of ownership, the dwelling-house has been occupied by a beneficiary as his only or main residence;

- the beneficiary has been entitled to occupy under the terms of the settlement;

- if the beneficiary has more than one residence, the trustees and the beneficiary jointly can elect that the trust property (or indeed the beneficially owned property) shall be treated as the main residence for purposes of the relief. Accordingly, it is not open for an individual for any period of time to be accruing relief on a property that he and/or his spouse owns and occupies at the same time as relief is being given on a property within a trust which he occupies. That said, the last 36 months rule (discussed at **5.26**) can, in appropriate circumstances, give relief on two properties concurrently occupied by the same individual, which can operate where the one property is owned outright and the other is owned by trustees. Similarly with the first 12 months rule.

One of the interesting factors about *s 225* is that there is no *pro rata* test. This means that, whether the trust is discretionary or interest in possession in form and whether there are a number of beneficiaries, occupation by just one of them will secure the relief for the whole of the gain arising on disposal.

The period of ownership

5.26   There is an interesting statutory 'concession' in *s 223(1)*. Relief is given automatically for the last 36 months of ownership (assuming that the property is not then used for business purposes) even if the beneficiary is not in occupation, providing that at some time the main residence relief applied.

Similarly, there is a non-statutory concession where for the first 12 months of ownership (or sometimes longer up to a further 12 months) the beneficiary cannot live in the house, either because of essential renovations or because the house is being built or reconstructed (HMRC extra-statutory concession D49). There are also further concessions, which give certain permitted periods of absence, some of which were given statutory effect in 2009.

Anti-avoidance rule for hold-over relief

5.27   An anti-avoidance rule was introduced on 10 December 2003, to counter an arrangement that had become common (see paragraph 2 of Example 5.11), which combined hold-over relief and main residence relief. Now, broadly speaking, for transfers into a discretionary trust on or after 10 December 2003 (since 22 March 2006, a 'relevant property' trust), a choice must be made between hold-over relief for the settlor on entry and main residence relief for the trustees on subsequent disposal. Under transitional rules, in a case where a property was already in a trust as at 10 December 2003, a subsequent sale by the trustees can attract main residence relief only for periods up to 9 December 2003.

Example 5.9—'Washing the gain'—in the past

The settlor of a discretionary trust made on 1 January 1993 owns a second property, which is used by the family as an occasional holiday home. The house is now worth £200,000 within which there is a gain of over £100,000. The children are aged 20, 18 and 16.

The settlor could have transferred the house to the trust, say on 9 December 2001, within his nil rate band for IHT purposes, holding over the gain under *TCGA 1992, s 260*. The trustees are therefore treated as acquiring the house at the date of settlement, for the original base cost. The trustees have power in the trust deed to allow a beneficiary to occupy a trust property. They allow the eldest child to occupy it as a residence from year to year, given that he also lives elsewhere. It is important that his occupation is more than occasional. The trustees and the beneficiary irrevocably elected within the two-year period that the trust property is treated as his main residence. The house was then sold two years later, on 9 December 2003, at a gain of £150,000, all of which is exempt under *s 225*.

If the house were instead to be sold on 9 December 2009, the anti-avoidance rule described in **5.27** would come into operation. Only one quarter of the gain would be exempt under *s 225*. The remaining three-quarters would be taxable (and, specifically, could not benefit from the last 36 months of ownership rule described in **5.26**).

If, since 10 December 2003, such a settlor is considering CGT mitigation possibilities for the house, the combination of hold-over relief into a discretionary trust and main residence relief within the trust is no longer open to him.

Up to 22 March 2006, it would have been possible to achieve much the same result through a combination of *s 165* hold-over (for business assets, including 'furnished holiday accommodation') and *s 225* relief. Suppose the husband owned a holiday home, which he gave to his wife on a no-gain, no-loss basis under *TCGA 1992, s 58*, she would then let the property as qualifying furnished holiday accommodation (within the meaning of *ITTOIA 2005, s 322* and following) after which she would give the property to an interest in possession trust for the children, excluding herself and her husband as beneficiaries. The gain would be held over under *s 165*. The trustees would allow one or more children to occupy the property as their only or main residence pursuant to powers in the settlement and on sale by the trustees the whole of the gain would be 'washed' under *s 225*.

Unfortunately, however, any new interest in possession settlement on or after 22 March 2006 falls within the 'chargeable transfer' regime and so any hold-over would be under *s 260* rather than under *s 165* (*TCGA 1992, s 165(3)(d)*). And of course the combination of *s 260* hold-over and *s 225* relief for the trustees has been precluded since 10 December 2003. Only if, within such an example, the parents were prepared for the property to become owned outright by the children, might the suggestion still be effective. *Section 165* hold-over would apply on the gift by mother to the children, who would then occupy and sell with the benefit of relief under *s 223*. And even this suggestion will not work following 5 April 2010, unless the mother is able to establish the existence of a trade under general income tax principles: Budget 2009 announced that with effect from 2010/11 the deemed trading treatment of furnished holiday accommodation would be removed for both income tax and CGT purposes.

ROLL-OVER RELIEF

5.28 The colloquially known roll-over relief is formally called 'relief on replacement of business assets' (*TCGA 1992, ss 151–158*). This allows a trader to defer CGT, triggered by a gain on a business asset, by deferring into acquiring a new asset used for the business. Complete relief depends on the investment of the total sale proceeds (net of incidental costs) into the new asset, though partial relief may be claimed. Roll-over relief does entail the loss of any accrued taper relief. A new asset must (subject to extension by HMRC) be acquired within 12 months before, or three years after, disposal of the old asset.

Trades: actual and deemed

5.29 The relief applies only to trades, ie not to property investment. However, certain non-trades, eg the occupation of woodlands on a commercial basis and (before 2010/11: see Example 5.9 at **5.27**, final paragraph) furnished holiday lettings, are treated as trades for this purpose.

Qualifying classes of assets

5.30 The old and the new assets must fall within certain specified qualifying categories including land and buildings, goodwill and certain quotas, though the old and the new assets do not have to fall within the same category, nor do the trades have to be the same.

The claim

5.31 The claim to relief may be made on a 'protective' basis, that is, even when the new asset has not been acquired, ie by stating an intention that the taxpayer will acquire the new asset within the qualifying time. When that time expires he can either confirm the claim on the basis that the new asset has been acquired, or simply withdraw it, in which case tax will fall due, plus interest in the normal way.

A trustee is a taxpayer like any other for the purposes of roll-over relief. The important thing is obviously that trustees carry on the trade whether as sole traders or in partnership. For this purpose they could be limited partners.

Example 5.10—Deferring the tax bill

The trustees are limited partners in a limited farming partnership. They have a one-third share in the capital of the firm. Among the assets is a barn, which has, throughout the family's ownership, been used for storing farm machinery and farm stocks. The barn is on the edge of the village and the partners have obtained planning permission for residential conversion. The barn is sold for £200,000, realising a gain of £180,000. The trustees, along with the other partners, will therefore have to pay CGT on the gain.

However, in the following three years, the partnership spends £205,000:

● as to £100,000, a further 40 acres;

● as to £30,000, extending the grain store; and

● as to £65,000, buying milk quotas; plus

● £10,000 on professional fees and disbursements.

The whole of the gain can, therefore, effectively be rolled over, subject to a claim.

ENTREPRENEURS' RELIEF

5.32   To compensate traders for the repeal of business assets taper relief from 2008/09, *FA 2008, Sch 3* introduced entrepreneurs' relief (*TCGA 1992, ss 169H–169S*). In broad terms, this relief reintroduces the provisions of retirement relief (for a brief description of which see the 2007/08 edition of this book at **5.32–5.34**). Gains qualifying for the entrepreneurs' relief are reduced by 4/9ths, up to a maximum of £1 million of qualifying gains over a lifetime, starting with 6 April 2008. With a uniform tax rate of 18%, the reduction produces an effective tax rate for entrepreneurs' relief of 10%.

Conditions

5.33   The relief is available on the following disposals:

- all or part of a trading business carried on by an individual whether alone or in partnership;

- a disposal of assets used for a business which has come to an end, within three years after cessation;

- a disposal of shares in or securities of a company where the individual was an officer or employee and had a minimum of 5% of the ordinary voting share capital of the company;

- under an 'associated disposal' there is a material disposal of business assets (whether in a partnership or in shares of a company) as part of a withdrawal by the individual from participation in the business of the partnership or the company.

Generally speaking, the conditions must be satisfied for a period of 12 months either ending with the disposal or in certain cases ending at a time which falls within three years after the disposal.

There is no minimum age or indeed working time requirement for an officer or employee of a company.

Extension to trustees

5.34   Gains realised by trustees can attract entrepreneurs' relief (*TCGA 1992, s 169J*). There must be an interest in possession (not including a fixed term) in the whole of the settled property or in part which contains the settlement business assets of which the trustees dispose. Those assets may be either shares or securities of a company or assets used for purposes of a business. Where the disposal is of shares of a company it must be the 'personal company' of the qualifying beneficiary who must also be an officer or employee. That is, the 5% minimum voting shareholding must be held by the individual not by the trustees; there is no minimum requirement for the trustees' holding. Where it is a business of which the trustees dispose, the business must be carried on by the beneficiary, whether alone or in partnership. Otherwise, the rules applying to disposals by an individual are applied to trustees.

Section 169O contains further provisions in the case where more than one beneficiary has an interest in the relevant settled property. An apportionment is made by reference to the proportional entitlement of the qualifying beneficiary to the income of the relevant settled property. Where the relief is to be claimed by the trustees, *s 169M* provides that there is a joint claim by the trustees and the qualifying beneficiary, which ensures that his £1 million maximum of qualifying gains is not exceeded.

TAPER RELIEF (FOR DISPOSALS BEFORE 2008/09)

5.35   Taper relief was introduced for disposals on or after 6 April 1998 (*TCGA 1992, Sch A1*). The relief has been withdrawn from 2008/09. Details of the relief can be found at **5.37** to **5.42** of the 2008/09 edition of this book. For greater detail, see the general guidance on HMRC's website at http://www.hmrc.gov.uk/cgt/shares/taper-indexation.htm.

THE ANNUAL EXEMPTION

5.36   The annual exemption, ie within which gains will be tax free, is £5,050 for most trusts for 2009/10 (or £4,800 for 2008/09). This is one-half of the individual's exemption. The individual's exemption is available to the trustees of a settlement for certain disabled persons.

The anti-fragmentation rule

5.37   An anti-avoidance rule operates in circumstances where the same settlor has made more than one 'qualifying settlement' since 6 June 1978. This is to prevent a person making a number of settlements, each benefiting from the £5,050 annual exemption (2009/10). If there is more than one qualifying settlement in a group, the annual exemption is divided between them, up to a maximum of five. That is, the annual exemption for a trust for 2009/10 can never be less than £1,010 (£5,050 ÷ 5 or £10,100 ÷ 10).

'Qualifying settlement'

5.38   The expression does not include charitable trusts, or trust death benefits of registered pension schemes (which are among 'excluded settlements' defined in *TCGA 1992, Sch 1, para 2 (7)(b)*. Otherwise, the expression will include almost every type of settlement, even settlements that do not realise a gain. This means that there could be a total of five qualifying settlements, only one of which is making a gain in the tax year, but it gets the benefit of an annual exemption of only £960, ie in 2008/09 £3,840 of annual exemption is wasted, forfeiting £691 in tax potentially saved and now payable. For disposals in 2009/10, the waste of annual exemption is £4,000 (£5,050 minus £1,050, forfeiting £720 in tax potentially saved, at 18%).

Beware

5.39   This rule needs to be watched very carefully, since under self-assessment it is up to the trustees to claim the right amount of annual exemption. If for some years they have always claimed the maximum exemption, but it then turns out that after a period of time that they should have claimed only, say, the minimum amount, issues of interest and penalties will arise, not to mention the consumption of professional and administrative time.

The problem is that it may be difficult for the trustees to discover the existence of qualifying settlements in any case. Indeed, the rule survives the settlor's death.

Example 5.11—Splitting the annual exemption

As well as an A&M trust for his grandchildren (which continues as such after 5 April 2008, with the capital vesting age reduced to 18), the settlor has also made the following:

- a discretionary settlement, in which his wife (but not the settlor) is a potential beneficiary;

- a £10 'pilot' discretionary settlement, in conjunction with his will. This is not uncommon, the will effectively 'tipping' a pot of money into the pre-existing discretionary trust (see **6.40**);

- a trust of a seven-year IHT protection policy, to guard against the possibility of IHT becoming payable within seven years after the making of a PET. This will be a qualifying policy only for such time as the seven-year period stays in being; and

- a small discretionary trust for his nephews and nieces, with the trust fund invested in a single premium investment bond.

There are therefore a total of five qualifying settlements and the annual exemption for any of the trusts which makes a gain will be only £1,010 for 2009/10.

THE SUB-FUND ELECTION

5.40   A new regime was introduced by *FA 2006* (found in *TCGA 1992, Sch 4ZA*). Where a single settlement has more than one 'sub-settlement' or 'sub-fund', even with separate trustees, the gains or losses on those sub-settlements or funds form part of the overall computation of chargeable gains, which is assessed on the trustees of the main settlement. In broad terms, the new regime allows trustees of the 'principal settlement' to elect that a fund or other specified portion of the settlement shall be treated for capital gains tax purposes as a separate settlement. The creation of a sub-fund will involve a disposal by the trustees of the principal settlement. And the election cannot take effect on a date earlier than that on which it is made.

Conditions

5.41 The four conditions are as follows:

- the principal settlement is not itself a sub-fund settlement;

- the sub-fund does not comprise the whole of the property in the principal settlement;

- there is no asset an interest in which is comprised both in the sub-fund settlement and the principal settlement; and

- no person is a beneficiary under both the sub-fund settlement and the principal settlement.

The four conditions must be satisfied when the election is made. And the last three conditions must be satisfied throughout the period from when the election is treated as taking effect and ending immediately before the election is made.

Procedure

5.42 HMRC have provided a form (SFE 1) for making a sub-fund election. No election may be made after the second 31 January after the year of assessment in which the effective date falls. The sub-fund election must contain certain declarations, statements and information and it may not be revoked.

Consequences of a sub-fund election

5.43 Following on the disposal which the trustees of the principal settlement are treated as having made, the trustees of the sub-fund settlement are treated as having acquired the relevant property at the date of the election taking effect and for a consideration equal to the then market value of the relevant assets.

For income tax purposes corresponding provisions were introduced by *FA 2006*, now found in *ITA 2007, s 477*.

Example 5.12—Sub-fund illustration

The London Trust, made some ten years ago, comprises a wide portfolio of rented property, quoted investments and a variety of shareholdings in private trading companies. The beneficiaries are, in broad terms, the grandchildren and remoter issue of the settlor. For various administrative reasons, the trustees want for 2009/10 to hive off into a separate settlement run by separate trustees (though this is not necessary under the legislation) the shares in the private trading companies.

So this they do, ensuring that the beneficiaries are restricted to the children of the settlor's elder daughter and that those beneficiaries cannot in future benefit under the principal settlement. Separate trustees are appointed. The trustees of the principal settlement are treated as making a disposal. However, regardless of the fact that the assets concerned are shares in trading companies, the gain can be held over by election by the trustees of the principal settlement under *TCGA 1992, s 260* because that settlement is a discretionary or 'relevant property' trust (as indeed is the sub-fund settlement).

ANTI-AVOIDANCE RULES

5.44   Trusts have a venerable history. While this book is about the tax aspects of trusts, some of the non-tax issues and advantages were summarised in **3.23–3.27**.

Avoidance perceived by HMRC

5.45   The very flexibility of a trust (as opposed to a company) has meant that over recent years they have been used as vehicles for tax planning. The most effective tax planning occurs where tax advantages are obtained within the context of overall family and/or commercial structuring. It is when tax saving becomes an end in itself and arrangements are made with no other purpose that the courts perceive taxpayers to have 'crossed over to the wrong side of the line' and will therefore try to redress the balance. This is the subject of numerous decided cases, which generally have prompted changes in the law.

A simple example of an anti-avoidance rule has been the settlor-interested trust regime (see **5.21–5.22**), which seeks to counteract any perceived advantage a person may gain by using the mechanism of a trust from which he or his spouse can benefit to trigger disposal. From 2004/05 to 2007/08 the CGT rate for all types of trust has been 40%. From 2008/09 the rate is 18%, along with all non-corporate taxpayers, and so it is no longer necessary to charge the gains of a settlor-interested trust on the settlor.

Tax mitigation, avoidance and evasion

5.46 Generally speaking, tax planning is permissible. The traditional distinction was between tax avoidance, which was permissible, and tax evasion, which involved a breach of the law (sometimes the criminal law). More recently (by way of summary categorisation only), tax avoidance has been divided into 'acceptable' tax mitigation and 'unacceptable' tax avoidance, which falls short of evasion.

On 1 August 2006 a disclosure regime was introduced for direct taxes. Arrangements with a view to tax avoidance which fall within one of seven prescribed descriptions, subject to exemptions, must be notified to HMRC within five days, failing which a fine of £5,000 will be levied.

HMRC continue to monitor types of transaction (sometimes sold as packages) whereby they perceive that the 'spirit' of the legislation is being undermined. Some of these 'tax avoidance schemes' have been legislated against in recent years, specifically in *FA 2000*, which attacked two UK trust schemes, two non-UK trust schemes and one scheme that applies wherever the trustees are resident; see below for examples.

Most recently, *FA 2004* has introduced wide-ranging anti-avoidance rules in relation to settlor-interested trusts. As from 10 December 2003, a gain arising on transfer into a settlor-interested trust cannot be deferred by hold-over relief (see **3.5–3.7**) and, also from 10 December 2003, the combination of hold-over relief on a gift into a discretionary trust and main residence relief for the trustees on a subsequent disposal is no longer possible (see **5.27**).

The following two arrangements were among five counteracted by *FA 2000*, whereas the third rule was introduced by *FA 2004*.

Disposal of interest in a settlor-interested trust

5.47 There has been a long-standing rule that no chargeable gain arises when a beneficiary disposes of his interest under a settlement (*TCGA 1992, s 76*). This must be an interest original to the settlement and will not protect a person who buys an interest in a settlement. It applies only to trusts which have always been UK resident.

A person might make a settlement in which he has an immediate life interest. He transfers to the trustees shares in a private trading company worth £1 million. He holds over the gain so that the trustees are treated as acquiring the shares with a base cost of, say, £100. The settlor is entitled to the income from the trust fund for life and the trustees also have power to advance capital to him. Both the settlor and trustees are UK resident.

Before 21 March 2000 the settlor might sell his interest in the settlement for say, £950,000. This would have been tax free. The purchaser would 'step into his shoes' in being appointed as a beneficiary. The shares could be advanced out under hold-over election and, the institution being exempt, would not attract CGT on ultimate disposal. This is no longer possible.

Restriction of losses

5.48   Prior to 2000/01 (see **5.22**: fourth bullet point under 'Effect of the rules') personal losses could not be offset against trust gains assessed under the settlor-interested rules on the settlor. Since 2003/04, but before 2008/09 (when the gains of settlor-interested trusts become assessed on the trustees), there is an automatic set-off.

Suppose that an individual not connected with the trust owns shares in a private company 'pregnant with gain'. He acquires an interest in the settlement and is added to the settlement as a beneficiary. He advances the shares to the trust under hold-over election, the trustees sell the shares and offset the gain against their losses. The proceeds of the sale are advanced to the new beneficiary. Where this occurs on or after 21 March 2000, ie someone has acquired an interest in a trust for consideration, the trustees cannot use their own losses to offset gains on the assets transferred by that person into trust under hold-over election.

No hold-over on transfers to a settlor-interested trust

5.49   Transfers into trust under hold-over relief have in the past been used for three specific tax planning purposes:

- as a device to get valuable non-business property down a generation without paying either IHT or CGT, under 'son of *Melville*' arrangements (see *Melville v IRC* [2002] 1 WLR 407) (see **6.20**);

- to mitigate the effect of the 'tainted taper' problem where an asset has changed its status from non-business to business; and

- in effectively 'doubling up' main residence relief for a second home as well as the individual's principal family home (see **5.25–5.27**).

New rules effective from 10 December 2003 have put paid to all of the above and, specifically in relation to private residences, a further set of rules prevents the combination of hold-over relief and main residence relief to achieve the tax advantage illustrated in Example 5.9 at **5.27**.

TAX PLANNING SUMMARY

5.50   You might give thought to any or all of the following possibilities:

- Annual exemption (see **5.36–5.39**): Do make use of it. Be aware of the circumstances where the anti-fragmentation rules apply and do make sure you claim the right amount each year.

- Losses (see **5.13–5.15**): Remember that current year losses must be set against current year gains, even if the effect is to 'waste' the annual exemption. Brought forward losses on the other hand, can be used only so far as is necessary to reduce the gains down to the annual exemption threshold. Losses arising on a disposal to a connected person can be set off only against a gain arising to the same connected person. Do remember to claim losses as they occur.

- If multiple disposals are made during the tax year, consider within a month or so of the end of it, ie early March, whether further disposals should be made to use the annual exemption or whether instead it might be worth triggering losses in appropriate cases to relieve tax liabilities. Remember that taper relief is up to the taxpayer to claim, ie in a case where there is the option 'where it has most effect'.

- Note that, from 2006/07 a settlement whose beneficiaries include the minor unmarried children of the settlor, not in a civil partnership, is now settlor-interested. This rule continues to be relevant where a person wants to give an asset standing at a gain to a trust, as he will not be able to hold over the gain (see **3.5**). Further, if within broadly six years after the end of the tax year in which the gift is made, the trust becomes settlor-interested, any hold-over relief previously claimed (on a disposal since 10 December 2003) is clawed back. There is no *de minimis* or *pro rata* let-out.

- Where the trustees own a property that is, or might be, occupied by a beneficiary so that main residence relief applies (see **5.25–5.27**), do ensure that the relief is maximised, ie you should not just think about it after you have sold the property. Consider the use of timely main residence relief elections where the trustees own what is manifestly not the beneficiary's main residence: the election must be made within two years after the property is occupied by that beneficiary. But bear in mind the anti-avoidance rules described in **5.27**.

- Base costs: Where, having sold an asset, you do not know the gain because the base cost has never been agreed, consider the IR 34 procedure (see **5.18–5.20**) with a view to agreeing the figures well before the time comes to pay the tax.

- EIS: By all means consider a subscription in qualifying shares as a means of deferring tax, but do not let the 'tax tail wag the investment dog'. Never make an investment just because it is tax efficient – you may lose your money (and the beneficiaries may be less than delighted).

- Payment of tax (see **5.53**): Do bear in mind following the end of the tax year what CGT will have to be paid on 31 January next, and budget for it. If the consideration is payable by instalments, consider the possibility of arranging with the inspector a deferred tax payment plan (see **5.6**).

THE TRUST AND ESTATE TAX RETURN

5.51   The form for returning capital gains tax is supplementary page SA 905 (to be included within the main trust and estate return): see **5.54–5.57**.

The only circumstances in which SA 905 need not be completed are (for 2008/09 and 2009/10):

- the total chargeable gains were less than, or equal to, the annual exempt amount (see **5.36–5.39**); and

- the assets disposed of during the tax year realise net proceeds of no more than four times the individual's annual exempt amount in total (ignoring exempt assets). For 2008/09, this amount is £38,400 and for 2009/10 £40,400.

That said, it is not a bad discipline to fill in the pages as part of the ongoing 'housekeeping' of the trust. In particular, it is important to use the form:

- to claim allowable losses which may be used in future;

- to make other claims or elections that require reference to, and completion of other HMRC forms, viz:
    - private residence relief: help sheet HS 283;
    - roll-over relief: help sheet HS 290;
    - entrepreneurs' relief: help sheet HS 275;
    - hold-over relief for gifts: help sheet HS 295;
    - EIS deferral relief: help sheet HS 297;
    - business transfer relief (where a business is transferred to a company in return for the issue of shares): column G on TC2;

– unremittable gains (asset disposed of outside the UK where exchange controls or shortage of foreign currency make the gain unremittable): column G on TC2;

– negligible value claims – see help sheet HS 286 and column G on TC2; or

– relief for foreign tax paid: if tax credit relief has not been claimed, the foreign tax ranks as a deduction against the chargeable gain. If tax credit relief is claimed, page TF3 on the trust and estates foreign pages should be completed and help sheet IR 390 referred to.

Tax year 2008/09: a compliance summary

5.52

Date for return	31 January 2010 if delivered online (or 31 October 2009, if delivered in paper form and where HMRC are to calculate the tax)
Payment of tax	31 January 2010 (or three months after the issue of the self-assessment return if later than 31 October 2009), subject to payment by instalments (see **5.6**)*
Interest and penalties	As for income tax (see **4.15–4.19**).

* CGT on gifts of certain assets (broadly those subject to instalment relief for IHT – see **11.92–11.95**) can on written election be paid by ten equal yearly instalments (TCGA 1992, s 281). The first instalment is payable on the usual due date, with any subsequent instalments payable on the subsequent anniversaries. Unpaid instalments carry any interest payable in the usual way. The instalment option is available also where assets leave a settlement and the disposal does not qualify for hold-over relief.

COMPLIANCE

Supplementary pages: Capital gains (SA 905)

5.53 The self-assessment of CGT operates in tandem with income tax (whereas compliance for IHT is entirely separate). The same tax district and reference deals both with income tax and CGT, whether for individuals or for trusts. SA 905 is the most complex of the supplemental pages. SA 905 has the benefit of substantive notes SA 905 (Notes) running to 20 pages and including 23 worked examples for 2008/09.

Gains and losses

5.54 SA 905 falls broadly into two parts – chargeable gains and allowable losses:

- The trustees must identify total chargeable gains (after any reliefs) and allowable losses for the year. These will be computed on pages TC2 and TC3 of SA 905. From the net gains will be deducted the relative annual exempt amount, which is basically £4,800 for 2008/09 (but could be less – see **5.36–5.39**), to produce the taxable gains to which the rate of 18% is applied.

- As to capital losses, losses for the current year, viz 2008/09 *must* be deducted from current year gains. Brought forward losses need be deducted only from current year gains to the extent that gains remain in charge over the annual exempt amount for the year. A loss arising on a transaction with a connected person (eg on a transfer from the settlor) can be offset only against gains made on disposals by the settlor to the trustees. Page TC1 enables notice to be given of a loss realised in tax year 2008/09 which may not be needed and can be carried forward. There is a time limit of five years and ten months from the end of the tax year for claiming losses (to be reduced to four years from 1 April 2010) and page TC1 performs this function.

CGT implications of events within the trust

5.55

- Death of a beneficiary with an interest in possession, provided the trust does not then fall within the relevant property regime for IHT purposes (see **9.10**).

- A person becomes absolutely entitled to trust property (see **9.10**).

- The trustees become non-UK resident (see **5.8–5.10**).

Example 5.13—Computation on property disposal

On 28 May 2009 the trustees sold for £150,000, a cottage which they acquired on 31 March 1982 for £40,000 (and which they had let on successive long tenancies). The calculation works as follows:

128

Disposal proceeds		£150,000
Less cost of acquisition	£40,000	
Less enhancement costs (May 1998)	£10,000	
Less incidental costs of acquisition	£1,000	
Less incidental disposal costs	£2,000	
Total costs	£53,000	(£53,000)
		–
Chargeable gain		£97,000
Less: annual exemption (say)		(£5,050)
CGT payable at 18%		£91,950
		£16,551

Additions of capital

5.56   Question 12 asks 'have any assets or funds been put into the trust?' The essence of a settlement or trust is that funds are contributed by way of 'bounty' or free gift. That is, the sale by the trustees of an asset included in the settlement for value would not be relevant to this question. However, if that sale were made at a gain, there would be a gain for the trustees.

HMRC need to keep track of the funds subject to the settlement and therefore if further assets are contributed there must be given:

● the settlor's name and address;

● a description of the asset; and

● the value of the asset.

Avoid contributing to someone else's settlement

5.57   There is no reason in principle why one person cannot contribute assets to a settlement made by another. However, this is generally a bad idea and it is best in practice to keep each settlement for assets contributed by a single settlor. The only exception could perhaps be joint husband and wife settlements, especially where the amounts contributed are the same, although even then there can be complications.

Such complications arise in particular with the anti-avoidance rules for settlor-interested trusts (see **4.26–4.29** for income tax and **6.16–6.21** for the reservation of benefit rules for IHT). One needs to be able to determine which property was contributed by which settlor and, unless very strict segregation of funds is operated, this becomes more and more difficult with the passage of time as assets are sold and reinvested.

One perceived advantage of having a single settlement with more than one settlor might be a saving in administrative and compliance costs. However, these could soon be outweighed. There is, further, a CGT advantage in having more than one settlement as each settlement will have its own annual exemption (subject to 'anti-fragmentation' rules; see **5.37–5.38**).

Example 5.14—The Adrian and Belinda A&M Trust

Adrian and Belinda were joint settlors of this trust, each contributing £125,000 at the outset. This settlement was made before the anti-avoidance rules for parental income were revised with effect from 9 March 1999. That means that income paid or applied for the benefit of any of Adrian's and Belinda's children will be assessed *pro rata* on Adrian and Belinda. As was pointed out in **4.24–4.29**, there is an interesting effect for income assessed on Belinda in so far as she is only a basic rate taxpayer.

Suppose that 10 years down the line, in 2009, ie after 9 March 1999, Belinda inherits some capital from her father's estate. The trust fund is now worth £500,000. She wants to add £100,000 to the trust fund. Although, for IHT purposes she does so by varying her father's will within two years after his death (see **13.1–13.4**), for income tax, and indeed, CGT purposes she is the 'settlor'. It has to be established what income accrues from her £100,000 addition (as opposed to the original £250,000 settled) for two purposes:

- following the 1999 change, income from Belinda's addition will be assessed on her, whether paid out or not; and

- for the purposes of the charge under *ITTOIA 2005, ss 629–632*, it must be clear which income is arising to Adrian (a higher rate taxpayer) and which to Belinda (only a basic rate taxpayer).

The easiest solution would be to retain the £100,000 addition as a segregated fund. However, this might not be so easy (and would not be welcomed by the stockbroker or investment manager). A sensible working solution might simply be to divide the income into 12 parts each year, assess two of those parts on Belinda in any event, and the remaining ten parts equally on Adrian and Belinda in so far as distributions are made to or for the benefit of the children.

Capital received from non-UK resident trusts

5.58   Question 16 on page 9 asks: 'Has the trust at any time been non-resident or received any capital from another trust which is or has at any time been non-resident?' If 'Yes', have the trustees made any capital payments to, or provided any benefits for, the beneficiaries?'

It is assumed in this book that the trust concerned has always been UK resident. What relevance, therefore, could there be, if a non-UK resident trust has paid any capital to our UK trust? The answer lies in *TCGA 1992, s 87*. A brief discursus is necessary into the anti-avoidance rules for non-UK resident trusts.

The CGT regime

5.59   The 'settlor charge' in *TCGA 1992, s 86* taxes a UK resident and domiciled settlor on gains made by non-UK resident trustees of certain settlements made by him.

Section 87 (the 'capital payments' charge) taxes UK resident and domiciled beneficiaries on capital payments received by them to the extent of the 'trust gains' (or, since 2008/09, the 'section 2(2) amounts') (*TCGA 1992, s 87A*)made by non-UK resident trustees (insofar as they have not already been attributed to 'capital payments'). From 2008/09 the capital payments charge applies even where the recipient UK resident beneficiary is domiciled outside the UK (although the trustees can by election ensure that trust gains realised or accrued before 6 April 2008 cannot be attributed to capital payments made to non-UK domiciled beneficiaries and, where the payment is received outside the UK, a remittance basis may apply).

Furthermore, the section has applied since 1998/99 even if the settlor of the trust was, and remains, non-UK domiciled. Nor does the horror end there. There can be a 'supplementary charge' on the beneficiary by reference to the time that has elapsed between making the trust gain and the capital payment, up to a maximum of six years, which increases the tax charge by 10% per annum. That is, the beneficiary could be facing a tax charge of up to 64% (in 2007/08), although in 2008/09 and 2009/10 the maximum rate falls to 28.8% (18% plus $6 \times 18\% \times 10\%$).

Scope of 'capital payment'

5.60   Most commonly, such capital payments charges might arise where the payment is made directly to the beneficiary. However, anti-avoidance rules mean that channelling the payment through another trust, including a UK-resident trust, would trigger the rules. Hence question 16. A Court of Appeal decision in *Billingham v Cooper* [2001] STC 1177, confirmed HMRC's view that the benefit of an interest-free loan is a capital payment. HMRC also take the view that rent-free enjoyment by a beneficiary of trust property is a capital payment.

If the question is answered affirmatively, the total capital payments or value of benefits provided must be given, together with their allocation between the beneficiaries, if more than one (whose names and addresses must be given). Equally, if the trust has received capital from any other trust that may have been non-UK resident, the name of the trust, the address of the trustee, the date of the establishment and the value received must be given.

Example 5.15—Beneficial loan is a capital payment

The Hector trust, being non-UK resident, makes a payment to the Albert discretionary settlement of £100,000. The Albert trustees decide to lend £50,000 to a beneficiary on 5 October 2008, interest-free, repayable on demand.

The beneficiary is treated as having received a capital payment of the interest forgone on £50,000 for six months. At the beneficial loan rate of 6.25% from 6 October 2008 to 5 April 2009 the capital payment is only £1,562. (For 2009/10 the beneficial loan rate is 4.75%, making the benefit of the capital payment of £50,000 £2,375 for the year.)

If, however, the other £50,000 were advanced to the beneficiary absolutely on 5 October 2008, the capital payment would become £51,562. The rate of tax in 2008/09 could be anything between 18% and 28.8% depending upon when the relative trust gains were realised by the Hector Trust – and this may not be easy to find out.

Chapter 6

Running a trust: inheritance tax

COMPLIANCE IN SUMMARY

6.1   We made the point in Chapter 3 (see **3.12–3.17**) that the principal distinction before 22 March 2006 was between:

- a potentially exempt transfer, viz principally a life interest trust and an accumulation and maintenance trust; and

- a chargeable transfer, viz a discretionary trust.

As from 22 March 2006, however, the creation of any non-charitable trust (other than a qualifying trust for a disabled person – see **2.10**) is a chargeable transfer. Accordingly, what was, in editions of this book before 2006/07, referred to as the 'discretionary trust regime' is now called the 'relevant property regime' (or 'the mainstream trust regime'). One must remember that, for trusts created before 22 March 2006, however, the above potentially exempt transfer/chargeable transfer distinction applied.

PETs (to a qualifying disabled trust or, before 22 March 2006, to an interest in possession or A&M trust)

6.2   In terms of ongoing compliance requirements, no action is required so long as:

- In the case of a life interest trust, the beneficiary remains alive and no capital leaves the trust (other than by advance to the life tenant). Because the life tenant is treated as owning the assets underlying the trust, an advance of capital to him is simply giving him unfettered ownership of property that he was treated for IHT purposes as owning already *(IHTA 1984, s 49(1))*. If the trustees exercise a power to transfer capital to any other individual (other than his UK-domiciled spouse or civil partner, which will be exempt) the life tenant will be treated as having made a PET himself, with no implications unless he dies within the following seven years.

- With an A&M trust, the basic conditions are satisfied (see **6.45**) and (see the last sentence below) capital vests at or before age 18. Once, or to the extent that the qualifying A&M conditions cease to be satisfied, the settlement leaves the favoured A&M regime and the asset will either become an interest in possession trust or will be owned outright. For A&M trusts in being at 22 March 2006, the options during the transitional period which came to an end on 5 April 2008 are set out at **6.50**. Any capital still left in the trust at 6 April 2008 is now subject to the relevant property regime (see **6.29–6.44**), *unless* the terms of the trust were changed (if necessary) before 6 April 2008 to ensure that absolute capital entitlement arises at age 18.

If a life interest settlement comes to an end because of the life tenant's death, IHT will be calculated on the combined total of his free estate and the settled estate and the trustees will bear their proportion of the tax (see **11.74–11.76**). If the life interest comes to an end within seven years before the life tenant dies, by capital being advanced to someone else, so that he is treated as making a PET, the transfer of value may well be within his nil rate band. To the extent that it exceeds the life tenant's nil rate band, the trustees will be primarily responsible for the tax, though the transferee of the capital and indeed the life tenant's personal representatives could also have a residual liability (*IHTA 1984, s 201(1)*).

Chargeable transfers

6.3   With a discretionary trust, on the other hand, not only might there have been IHT implications at outset (see **3.17–3.20**), there can be implications thereafter, both as to giving notice to HMRC Inheritance Tax, and may be as to payment of tax during the lifetime of the trust. These are explained in more detail in **6.30–6.44**. All lifetime trusts made on or after 22 March 2006 (except for a disabled person) will be chargeable transfers.

Example 6.1—Discretionary trust

Albert's discretionary trust (see Example 2.1 at **2.8**) was made on 1 January 1998, that is, at a time when the nil rate band was £215,000. The value of the assets given to the trust was £220,000. Albert had used his £3,000 annual exemption in 1995/96 but had not otherwise made any transfers of value in the seven years ending on 1 January 1998. He had available his annual exemptions for 1997/98 and 1996/97 and therefore a chargeable transfer of £214,000 to the discretionary trust did not cause him to exceed his nil rate band. Given that the whole of the trust fund was neither agricultural nor business property, there will be no exit charges on an exit within the first ten years. The question of a ten-year anniversary charge will depend on the amount in the trust at that time (viz, 1 January 2008).

Example 6.2—Accumulation and maintenance trust

The Adrian and Belinda Settlement (see Example 2.2 at **2.8**) was a qualifying A&M trust. However, it is better to think of a trust satisfying the A&M conditions (at any relevant time). This it will do so long as no part of the trust fund is subject to an absolute interest or interest in possession and at least one beneficiary remains who has not yet become entitled to such an interest. There is a 21-year period of accumulation, which expires on 1 January 2020. At that point, Caroline, aged five when the settlement was made, must have become entitled to at least an interest in possession. David, then aged two, will be aged 23 and must become entitled at that time, if not hitherto. Accumulation could continue in respect of the prospective share of a beneficiary still under the age of 18. Failing any, however, the A&M regime will end and an interest in possession will commence.

Of course, this is a classic case of a type of settlement which is adversely affected by the new IHT regime for trusts that took effect on 22 March 2006. Unless the terms of the trust were changed before 6 April 2008 (see **6.50**) to provide that the capital vests outright in the children at age 25 at latest, the trust fund will have entered the 'relevant property' regime on 6 April 2008 (if not before, once an interest in possession arises). If the trust was changed so that capital vests absolutely at age 25, the advantage is that, although the special charging regime for 'age 18–25 trusts' will apply to the presumptive share in capital while the relevant child is between the age of 18 and 25, that special charging regime will not apply to any such share until the relevant child attains age 18. Had changes to the trust been effected before 6 April 2008 to make the vesting age 18, the trust fund will be preserved from any IHT charge, as the A&M status will continue.

Example 6.3—Interest in possession trust

The settlement for Alistair made on 1 January 2006 (see Example 2.3 at **2.8**) was an interest in possession settlement. During Alistair's lifetime, the trustees have the power to appoint income away from him. If they do this in favour of any individuals absolutely or (before 6 October 2008) in trust as a TSI (see **6.58**) or as a disabled person's interest (see **2.10**), this will cause Alistair himself to be treated as making a PET, that is with no IHT implications if he survives for seven years. On the other hand, if the appointment created any other type of settlement, this will be a chargeable transfer by Alistair and could, depending upon the value involved and Alistair's own gifts history within the seven preceding years, have positive IHT implications.

THE TERRITORIAL LIMITATION OF IHT

6.4   The basis of inheritance tax differs from that of income tax and CGT. Income tax and CGT broadly catch the income and gains of a person (including trustees) who is resident or ordinarily resident in the UK at some time during the tax year. There is also an income tax liability on the UK source income of a non-UK resident. There is some limitation (called the 'remittance basis'), in that the income and gains outside the UK of a person resident but not domiciled in the UK may escape UK tax, insofar as the income or proceeds of sale are not brought to this country, directly or indirectly. *FA 2008* has introduced an annual income tax charge of £30,000 on a person aged 18 or over who claims the remittance basis and who has been UK resident in at least seven of the preceding nine years, subject to a *de minimis* of £2,000 for unremitted income and gains, and has made various technical clarifications to the concept of remittance.

Actual domicile

6.5   IHT is different, in working largely on the basis of domicile, ie residence is irrelevant. A person is domiciled in the jurisdiction in which he intends to make his permanent home. Each individual has at birth a domicile of origin, which will generally be where he is born if that is the domicile of his parents, or he may have a domicile of dependency up to age 16, which will follow the domicile of his father. A domicile of origin may be displaced by the acquisition later on of an independent domicile of choice. If a domicile of choice is abandoned without a new domicile of choice being acquired, the domicile of origin will revive.

A person may be resident in more than one country during the tax year, but he can have only one domicile.

Deemed domicile

6.6   In addition, there is a special 'deemed domicile' rule for IHT purposes where a person who is not domiciled in the UK under the general law is treated as domiciled for IHT (only), if (under *IHTA 1984, s 267*):

- he has been resident in the UK for at least 17 out of the last 20 tax years, when the deemed domicile will arise at the beginning of the 17th year; or

- he has been domiciled in any part of the UK at any time during the previous three calendar years.

Note the (current) HMRC and Treasury review of residence and domicile launched in 2003 (see **4.3**).

The scope of IHT

6.7   How far does IHT bite? Generally, subject to a double tax treaty, IHT will apply to:

- the worldwide estate of a person actually, or deemed, domiciled in the UK; and

- the UK-situated estate of a person, not UK domiciled and not deemed domiciled here, subject to some exceptions.

Excluded property

6.8   IHT does not apply to excluded property, viz:

- property situated outside the UK if it is owned by a person domiciled outside the UK for all IHT purposes (*IHTA 1984, s 6(1)*);

- certain government securities (known as FOTRA, ie 'free of tax to residents abroad') owned either by non-UK domiciliaries or individuals not 'ordinarily resident' in the UK, or by the trustees of an interest in possession if the beneficiary is non-UK domiciled and there would be excluded property in relation to him. Similarly, with FOTRA securities owned by discretionary trustees and all possible beneficiaries falling into that category (*IHTA 1984, s 6(2)*);

- the reversionary interest to a settlement, ie the interest that comes into being when a qualifying interest in possession expires. This is the corollary of the rule that the life tenant is treated as beneficially entitled to the trust property, in a case where the relevant property regime does not apply. The only exception is an anti-avoidance one where it is the settlor or spouse who owns the reversionary interest (*IHTA 1984, s 48(1)*);

- property outside the UK owned by trustees (wherever resident) of a settlement made by someone domiciled outside the UK, even if the settlor has since become UK domiciled, provided (and to the extent) that there has been no purchase of an interest in the settled property on or after 5 December 2005 (*IHTA 1984, s 48(3)–(3C)*).

Traditionally, HMRC Inheritance Tax have taken the view that the excluded property rules take precedence over the reservation of benefit regime (see **6.16–6.21**).Though there have been recent indications that they may be rethinking this issue, that traditional view currently remains in force.

PAYMENT OF TAX

6.9　　While a trust continues, there will be no IHT implications if it is interest in possession or A&M in character. Note that, even after 5 April 2008, a trust can be A&M, if the age of absolute entitlement to capital is 18 (see **6.50**). However, this will not be true of a 'relevant property' trust (see **6.27– 6.44**), when there may be:

- a charge on the first and each subsequent ten-year anniversary of making the settlement; and

- a charge on the exit from the trust of all or any part of the trust property.

In respect of either event, the trustees must:

- submit a tax return, called an 'account', which will be on form IHT 100; and

- pay any tax due.

On the assumption that notice of the settlement was given to HMRC Inheritance Tax in the first place, HMRC Inheritance Tax will have knowledge of the settlement and the names and addresses of the trustees. However, in cases where HMRC Inheritance Tax suspect there may be a settlement but do not have the information, they have a statutory power to serve notice, whether on the trustees or anyone else, eg a bank or stockbroker. HMRC Inheritance Tax do first have to obtain the consent of a special commissioner to serve such a notice. Once the notice has been served, a response must be given within 30 days (*IHTA 1984, s 219*).

As to the liability to pay tax, whether on the ten-year anniversary or on exit, much will depend upon the character of the trust property. If it is illiquid, viz invested in land or shares that do not produce income, the trustees may find themselves with some financial embarrassment. Happily, there are provisions (see **11.92–11.96**) whereby any tax due in these circumstances may be paid by instalments, the first one falling due on the date when the whole of the tax should have been paid and the other nine instalments following at annual intervals (*IHTA 1984, ss 227–229*).

Due dates

Delivery of account

6.10   The account must be delivered:

- within 12 months after the end of the month in which the occasion of charge took place; or
- alternatively, if later, at the end of a three-month period beginning from the date on which the trustees become liable for tax (*IHTA 1984, s 216*).

Payment of tax

6.11   By contrast, the tax will usually become due earlier (*IHTA 1984, s 226*), viz:

- If the chargeable event takes place after 5 April but before 1 October – the tax is due on 30 April of the following year.
- If the chargeable event occurs after 30 September and before 6 April – the tax is due six months after the end of the month in which the event occurred.

THE INTEREST AND PENALTY REGIME

Interest

6.12   IHT paid late attracts interest, which is not deductible for income tax purposes (*IHTA 1984, s 233*): see **6.14** for the rates. Sometimes, of course, the value of the property attracting the tax may not be known and, therefore, the tax is not known at the due date. An amount can be deposited on account. If excessive, and therefore some repayment is due, that repayment will attract repayment supplement. The trustees can also buy certificates of tax deposit. Interest will be received on any overpayment and will be tax exempt.

Penalties

6.13   A new penalty regime for IHT took effect on 1 April 2009 for deaths and other chargeable events occurring on or after that date (where the return is due to be filed on or after 1 April 2010). This is the impact of *FA 2008, Sch 40* extending to IHT among other taxes the new regime introduced by *FA 2007, Sch 24*. Readers are referred to the discussion at **4.15** under income tax for a summary of the new system, maximum penalties and the mechanism of statutory reductions for disclosure. While the new regime looks considerably more 'fierce' than that which applied before, HMRC do say at question 32 of their frequently asked questions on the regime published on 19 March 2009:

> 'HMRC recognise that IHT applies to a single event and concepts such as reasonable care will be somewhat different under these circumstances than for taxes where people have to make returns more regularly. HMRC also recognise that the position of personal representatives is different from other individuals and trustees who may make a transfer that is liable to IHT'.

For the position on penalties in relation to deaths and other chargeable events before 1 April 2009 readers are referred to **6.13** of the 2008/09 edition of this book.

Separately, a system of penalties has been introduced by *FA 2009, Sch 56,* for failure to make payments on time to take effect from a date to be appointed by Treasury order, possibly 1 April 2010. In broad terms, failure to pay IHT by the filing date (in the case of death, 12 months after the end of the month of death) carries a penalty of 5% of the unpaid tax, with a further 5% due on tax remaining unpaid five months after the penalty date and a further 5% on the unpaid 11 months after the penalty date. Special provisions apply to tax payable by instalments.

Interest rates over the last four years

Underpaid and overpaid tax

6.14

6 September 2005–5 September 2006	3%
6 September 2006–5 August 2007	4%
6 August 2007–5 January 2008	5%
6 January 2008– 5 November 2008	4%
6 November 2008–5 January 2009	3%
6 January 2009–26 January 2009	2%
21 January 2009–23 March 2009	1%
24 March 2009 to date	0% (subject to a minimum of 0.5% on tax repayments announced by HMRC on 29 July 2009, to take effect from a date in September 2009)

Professional obligation to notify

6.15   There is a further obligation to be taken seriously by solicitors and other professional advisers. If a UK-domiciled settlor makes a settlement with non-UK resident trustees (or gives a professional person concerned with the making of a settlement cause to think that non-UK resident trustees will be appointed), there is a stand-alone obligation (ie whether or not requested by HMRC Inheritance Tax) for that professional person, though not a barrister, to give notice within three months (*IHTA 1984, s 218*).

GIFTS WITH RESERVATION

6.16   The reservation of benefit rules were introduced for IHT in 1986 (*FA 1986, s 102* and *Sch 20*). They apply to any type of gift, not just a gift into trust. However, so far as gifts into trust are concerned, they may be regarded as the equivalent of the settlor-interested rules for income tax (see **4.26–4.29**) and for CGT (see **5.21–5.22**). They are narrower in scope, however, in that:

- they do not apply to gifts before 18 March 1986; and also

- settlements from which the settlor but not his spouse are excluded do not come within the ambit of the rules.

It is usually sensible that settlor and spouse are irrevocably excluded from benefit, though the income tax and CGT rules (or, of course, the reservation of benefit rules) will not apply if there is a possibility of the widow or widower of the settlor benefiting after the settlor's death. That said, there could be examples where a settlor-included settlement is useful, eg to secure the main residence relief for trusts and an IHT benefit is not envisaged, so that the settlor and spouse might be included (but this will be unusual).

Effects

6.17

- If the reservation of benefit continues until death, the settlor is treated as if the subject-matter of the gift were comprised in his estate at its then market value (*FA 1986, s 102(3)*).

- If the benefit was released within the seven years before his death, the settlor is treated as having made a PET at that time of its then value (*FA 1986, s 102(4)*).

Double charges

6.18 There could, however, be double taxation in so far as a gift to discretionary trustees from which the settlor is not excluded from benefit will be both a chargeable transfer and a gift with reservation of benefit. The *IHT (Double Charges Relief) Regulations 1987* contain provisions whereby, broadly speaking, the IHT payable separately on the chargeable transfer and the reservation of benefit is computed and only one charge, not surprisingly the higher one, is applied.

Anti-avoidance rules from 2005/06: the 'pre-owned assets' regime

6.19 With effect from 6 April 2005, *FA 2004, Sch 15* has introduced a savage new income tax charge on (broadly) IHT mitigation arrangements made since 18 March 1986 under which, in relation to all of land, chattels and certain settlor-interested trusts, an individual continues to enjoy the free benefit of an asset that he or she has given away. The income tax charge can be avoided by:

- paying an annual amount prescribed by the legislation;

- terminating the benefit before (ideally) 6 April 2005 or before the beginning of any subsequent year (though the charge remains in force for any preceding years from 2005/06); or

- making an irrevocable election to opt back into the reservation of benefit regime.

See **4.44–4.54**.

Releasing the reservation – concept of 'settlement power' blocks avoidance arrangement

6.20 In *Melville v IRC* [2002] 1 WLR 407, the Court of Appeal affirmed on 31 July 2001 the effectiveness of a scheme designed to make use of hold-over relief from CGT for non-business property worth more than the nil rate band.

Assume that a person owns very valuable investment property, say worth £1 million, which he wishes to give to his children. The assets carry a large gain. If he makes the gift to a discretionary trust and holds over the gain, he will have to pay 20% lifetime IHT. If, however, he can reduce the transfer of value amount to within the nil rate band, he could at least make the gift to a discretionary trust and hold-over the gain with a liability to IHT.

The way he might make such a large reduction in value is by reserving a valuable benefit, viz a right after 90 days having elapsed to require the trustees to return the assets to him.

He makes the gift, holds over the gain and because of the right, the transfer of value is worth very much less than the original £1 million. Once 90 days have expired, he releases the benefit, which treats him as making a potentially exempt transfer, which he survives by seven years, ie it becomes exempt.

What the Court of Appeal did was to confirm that the valuable right retained by the settlor was 'property' to be taken into account in computing the amount of the transfer of value.

In response to the *Melville* decision, *FA 2002, s 119* introduced the concept of a 'settlement power', which does not constitute property for IHT purposes. This specifically counters the effect of the *Melville* arrangement by ensuring that the transfer of value made by the settlor equates to the market value of the initial trust fund with no reduction for the valuable right. Interestingly, however, it remains possible to avoid the ambit of the new rule, for example by having an initial discretionary trust for say 12 months, after which there is a reversion to the settlor. The settlor simply gives away his reversion during the 12-month period to a second settlement from which he is excluded from benefit. The existence of the reversionary interest devalues the initial transfer of value and hold-over relief is obtained both on that initial gift and on the subsequent transfer of funds from the first to the second settlement. Further anti-avoidance legislation has been enacted to counteract the so called 'sons of *Melville*'. See **5.49**.

FA 2006 blocks gift with reservation avoidance device using life interest settlements

6.21   A common spousal will structure over recent years has been to put the deceased's share of the family home into a life interest trust for the benefit of both spouse and children. While the children would, if adult, typically not chose to live in the matrimonial home, they could do so nonetheless under the trust and, under the *IHTA 1984, s 49(1)* regime, their *pro rata* share of the house was treated as comprised in their estates and not in that of the surviving parent. The proportion of the deceased's interest in the house that could be left within his nil rate band on life interest for the children, the balance for the surviving spouse, would depend on both the value of the house and the extent of chargeable transfers made in the seven years before death plus any other chargeable transfers under the will. But suppose the surviving spouse were left say, a 50% interest in the deceased's half share. The trustees might, in exercise of their powers of appointment, reduce the survivor's interest to 10% and increase those of the children to 90%. This would be a potentially exempt transfer by the survivor, ie exempt for IHT purposes on survival for seven years. But there would be no gift with reservation because the transfer of value had been engineered by the trustees, not created by the beneficiary.

This effect is changed from 22 March 2006, to provide that in such circumstances, that is treated as a gift by the beneficiary in which he reserves a benefit for so long as he continues to occupy the house rent-free or for less than full consideration (or enjoys a benefit from any other trust asset). (*FA 1986, s 102ZA.*)

AGRICULTURAL AND BUSINESS PROPERTY RELIEF

6.22 BPR and APR are reliefs that differ from each other, though they operate in much the same way (*IHTA 1984, ss 103–114* for BPR and *ss 115– 124C* for APR). They are given either at 100% or at 50% in reducing the chargeable transfer for IHT purposes. This could be:

- with an interest in possession trust, on the death of the life tenant; or

- with a discretionary trust, either when the property enters the trust or on the ten-year anniversary, or when the property leaves the trust.

Business property relief

6.23 Business property relief will apply when the trust owns (*inter alia*):

- a business or an interest in a partnership business (100% relief);

- unlisted shares in a trading company (100% relief);

- fixed assets, premises or plant held outside the business carried on by the trustees in partnership or a business carried on by the life tenant (50% relief).

The above represents a summary of the six categories of 'relevant business property' defined at *IHTA 1984, s 105(1)*.

Agricultural property relief

6.24 APR will apply to agricultural land and (subject to some restrictions), farmhouses, farm cottages and farm buildings (defined as qualifying 'agricultural property' at *IHTA 1984, s 115(2)*). Relief will be given at 100% if the trustees own and farm the land themselves or if they let the land on a farm business tenancy. The trustees will get only 50% relief if they let the land and cannot recover vacant possession within 12 (or by concession 24) months.

Further details of APR and BPR may be found in **11.54–11.66**.

The clawback rules

6.25 There are 'clawback' rules, which need to be watched where property was put into trust with the benefit of APR or BPR and the settlor dies within seven years. To avoid a retrospective withdrawal of relief it must be shown that the trustees continued to own the original or qualifying replacement property and that it continued to attract APR or BPR in their hands (*IHTA 1984, ss 113– 113B* for BPR and *ss 124–124C* for APR).

Example 6.4—The 'clawback trap'

In 2002 Jack who farmed as sole trader an agricultural estate of 1,000 acres put into a discretionary trust 200 acres plus two cottages, all of which had development potential. The transfer attracted business property relief (on the authority of the High Court decision in *HMRC v the Trustees of the Nelson Dance Family Settlements* [2009] EWHC 71 Ch 22). Jack died in 2008, by which time he was paying a rent to the trustees for the land and cottages which had not yet been sold. There is a clawback of the relief, with a positive IHT effect insofar as the gross value of the assets settled exceeded Jack's nil-rate band on death.

By contrast, had Jack taken the trustees into a (perhaps, limited) partnership and the trustees had contributed the land and cottages to the partnership, there would have been no clawback of relief.

The 'first ten years exit' trap

6.26 There is a trap with discretionary trusts and an exit in the first ten years where agricultural or business property is concerned; this is explained at **6.35**.

'RELEVANT PROPERTY' TRUSTS

Estate duty

6.27 Under estate duty (which was replaced by capital transfer tax in 1975) it was possible for a discretionary trust to be a family's 'tax-free money box' insofar as gifts, taxation and death duties were concerned. This assumes that the trust was made at least seven years before the settlor's death as, if not, it would have come into charge for estate duty on that death.

The CTT regime

6.28   1975 saw the introduction of a new regime for discretionary settlements under capital transfer tax, which was thought to be excessively draconian (which in a sense it was, when compared with the previous regime). Since then, however, the regime has come to be seen as relatively benign if viewed in the broader context of things. It has to be said that much of the legislation is fairly complex; the spirit behind it, however, is as follows.

Taxing the trust

6.29

- The ten-yearly charge: the thinking behind the legislation is to treat each discretionary trust as a separate taxpayer and to subject it to IHT as if the property in the settlement had been the subject of a lifetime gift made every generation. The rate of IHT on death is 40%, whereas the rate on chargeable lifetime gifts (which the donor survives by more than seven years) is 20%. A generation is assumed to be 33 and ⅓ years. HMRC Inheritance Tax want to collect the money rather more regularly than three times every 100 years, so the charge on property in the settlement is collected every ten years at a maximum rate of 6%, which equates to 20% every 33 and ⅓ years. However, 6% is a maximum rate and in very many cases the effective rate will be much less than this given the effect of the nil rate band. The method of calculation is explained in **6.30–6.33**.

- In addition there is an 'exit' charge (see **6.34–6.36**) charged on the value of the property leaving the trust.

The vast majority of discretionary settlements are within the nil rate band and the charges to tax may be very small or nothing at all. Very often, the reason for using a discretionary, rather than any other type of settlement, are the CGT advantages of hold-over relief. (However, note the rule effective from 10 December 2003, which prevents hold-over relief on a transfer to a settlor-interested settlement (see **3.5**).)

Example 6.5—IHT impact of capital advance

Albert's settlement, made on 1 January 1998 was within his nil rate band. By the time of the first ten-year anniversary on 1 January 2008, the trust fund had, with successful investment management, grown to £800,000. A capital

146

advance of £50,000 was made on 1 January 2006. The rate of tax charged on this exit was nil (see **6.35**).

However, on the first ten-yearly charge on 1 January 2008 there was a positive charge, as the value of the trust fund exceeded the then nil rate band. The detailed calculation is shown in Example 6.6 at **6.33**.

Any exit of capital in the ten years following 1 January 2008 will, for its rate, be related back to the rate on the first ten years, subject to possible adjustment for any increase in the nil rate band (see **6.36**).

THE TEN-YEAR CHARGE

6.30   The ten-year anniversary charge is the main IHT charge for discretionary (or 'relevant property') settlements.

Date of charge

6.31   The first ten-year charge arises on the tenth anniversary of the date when the settlement began, which is the date on which the property first became settled (*IHTA 1984, s 61*). Therefore, if the settlement was established first with £10 and then six months later, the main trust fund advanced, it is the date on which the £10 went into the trust that fixes the commencement.

Where property is left under a will on discretionary trusts, the date of death is the commencement of the settlement (regardless of how long it takes to administer the estate).

Two elements

6.32

● The chargeable amount (*IHTA 1984, s 64*). This is the value of all 'relevant property' (see **6.37**) contained in the settlement immediately before the ten-year anniversary, subject to adjustment where property has changed its character during the ten years (see **6.42**). 'Relevant property' will include the capital, and accumulated income, but not undistributed income. Contingent CGT is not a valid deduction, although liabilities secured on the property would be. Applicable BPR and APR are available to reduce the amount chargeable to tax.

- The rate of tax (*IHTA 1984, s 66*), which is 30% of the 'effective rate' applicable to a lifetime charge made by a hypothetical transferor with a gifts history equal to that of the settlor in the seven years before he made the settlement, but excluding the date of settlement, plus any amounts on which an exit charge have been imposed in the last ten years.

This means that the seven-year gifts history of the settlor will persist in being relevant to the calculation of each ten-year anniversary charge within the settlement.

Taking our hypothetical transferor, his gifts history is assumed to be the aggregate of gifts made by him in the seven years before the settlement plus any amount on which exit charges were imposed in the ten years before the particular ten-year anniversary (*IHTA 1984, s 66(5)*).

Calculating the IHT payable

6.33 Having calculated the deemed chargeable transfer and the deemed cumulative total, the lifetime rate, ie 20%, is used to discover the tax appropriate. This divided by the deemed chargeable transfer gives an effective rate, which is multiplied by 30% to discover the rate payable and then applied to the chargeable property to discover the tax payable. An example is given below.

Example 6.6—Ten-year charge illustration

There was a ten-year charge on 1 January 2008 on Albert's settlement.

The value of the trust fund at that date, after an advance of capital of £50,000 made on 1 January 2006, was £800,000. That is called the 'relevant property'.

The rate of tax is 30% of the 'effective rate' applied to a lifetime gift made by a hypothetical transferor with a gifts history equal to that of Albert in the seven years before he made the settlement, plus the advance of capital in 2006. Albert, being well advised, had a nil chargeable transfers history during that seven-year period. However, the deemed cumulative total of the hypothetical transferor includes any amounts on which exit charges were imposed (even if at the nil rate) in the previous years (*IHTA 1984, s 66(5)(b)*). This is achieved in computing the rate below by deducting the capital advance of £50,000 from the nil rate band.

The nil rate band in 2007/08 was £300,000. The lifetime charge would therefore have been:

		£800,000
Nil rate band	£300,000	
Less capital advance	(£50,000)	(£250,000)
		£550,000
Tax @ 20% (lifetime rate)		£110,000

The 'effective rate' is £110,000 divided by 800,000 = 13.75%, of which 30% is 4.125%.

The tax on the ten-year anniversary, therefore, is 4.125% of £800,000 = £33,000.

EXIT CHARGE

6.34 The exit charge arises when property leaves the discretionary regime, by way of gift (*IHTA 1984, s 65*). Therefore, it would not apply to the sale or purchase by the trustees of trust property nor indeed to the payment of professional costs or other expenses. Likewise, if the property was paid to a charity or other tax relieved body, eg the National Trust.

There is no exit charge if the event happens in the first quarter (three months) following either creation of the settlement or the last ten-year anniversary (*IHTA 1984, s 65(4)*). If the discretionary trust was created by will, there is no exit charge if the event happens at least three months but within two years after the death (see **13.9**).

The exit charge taxes the fall in value of the relevant property (the 'estate before less estate after' principle). If the tax is paid out of the residual trust fund rather than by the recipient of the property, the amount must be grossed up.

A distinction should be drawn between the exit charge in the first ten years and the exit charge following the first or subsequent ten-year anniversaries.

Exit in the first ten years

6.35 Like the ten-yearly charge, the exit charge in the first ten years (*IHTA 1984, s 66*) requires a deemed cumulative total of the hypothetical transferor, which is that of the settlor in the seven years before the settlement began. This is applied to the value of the settled property at commencement (not at exit) taking into account related settlements and added property discussed in **6.39–6.41**.

The lifetime rates are then applied to the deemed chargeable transfer on the basis of the deemed cumulative total, with 30% applied, ie just like the ten-year charge. However, there is then a reduction to take account of the number of completed quarters that have elapsed since commencement.

If, however, the rate is nil (even if a day before the ten-year anniversary), then whatever the value of the trust fund at exit, no IHT is charged.

There is a trap, however, with agricultural and business property when working out the exit charge the *gross* and not the relieved value of the property is taken (*IHTA 1984, s 68(5)(a)*). Unless therefore the gross value is within the nil rate band on exit, *or* the property continues to attract APR or BPR in the hands of the trustees, there could conceivably be a positive charge on exit, whereas there would have been a nil charge on entry.

Exit after the first ten years

6.36   The exit charge between ten-year anniversaries adopts the rate charged on the last ten-year anniversary, scaled down by reference to the number of quarters that have elapsed since then. If, since that ten-year anniversary, the nil rate band has increased, that higher figure is used instead of the nil rate band prevailing at the ten-year anniversary, in effect to give a lower rate of exit charge (*IHTA 1984, Sch 2, para 3*).

Example 6.7—Exit charge

The trustees of Albert's trust decide to appoint capital of £100,000 on 1 January 2009 equally between the children of the settlors: Charles, Debbie, Edward and Fiona. This is a charge following the first ten-year anniversary when the rate of tax was 4.125%. But the rate is recalculated to take into account the higher nil rate band of £312,000 in 2008/09: this reduces the rate to 4.035%.

This rate is applied to the capital leaving the trust, viz £100,000 to produce tax of £4,035. However, of the 40 three-month quarters in the ten-year period, only four have expired since the last ten-yearly charge. This figure is therefore multiplied by four and divided by 40 to produce a tax charge of just £403.50. The tax is payable out of the appointed funds. If the trustees were to pay the £403.50, then although *de minimis*, grossing up would have to be applied as this would increase the value of the appointment being tax free.

RELEVANT AND NON-RELEVANT PROPERTY

6.37   The legislation uses the expression 'relevant property' generally to mean property subject to the discretionary (or 'mainstream') trust regime. The expression is defined in *IHTA 1984, s 58* as settled property in which there is no qualifying interest in possession. However, there are further exceptions, which are the standard favoured trusts, viz in particular:

* charities;

* A&M trusts (so long as, following 5 April 2008, the age of capital vesting is 18);

* disabled person's trusts;

* qualifying employee trusts, maintenance funds for historic buildings, pension funds etc; and

* excluded property trusts (see **6.8**).

Mixed property settlements

6.38   There is a trap where a non-UK domiciliary sets up a relevant property trust containing both UK and non-UK property. The non-UK property is clearly excluded property. However, the existence of the non-UK property (and specifically its value after commencement of the settlement) is taken into account in computing the rate of tax either on exit or at each ten-year anniversary – as part of the settled property which is not specifically excluded from the calculation. It is, therefore, essential that a UK property settlement made by a non-UK domiciliary should not be tainted in any way with excluded property.

The above principle applies in any case where within the one settlement there is both relevant and non-relevant property. What the legislation does is bring the non-relevant property into the deemed chargeable transfer to fix the rate, even though that non-relevant property does not itself attract tax.

There could be a situation where a discretionary settlement began with 100% relevant property, but during the ten-year period an interest in possession arose in part. For example, HMRC Inheritance Tax consider that if discretionary trustees allow a beneficiary to occupy a dwelling-house on terms and in circumstances that it is anticipated to be the beneficiary's permanent home, the exercise of that power converts the settlement from discretionary into interest in possession (Statement of Practice SP 10/79). If subsequently the beneficiary leaves the dwelling-house, the property reverts to being relevant property. The matter is handled by adjusting the rate on the ten-year anniversary and not the deemed chargeable transfer. If, by contrast, all the trust fund is appointed out

151

of the settlement, there will have been an exit charge and no relevant property left to be taxed at the next ten-year anniversary.

With the 'alignment' of IHT for trusts on 22 March 2006, this rule ceases to have such an impact in calculating IHT. This is because (subject to the rules for 'transitional serial interests' – see **6.58**) an interest in possession created since 22 March 2006 out of a discretionary trust in circumstances described in the previous paragraph will be a non-qualifying interest in possession and so the capital concerned will remain within the relevant property regime. The only impact, with income-producing property, might be an income tax one, where the special trust rates described at **4.32** would not apply if there were an interest in possession, albeit non-qualifying for IHT purposes.

RELATED SETTLEMENTS

6.39   The concept of 'related settlement' is relevant only to the discretionary trust (or 'relevant property') regime (*IHTA 1984, s 62*).

On commencement, a discretionary (or 'relevant property') settlement has a settlement related to it if the settlor is the same and the two settlements begin on the same day. The only exception is an exclusively charitable settlement. If, however, a settlor makes on the same day both a discretionary settlement and (before 22 March 2006) an A&M trust, for example, the A&M trust will be related to the discretionary settlement.

Because, in calculating the settlor's cumulative total, transfers made on the day on which the discretionary settlement commences are disregarded, a related settlement could be an avoidance device. Therefore, the calculation of both the exit charge and the ten-year charge brings in related settlements. Otherwise, a settlor could create a number of small settlements all on the same day to produce a lower overall rate of tax. Ten settlements each with £10,000 all sharing the same deemed cumulative total would obviously be preferable to one with £100,000, were it not for the aggregation of related settlements. To counter all this, the legislation requires the calculation of the chargeable value for both the ten-yearly and the exit charge to include related settlements made on the day of the discretionary trust (see, for example, *IHTA 1984, s 66(4)(c)* for the ten-yearly charge).

An alternative might be to create a number of discretionary settlements all on consecutive days and then subsequently on the same day to add the substantive trust property to each of the settlements. This on the face of it avoids the rules. However, there are 'associated operations' provisions whereby HMRC Inheritance Tax might treat a series of settlements made in such circumstances as a single transfer of value. HMRC have been known to attack a series of as few as four or five settlements in the past in such circumstances: however, they were unsuccessful in the Court of Appeal in January 2003 in *IRC v Rysaffe Trustee Co (CI) Ltd* [2003] STC 536, where there was a series of five identical settlements made by each of two brothers on successive days with nominal initial trust funds, the substantive trust property being added to each of the settlements on a subsequent day.

Related settlement by will

6.40   Suppose a person wants under his will to provide both a discretionary trust and some other settlement, eg a life interest trust which, as an 'immediate post-death interest', falls outside the relevant property regime (*IHTA 1984, s 49A*): see **6.61**. Because a will 'speaks from' death, the life interest trust would necessarily be related to the discretionary trust. Common practice to avoid the related settlement issue in such circumstances is as follows: on the day he makes his will, the settlor makes a £10 'pilot' discretionary settlement and then has his will 'tip' into the pre-existing settlement, the substantive trust fund. As a settlement commences when property is first included in it, the discretionary trust will have commenced on the day of making the will, not on the date of death, thereby avoiding the related settlement problem.

There is an exception to the related settlement rules where the other trust is an immediate post-death interest or IPDI (or a disabled person's interest) for the settlor's spouse. This is expressly provided by *IHTA 1984, s 80*, as amended by *FA 2006*. In other words, if under his will a man leaves a discretionary nil rate band trust and an IPDI of the residue to his wife, the related settlement provisions will not apply to the discretionary trust. However, *s 80* goes on to provide that if on the death of the wife discretionary trusts arise, ie under the husband's will, that discretionary trust is treated as made by the wife. If therefore under her will there is, for example, an IPDI for her daughter, the daughter's fund (at its initial value) will be related with the discretionary trust, which arises under the husband's will when the wife dies, for purposes of the related settlement rules: this will affect the computation of future ten-year anniversary and exit charges.

The moral, with regard to will planning, is always to consider the wills of two spouses taken together when exploring the possible application of the related settlement rules.

ADDITIONS OF PROPERTY

6.41   The general advice to a settlor proposing to add property to an existing discretionary settlement is: *Don't*. The reason is that, except where a transfer is exempt, eg within the annual £3,000 exemption, there is or can be a recalculation of the trustees' deemed cumulative total in any case where the addition by the settlor increases the settled capital (*IHTA 1984, s 67*). This recalculation means that if the settlor's cumulative total before the addition is greater than his total before the settlement; the greater figure is used in subsequent calculations of the ten-year charge.

For example, if a settlor takes out a life policy on his own life and settles the benefit on discretionary trusts, continuing to pay the premiums, the payment of each premium will be an addition to the settlement, unless the premiums fall within, for example, his normal expenditure out of income exemption or the annual £3,000 exemption.

There is a *de minimis* rule for transfers that are not primarily intended to increase the value of the settled property and do not in fact increase it by more than 5%.

If on a person's death, his will adds property to an existing discretionary settlement the addition is treated as having been made on the date of the death.

As in life, so in death, the advice must be generally not to add property to an existing discretionary settlement unless one is absolutely clear that there are no adverse effects, viz because the settlor's cumulative total before the addition is no greater than it was before the date of the original settlement.

Example 6.8—Effect of addition of property on ten-year charge

Referring once again to Albert's Trust (see Example 6.6 at **6.33**), let us suppose that on 1 January 2006, instead of the trustees appointing £50,000 out of the trust, Albert had added another £50,000 to the trust. On 1 January 2003, he had made an accumulation and maintenance settlement for his grandchildren in the sum of £100,000 (having used his annual exemptions for both 2001/02 and 2002/03). This was a PET, ie assumed to be exempt except in the event of Albert's death within the following seven years. Unfortunately, Albert died on 1 January 2009, making the gift to the A&M trust on 1 January 2003 a chargeable transfer.

This means that, even though it is after the first ten-yearly charge on 1 January 2008, the tax has to be recalculated, because it is now seen that the gifts history of Albert in the seven years before he made the addition is greater than that in the seven years before he made the settlement.

Therefore, the ten-yearly charge on 1 January 2008 is calculated as follows, remembering that the tax attributable to the addition of £50,000 is reduced by 32 fortieths, as having been comprised in the settlement for only two years (*IHTA 1984, s 66(2)*):

Trust fund	£800,000
Add settlor's gifts history	£100,000
	£900,000
Less nil rate band	(£300,000)
	£600,000
Tax at 20% lifetime rate	£120,000
Ten-yearly charge (£120,000 × 30%)	£36,000
Less: 32/40 × 50,000/800,000 × 36,000	(£1,800)
IHT payable	£34,200

Furthermore, this rate of 4.275% (£34,200/£800,000) will be the rate governing exit charges within the following ten years (subject to the relieving provision mentioned at **6.36**): see Example 6.7 at **6.36**. Indeed, on any future calculation of tax within the trust it will always be Albert's cumulative total before he made the addition which will be taken into account.

PROPERTY CHANGING CHARACTER

6.42 The possibility that relevant property in the settlement at a ten-year anniversary might not have been relevant property throughout the preceding ten years is taken into account in reducing the rate of tax (see **6.37**).

However, double counting could arise because any value subject to an exit charge is added into the deemed cumulative total. This could happen if there had been a life interest (which was not relevant property) in part of the property for part of the ten-year period. This would have triggered an exit charge and yet, if the property was still in the settlement and had become relevant property at the ten-year anniversary, it would form part of the deemed chargeable transfer.

To meet this problem, the deemed cumulative total is reduced by the lesser of two figures:

- the amount subject to the exit charge; and

- the value included for that property for the deemed chargeable transfer (ie the value immediately before the ten-year anniversary of the property which for a time had been subject to a life interest).

Example 6.9—Illustration of property changing character

A discretionary settlement was made on 1 January 1999 with initial capital of £200,000.

On 1 January 2001 certain funds were appointed to Charles for life, with reversion to the main trusts of the settlement, valued at £100,000.

Charles dies on 1 January 2005 and the property reverts.

On 1 January 2009, the settlement property is valued as follows:

The previously appointed funds	£240,000
Other assets	£150,000
Total	£390,000

The deemed chargeable transfer in calculating the ten-yearly charge is:

Per valuation	£390,000
and the deemed cumulative total is:	
Settlor's seven-year cumulations, say	£20,000
Amount added to exit charge	£100,000
Adjustment: the lesser of £100,000 and £240,000	(£100,000)
Deemed cumulative total	£20,000

PROPERTY MOVING BETWEEN SETTLEMENTS

6.43   An ingenious person might think of:

● avoiding or deferring a ten-year anniversary; or

● benefiting from a lower rate applying to one settlement rather than another, by moving property between settlements.

As we have seen already, the rate calculation includes non-relevant property within a particular settlement (see **6.37**). Accordingly, no protection is needed for HMRC Inheritance Tax if the movement is within the settlement, eg an appointment to a sub-trust. The problem occurs when property leaves one settlement and enters another. There could be CGT to consider at that point (see **9.5**), though there would not be a problem with sterling cash.

Although the tax at stake is unlikely to be substantial, there is some protection for HMRC. For purposes of the ten-year charge the property that has moved is treated as remaining within the first settlement (*IHTA 1984, s 81*).

Example 6.10—Illustration of property moving between settlements

A settlor makes a will under which the nil rate band is shared equally by his two children with the remainder left to his wife. When his wife dies in 2009/10, the trust fund subject to tax at her death is left to the two children. Both children anticipate receiving £300,000 each on their mother's death.

The children resettle their interests on (settlor and spouse excluded) discretionary trusts while their mother is still alive (as excluded property), in the expectation that this would create a nil rate band settlement made by each of them. However, the £600,000 must be treated as a single settlement and not two settlements for purposes of the relevant property regime.

The rule would not have applied had the children waited for their mother's death and settled their inheritances at that point (outside a deed of variation), since the property concerned would have belonged to each of them outright and would not have been subject to trust.

RELEVANT PROPERTY TRUST PLANNING POINTS

6.44   The moral in advising on making a lifetime relevant property settlement is to ensure that the settlor always has as 'clean' a gifts history as possible.

Further, before 22 March 2006, if a settlor was minded to make a PET (eg an A&M settlement) and also a chargeable transfer (eg a discretionary settlement) at about the same time, he should always have been advised to make the chargeable transfer first. This was to protect against the possibility that he might die within seven years after the PET making it chargeable, which would therefore be part of his gifts history.

There is a subsidiary point in relation to allocation of the annual exemption: HMRC Inheritance Tax take the view that the annual £3,000 exemption is given to gifts according to the order in which they are made during the tax year (see **3.18**). Thus, according to HMRC Inheritance Tax, the £3,000 annual exemption could be 'wasted' if a PET were made before a chargeable transfer and the PET subsequently became exempt through the settlor's survival for seven years.

Example 6.11—Order of gifts

George, being well off and generously disposed towards his family, wanted before 22 March 2006 to make both an A&M settlement for his grandchildren and a discretionary settlement for a wider class of beneficiaries, each to have a trust fund of £500,000.

He should have made the discretionary settlement at least one day before the A&M settlement:

- to get the benefit of the current year's and the previous year's annual £3,000 exemptions; and

- so that, if he dies within seven years, the consequential chargeable transfer on making the A&M trust does not have to be taken into account in calculating the tax both on making and within the discretionary settlement.

A&M TRUSTS (MADE BEFORE 22 MARCH 2006)

Maintaining the s 71 conditions

The s 71 conditions

6.45 We have already noted (see **2.7**) that an A&M trust is a 'privileged' type of discretionary trust introduced in 1975, albeit largely brought to an end on 22 March 2006 (subject to transitional rules for such trusts in being at that date). No new A&M trusts can have been made since then. The aim behind this category of settlement was to give favoured treatment where the beneficiaries are all children or grandchildren of a particular family, ie with no possibility of benefiting anyone outside those categories so long as the A&M regime lasts. Hence, it is better to think in terms of accumulation and maintenance trusts as being not so much a type of settlement as a particular IHT favoured regime. This is because, when or to the extent that the regime ends, if the settlement continues, it will then become some other type of settlement, typically an interest in possession trust.

The conditions that have to be satisfied are set out in *IHTA 1984, s 71* and fall into two parts. The first set of conditions is:

- at any time, that is when the settlement is tested, eg when there would otherwise be an exit charge, there is no interest in possession;

- the income from the settlement is to be accumulated, insofar as not paid out for the maintenance, education or benefit of the beneficiary; and

- one or more beneficiaries *will* become entitled to the trust fund, or to an interest in possession in it before attaining a specified age which must not exceed 25 years.

The second set of conditions is, *either*:

- not more than 25 years have passed since the settlement was created or, if it has been some other kind of settlement and has been converted into an A&M, not more than 25 years have passed since it became such a settlement (see **6.46–6.48** for the fixed charge trap following 15 April 2001); *or*

- rather more commonly, all the persons who are or have been beneficiaries are, or were, grandchildren of a common grandparent. Children includes step-children and adopted children. Where a grandchild has died before attaining an interest in income or capital then his children, widows or widowers may take his place as beneficiaries.

If there is any possibility of either set of conditions being breached, the settlement will not have A&M status and will therefore be treated as an ordinary discretionary trust with its exit and ten-yearly charges. The important point, obviously, is to ensure that the *s 71* conditions are maintained.

Example 6.12—Analysing the 'lives' of an old A&M trust

When Adrian and Belinda made their A&M trust for their children on 1 January 1999 they had just two children, Caroline, then aged five and David, aged two. Edward was born on 1 January 2004.

For the first five years of the settlement there were two beneficiaries and therefore two prospective shares in capital (and income). The word 'prospective' is used because those shares could be defeated by subsequent appointment of the trustees.

Insofar as income is not paid out, it must be accumulated, that is, added to capital. However, it would be helpful for the accumulations to be shown separately in the accounts as, in particular, the trust deed gives power to the trustees to pay out accumulations of a previous year as if they were income of a current year.

The income for the first three years is £6,000 and in the absence of any payments of income (given the parental settlement rules: see **4.30–4.31**) each of Caroline and David will have an accumulations account of £3,000 per annum.

Once Edward is born, there are three prospective shares and, therefore, income from that moment on must be divided into three, ie £2,000 per annum. However, this will not defeat the existing shares in the accumulations built up for Caroline and David.

Example 2.2 at **2.8** summarises the options for the trustees on or before 5 April 2008.

The 25-year trap

6.46 Most settlements will satisfy the *s 71* conditions by having all the beneficiaries restricted to children of a common parent or a common grandparent. However, as explained in **6.45** there is an alternative, viz that no more than 25 years have elapsed since the commencement of the settlement or from 15 April 1976, if later. The '25-year trap' is that, if an A&M settlement qualifies as such through the 25-year condition, and no action has been taken before those 25 years expire to remove the settlement from the A&M regime, an automatic charge to IHT arises. The first date on which such a charge could arise would be 15 April 2001. It is quite clear that, although comparatively rare, there are or have been in existence a number of settlements, which owe their qualifying status to the 25-year condition. The trap could arise even after 5 April 2008, with property within an A&M trust which has 18 as the age of absolute entitlement and which was made at least 25 years before and with no common parent or grandparent for the beneficiaries.

The tax charge

6.47 If a settlement is caught by the 25-year rule, tax is charged at rates that depend upon the number of quarters for which the settlement has lasted (ignoring periods before 13 March 1975) the rates are:

- 0.25% for each of the first 40 quarters, plus

- 0.20% for each of the next 40 quarters, plus

- 0.15% for each of the next 40 quarters, plus

- 0.10% for each of the next 40 quarters, plus

- 0.05% for each of the next 40 quarters.

A settlement that has lasted five years, has a tax rate of 5%. After ten years, it rises to 10%, after 20 years 18% and after 25 years 21%. The particular harshness of this rule is that, unlike the calculation of the exit charge for discretionary trusts, no allowance is made for the nil rate band.

The solution to the trap

6.48   The automatic IHT charge may be avoided if an interest is given to qualifying beneficiaries before the end of the 25-year period. This interest may be an interest in possession or an absolute interest. There would, of course, be no difficulty if all the beneficiaries had already received a right to income, eg on attaining the age of 18, because the settlement would then have ceased to qualify as an A&M settlement. Equally, there would be no problem if the permitted accumulation period had expired and therefore all the beneficiaries had obtained a right to receive all the income.

Provided the problem is spotted in advance, there is unlikely to be a difficulty as there will be powers in the settlement to end or vary it before the 25-year limit expires. In the absence of such a power, it may be necessary to consider an application to the court to vary the trust. If the amount of the IHT charge does not justify such an application it would be sensible to consult adult beneficiaries and carefully minute the decision of the trustees to show that the issue had been considered.

Example 6.13—The 25-year trap illustrated

A qualifying A&M settlement was made on 30 January 1983 for the benefit of a nephew and unborn grandchildren on attaining the age of 25. Grandchildren were born in 1986, 1989 and 1990. On 30 January 2008, the 25-year limit ran out before any of the grandchildren had become entitled to the income at a time when the settlement property was worth £500,000. The trustees pay the tax. The tax due on 30 January 2008 is £500,000 × 21% = £105,000.

Suppose, by contrast, that all the beneficiaries had become entitled to all the income before 30 January 2008, eg because the settlor had died more than 21 years ago and all the beneficiaries had reached the age of 18, that is, no permitted accumulation periods continued, there would not have been a problem.

Transitional provisions from 22 March 2006

6.49   The effect of the surprise Budget 2006 announcement on 22 March 2006 on the 'inheritance tax alignment for trusts' is that no new A&M settlements can be created after 21 March 2006.

The regime for A&M trusts in being at 22 March 2006

Periods from 22 March 2006 to 5 April 2008

6.50 The A&M regime continues to apply insofar as the *s 71* conditions are satisfied, ie there will be no ten-yearly or exit charges within the 'relevant property' regime. If an interest in possession arises before 6 April 2008, the 'relevant property' regime will apply to the extent of the underlying capital. If the terms of the A&M trust were changed (if necessary) before 6 April 2008 to provide that capital vests outright at or before age 18, the A&M regime will continue to apply. Alternatively, if before 6 April 2008 the trusts were changed so that capital arises at some point between 18 and 25, the A&M regime will not cease to apply in respect of a presumptive share of capital until the beneficiary attains 18, but there will then be an exit charge on vesting (calculated as illustrated in Example **6.14**).

Example 6.14—Exit from an 'age 18-to-25' trust

Harold made a settlement for his children on 1 January 1980. Under the terms of the settlement there was a direction to accumulate income for 21 years (now therefore expired) with children becoming entitled to income at age 18 and capital deferred broadly until grandchildren attained 18, with wide powers of advancement of capital before that age. Harold has three children: Arabella, Bertha and Charles. Each of Arabella and Bertha is in line for substantial inheritances from godparents, and so before either attained an interest in possession under the settlement they were effectively excluded, leaving Charles as the sole prospective beneficiary. Charles becomes 18 on 1 January 2011. Before 6 April 2008, the terms of the trust are changed to become compliant with *IHTA 1984, s 71D*.

In the seven years before he made the settlement Harold had cumulative chargeable transfers of £100,000 and there were no related settlements. The initial value of the settlement was £200,000. The trust assets are now worth £500,000. When Charles becomes 25 on 1 January 2018 when, let us suppose, the fund is worth £1m and that the rates of tax are as in 2008/09 but with a nil rate band of £630,000, the calculation under *s 71F* of the *s 71E* exit charge proceeds as follows:

The tax is calculated as: chargeable amount × relevant fraction × settlement rate (*s 71F(3)*). The 'chargeable amount' is £1m (assuming that any tax is paid out of it and not out of any property remaining subject to *s 71D* trusts, in which case there would be grossing up (*s 71F(4)*). Although the 'chargeable amount' is expressed as a bare value, HMRC have indicated that any available agricultural or business property relief will go to reduce the amount, the charge falling within *Ch III* of *Pt III* of *IHTA 1984*. The 'relevant fraction' is 3/10 ×

28/40 (the number of complete successive quarters in the period, viz 0.21, expressed as a decimal (*s 71F(5)*). The 'settlement rate' is the effective rate found under *s 71F(7)–(9)* as follows:

Deemed chargeable transfer (*s 71F(9)*)	£200,000
Add: settlor's chargeable transfer total (*s 71F(8)(b)*)	£100,000
	£300,000
Less nil rate band	(£630,000)
Deemed taxable amount	0

Therefore the settlement rate is 0%

So, in this case, the IHT is zero: £1,000,000 × 0.21 × 0.

Suppose that Charles had a brother, David, whom the trustees also wanted to benefit. David was born two years after Charles and so the capital of around £1 million is divided between them, David inheriting his share on 1 January 2020. The calculation of the rate of tax applicable on the exit would be exactly the same for David as it is for Charles.

The regime on or after 6 April 2008

6.51   Subject to taking advantage of the two transitional rules mentioned at **6.50**, any property left within what was the A&M regime will fall within the relevant property regime, that is with the system of ten-yearly and exit charges as described in **6.30–6.36**. It will become necessary to ascertain the date on which the settlement commenced, so as to identify the first ten-year anniversary which falls after 6 April 2008 and indeed to confirm the seven-year chargeable gifts history of the settlor up to the date of commencement, plus the existence of any related settlements on that day and any additional property since. This information may be hard to obtain in certain cases.

The new regime introduced by *FA 2006* is applied below to Examples 6.15, 6.16 and 6.17.

Example 6.15—A&M becoming relevant property trust

Given that no action was taken by the trustees before 6 April 2008, Adrian and Belinda's A&M trust made on 1 January 1999 fell into the relevant property regime on that date. The first ten-year anniversary arose on 1 January 2009 and there was a ten-year anniversary charge on the value of the property comprised in the settlement at that date. The rate of tax would be found as stated in **6.30–**

6.33. In fact two settlements would be treated as having been made, one by each of Adrian and Belinda, each of whose seven-year cumulative total up to 31 December 1998 will have to be ascertained. Because the trust fund will have been relevant property for only two completed quarters out of 40, the charge will be reduced accordingly.

Example 6.16—Flexibility lost by the FA 2006 regime

Father died in 1982, leaving mother with a life interest. On her death on 1 February 2006 the capital was divided equally between brother and sister, who were then aged 30 and 25 respectively. Sister Anne is married, with one son and one daughter. Brother John is not then married, though he feels he will do so and wishes to provide for his future children. Because he had a niece and nephew, John created an A&M settlement on 1 February 2006 settling the assets which fell to him on his mother's death. As and when John marries and has children, his thinking was that those children, because of the class gift, would automatically be beneficiaries. Given that none of the shares of his nephew, niece or future children of Anne had by then vested, the shares in the capital could be varied in favour entirely of John's own children. Even if this were to happen after an interest in possession had arisen to his nephew or niece before 22 March 2006, there could be power in the settlement to take it away from them, thus causing them to make a PET if an absolute gift. All this, of course, now operates subject to the *FA 2006* regime, described above.

Example 6.17—Business property relief to the rescue

The fiscal luxury that Adrian and Belinda thought they had when making their A&M trust in 1999 was taken away from them on 6 April 2008. Given the circumstances, that is the age of the children and the prospective inheritance of shares in the family company, they were unlikely to 'accept the carrot' of the government in advancing the age of entitlement to capital at age 25, though it does at least seem if they were to do this and thus preserve freedom from the 'relevant property' regime they could still 'chop and change' prospective shares among their children up to 6 April 2008. But it may be thought that it is simply too early to make a decision – and in any case, age 25 is thought too young to vest valuable assets in the children. Happily in this case they have the advantage of business property relief at 100% (at least, for the time being), which removes any IHT burden of the new regime. It would of course be otherwise if the trust fund were comprised of quoted stocks and shares.

Wills and intestacies: bereaved minor trusts and 'age 18-to-25 trusts'

6.52 If at any time, whether before 6 April 2008 or after 5 April 2008, the trust qualifies as a 'bereaved minor trust' under *IHTA 1984, s 71A*, the relevant property regime will not bite. In broad terms, the *s 71A* regime applies to property left under the will of a parent, step-parent or person with parental responsibility for a child who will become absolutely entitled by the age of 18, with any income or capital applied under that age only for the benefit of that child (though see the next paragraph). Under the 'age 18-to-25' regime introduced by *IHTA 1984, s 71D*, capital to which a person is presumptively entitled must vest on or before the age of 25 and the relevant property rules will apply to the capital in the trust between age 18 and the age of absolute entitlement will suffer an exit charge on that entitlement (see **6.50** and Example 6.14 for an illustration of how the rules work).

HMRC do allow some latitude in applying the strict statutory conditions for both bereaved minor trusts and age 18-to-25 trusts. In particular, a prospective share can be varied while the beneficiary is under the age of 18 or (with age 18-to-25 trusts) 25. But the class of beneficiaries must be closed when the relevant trust comes into being. A power of advancement may be exercised to keep the property in trust beyond age 18 or 25, as appropriate, at which point the trust property will enter the relevant property regime. For HMRC's answers released on 29 June 2007 to three questions put to them by STEP/CIOT on trusts for children, see www.tax.org.uk/show article.pl?id=5668;n=9999.

INTEREST IN POSSESSION TRUSTS

The s 49 fiction for pre-22 March 2006 trusts and transitionally protected trusts

6.53 A person entitled to an interest in possession on (or before) 22 March 2006 is treated as beneficially entitled to the underlying property in the trust fund (*IHTA 1984, s 49(1)*). This is technically a 'qualifying' interest in possession and within the professions is generally known as an 'estate' interest in possession.

Therefore, for so long as a beneficiary stays alive, and the interest in possession continues, there is no chargeable event for IHT purposes. On the death of the beneficiary, however, there will be a transfer of value, which will be chargeable, subject to the spouse and charities exemptions. The value in the life interest trust is aggregated with his free estate, and the combined total is subjected to IHT at the appropriate rate, known as the 'estate rate'. The trustees are liable for the IHT in respect of the trust fund and the executors for the tax on the free estate.

If the interest comes to an end during the lifetime of the beneficiary (other than by outright advance to him), he will be treated as having made a transfer of value. This will be either:

- a PET if the capital is advanced to an individual or to trustees for a disabled person or (before 22 March 2006) passes on life interest or A&M trusts—and will become exempt if the life tenant survives for seven years; or

- a chargeable transfer by the life tenant if the capital becomes subject to discretionary trusts or (on or after 22 March 2006) is held on any form of continuing non-charitable trust (which is not a disabled trust and subject to the rules for transitionally protected trusts set out at **6.57– 6.60**).

Example 6.18—IHT due where both settled and free estate

Alistair dies on 1 January 2017. Suppose that the value in the life interest trust made for him by his father in 2006 was then £1.8m. His free estate is £600,000. No APR or BPR is available. Let us imagine that the nil rate band is £600,000. Under the terms of the trust, the trust fund passes to Alistair's children in equal shares. Alistair's will leaves two-thirds to his wife and one-third to his children.

The chargeable transfer on death therefore is:

Free estate: one-third of £600,000 (two-thirds being spouse exempt)	£200,000
Settled estate	£1,800,000
	£2,000,000

Calculation of IHT
£600,000 @ 0%

£1,400,000 @ 40%	£560,000
Estate rate £560,000 divided by £2,000,000	28.00%

IHT payable by the executors will therefore be £200,000 × 28% = £56,000.

IHT payable by the trustees will be £1,800,000 × 28% = £504,000.

Lifetime termination

6.54   There will be no positive IHT liability (though the first situation below may carry a reporting obligation) to the extent that:

- the trust fund consists of assets attracting APR or BPR at 100%;

- there is a capital advance by the trustees to the life tenant (ie technically from the deemed owner to himself) – *IHTA 1984, s 53(3)*;

- the termination is a PET, ie there is an advance of capital to one or more children of the life tenant and he survives for seven years (*IHTA 1984, s 3A*);

- there is a transfer whether during lifetime or in death by the life tenant to his spouse – *IHTA 1984, s 53(4)*; or

- the life interest derives from an old estate where the trustees are entitled to the estate duty surviving spouse exemption and there is an advance of capital to the surviving spouse or life tenant. This assumes that under estate duty a person died before 13 November 1974 leaving a life interest in his will to his surviving spouse. Under estate duty, tax was paid on the first death with the spouse exemption given on the death of the second provided that a life interest had come into being under the will of the first spouse to die. Both CTT and IHT have continued, on a transitional basis, this old estate duty relief (*IHTA 1984, Sch 6, para 2*).

Valuation

6.55   Where there is a chargeable transfer within a qualifying or 'estate' interest in possession trust on death of the life tenant, the rule is quite straightforward (see **6.53**), in that IHT is calculated on the value of the settled property and the free estate taken as one fund.

What happens, however, where the interest in possession comes to an end during the life tenant's lifetime, but is a chargeable transfer, either because a discretionary trust (or, following 21 March 2006, other 'relevant property' trust) arises or because the life tenant dies within seven years?

The general rule for IHT in valuing a transfer of value made during a lifetime is on an 'estate before, less estate after' basis. That is, the value is taken of the individual's estate before the transfer and then again after the transfer – the difference is the amount of the transfer of value. Note that this is not necessarily the same as the value of what is received by the donee.

For example, consider a company whose shares do not attract business property relief because it is, say, an investment company. The value of the shareholding depends upon the size of the shareholding and thus the extent to which they can carry votes. The critical threshold will be the 51% threshold carrying voting control, although there will be other significant thresholds of 90% and 75%, 25% and 10%, all based on company law principles. A gift of 2% out of a 51% shareholding will put the recipient in possession of a relatively small 2%, though its significance on the estate of the donor may be very great, depending on the circumstances.

Originally, HMRC inheritance Tax took the view that this 'estate before, less estate after' principle applied in relation to life interest trusts where the interest came to an end during the lifetime of the beneficiary. They then changed their view in March 1990 and agreed that the settled property could be valued in isolation, subject always to the application of the associated operations provisions of *IHTA 1984, s 268*.

More recently, however, it appears that HMRC may have reverted to their pre-1990 stance, given the following sentence from IHMT 16063: 'The effect of IHTA 84/S49 is that for all practical IHT purposes – and especially on valuation matters – the person having the interest in possession is treated as the absolute owner of the property.'

Planning points

Uses of life interest trusts

6.56 The *FA 2006* 'alignment of IHT for trusts' substantially put paid to planning advantages of lifetime interest in possession trusts: see, for example, **6.56** of the 2008/09 edition of this book which summarises six possibilities for trusts made before 22 March 2006, albeit subject to the TSI regime (see **6.58**).

For the future, however, there are distinct advantages of an IPDI structure as against outright gifts (rather than relevant property trusts) in wills, which is the subject of **6.20** below.

Example 6.19—Pre-22 March 2006

Husband and wife together own Grey Gables, their matrimonial home, in equal shares. Grey Gables is worth £450,000. The husband dies in 2005/06. He wanted to use his nil rate band but had no suitable assets other than his share in Grey Gables. He also wanted to ensure his wife's security of tenure. That seems to call for a trust, rather than an outright gift to the children.

If the husband were to make a gift to the children on interest in possession trusts, that would give them a right to live in Grey Gables, which is fine as the family get on and each of the children lives elsewhere. However, if the trustees and the wife were to sell Grey Gables at a gain, the trustees' share would be subject to CGT. The gain could be made free of tax if a beneficiary entitled under the settlement occupied the property. Realistically, this is only going to be the wife.

The husband has made chargeable transfers of £235,000 in the seven years before he died. What he might do, therefore, is under his will, create a life interest trust of his share in Grey Gables with 90% going to his wife and 10% to his two children: £235,000 plus £22,500 is still within the nil rate band of £275,000. (Husband's half share is £225,000 multiplied by 10% = £22,500 + £235,000 = £257,500). After six months the trustees could use their powers under the trust to reduce the wife's share to 10%, increasing the children's share to 90%. The situation would still be protected by main residence relief, as the share of the occupying beneficiary is immaterial. The wife continues to live in the house without paying any compensation. The children will become entitled to capital on her ultimate death.

However, assuming that the wife survives the change in shares by at least seven years, the value of 80% of a half share in the house will have left her estate without any IHT implications. There will be no reservation of benefit as the PET was not caused by a disposition made by her.

Example 6.20—Post-21 March 2006

Assume the facts of Example 6.19, but on or after 22 March 2006. The tax effect is different from Example 6.19 in one major respect. The analysis in the final paragraph no longer holds good as, under *FA 2006, s 102ZA*, the exercise by the trustees of their power of appointment is treated as a gift by the widow and, as she continues to occupy Grey Gables, a gift with reservation of benefit, chargeable on her death assuming that she continues to occupy the property. The interest to the widow under the will will be treated as an 'immediate post-death interest' (see **6.61**) treated under *IHTA 1984, s 49A* as if the widow were entitled to the underlying capital; no change there, therefore.

To avoid the problem presented by new *FA 1986, s 102ZA*, what is wanted for the husband's will trust is a discretionary structure. However, it is essential that the widow does not acquire an interest in possession in a will trust which was initially discretionary, within two years after the death. This is because an immediate post-death interest will then be 'read back' into the will under *IHTA 1984, s 144(3)*, so destroying the planning. If, therefore, it is possible to ensure a genuinely discretionary trust established by the husband's will, the *s 102ZA* point will not cause a problem – even if a right to income constituting an interest in possession were to arise more than 24 months after the husband's death.

Transitional rules for trusts in being at 22 March 2006

6.57   The *s 49(1)* 'fiction', whereby the underlying trust capital is treated as beneficially owned by the life tenant, is preserved for interests in possession in being at 22 March 2006, so long as the interest is not a 'bereaved minors trust' under *IHTA 1984, s 71A* (see **6.52**). These are commonly called 'estate' interests in possession. What happens when that interest comes to an end? If during the beneficiary's lifetime, it will be a potentially exempt transfer only if the capital passes to an individual outright, or if it is a gift to a disabled person's trust (*IHTA 1984, s 3A(1A)*), or if it is followed by a transitional serial interest (TSI): see **6.58**. Otherwise, it will be a chargeable transfer, ie creating a 'relevant property' trust (see **3.17**) and the regime of ten-year and exit charges (see **6.30–6.36**) will apply.

If the interest comes to an end on the life tenant's death, there will be a transfer of value, exempt only if the capital passes absolutely to a surviving spouse or to a charitable trust. That is, subject to the next sentence, there will be a chargeable transfer (as indeed before 22 March 2006), if the interest passes to any other beneficiary absolutely or to a continuing trust (except for a disabled person). While, generally, the 'relevant property' provisions (see **6.30–6.36**) will apply to a continuing trust, there is a special rule for TSIs (see **6.58**).

Transitional serial interests ('TSIs')

6.58   There are three types of category of trusts where the *s 49(1)* 'fiction' continues to apply. These require a 'prior interest in possession' to exist at 22 March 2006 and, first, for that interest to come to an end (whether by lifetime termination or in death) before 6 October 2008 and to be replaced by a 'current interest'. *IHTA 1984, s 49C* treats that current interest as in being at 22 March 2006. Secondly, if the prior interest comes to an end on the death of a spouse after 5 October 2008 and is replaced by an interest in possession for the surviving spouse, that also is a TSI (*IHTA 1984, s 49D*). This rule does not apply either to a bereaved minor's trust or to a disabled person's trust (see **2.10**). Thirdly, contracts of life insurance written under life interest trusts before 22 March 2007 also have their own TSI regime in *IHTA 1984, s 49E*. The creation of a TSI is a PET under *IHTA 1984, s 3A*. The end of the transitional period for type one TSIs was originally 5 April 2008, though *FA 2008* extended it by six months to 5 October 2008.

In applying the TSI regime, it becomes important to know what is an interest in possession and when a new one arises (even if for the same beneficiary). In broad terms, HMRC accept that where a beneficiary's interest arises under the terms of the settlement (and not from the exercise of the trustees' powers), the same interest in possession continues, even though it might arise under a different provision. For example, at 22 March 2006 X had an interest in possession by reason of *Trustee Act 1925, s 31* (having attained age 18) and then becomes entitled to an express interest in possession on attaining the age of 25. This is the same interest, relevant to two issues: first, whether a TSI can be created before 6 April 2008 once X becomes 25 before that date and, secondly, where X reaches 25 after 5 April 2008, whether the *s 49(1)* fiction continues to apply at that point and the trust property will not enter the relevant property regime. The answer to both is affirmative. For various different scenarios on this theme and HMRC's answers to certain other questions (released on 29 May 2007) see http://www.tax.org.uk/showarticle.pl?id=5503.

The fourth exchange of correspondence between STEP/CIOT and HMRC was released in late November 2007. This concerned the application to the TSI regime of the principle under HMRC's statement of practice SP10/79, whereunder the exercise of a power by trustees of a discretionary settlement in relation to a dwelling house can give rise to an interest in possession. The agreed text can be found on http://www.tax.org.uk/showarticle.pl?id=6274&n=3794.

Example 6.21—TSI illustration

Edwin was the beneficiary under an interest in possession trust made by his father in 1988. The trust comprises wide powers of appointment. On 31 March 2008, using those powers the trustees replace Edwin's interest in possession with a successive interest in favour of Edwin's daughter Frieda aged 13.

On exercise by the trustees of their powers of appointment, Edwin ceases to be treated under *s 49(1)* as beneficially owning the trust fund. Under *FA 2006, Sch 20, para 9*, amending *IHTA 1984, s 3A*, Edwin is treated as making a potentially exempt transfer, which becomes exempt on his survival by seven years.

Frieda's interest is a TSI within *IHTA 1984, s 49C* and she is treated as entitled to the underlying capital for IHT purposes. The IHT implications on termination of that interest are set out at **6.60** below.

For capital gains tax purposes, there is no disposal.

For income tax purposes, the income arising to Frieda does not come from a 'parental settlement' as such for purposes of the anti-avoidance income tax rule (see **4.30–4.31**) and so the income is assessed on Frieda alone for tax purposes.

Post-21 March 2006 interests

6.59   Apart from the continuing special treatment given to TSIs (see **6.58**), gifts to interests in possession arising on or after 22 March 2006 (being 'non estate' interests in possession) are deprived of the PET treatment. This means that on creation there will be a chargeable transfer (see **3.17–3.20**) whatever the type of trust (except for a disabled person – see **2.10**), including one where the settlor creates a life interest for himself or his spouse or indeed where following a life interest there is a successive life interest for the beneficiary's spouse.

Termination of life interest following 21 March 2006 in favour of continuing non-TSI trusts

6.60   The life tenant will be treated as making a chargeable transfer. If the value is within his nil rate band (£312,000 for 2008/09 and £325,000 for 2009/10) there will be no IHT to pay, though form IHT 100 should be submitted by the beneficiary (see **3.20**). To the extent that the transfer of value exceeds his nil rate band, IHT will be payable at the lifetime rate of 20%, subject to increase to 40% in the event of death within seven years.

Should the trust be already within the chargeable transfer regime prior to the new life interest (as either a discretionary trust or a life interest created on or after 22 March 2006, which is not a TSI or a disabled trust), the trust will already be within the 'relevant property' regime and there will be no immediate IHT implications, given that no new trust is created for IHT purposes (see **6.43**).

Will trusts

6.61   A person's will might establish an interest in possession. If it is an 'immediate post-death interest' (IPDI) within *IHTA 1984, s 49A* (as almost every interest in possession will be), the underlying capital will be treated as part of the life tenant's estate under *IHTA 1984, s 49* so long as it is neither a bereaved minor's trust (see **6.52**) nor a disabled person's interest (see **2.10**).

If the IPDI comes to an end during the lifetime of the beneficiary, tax is charged as if he had made a transfer of value, which will be a potentially exempt transfer only if it passes to an individual outright or creates a disabled person's interest or (given a termination before 6 April 2008) a TSI (see **6.58**). Otherwise, if successive trusts arise, the beneficiary will be treated as making a chargeable transfer.

Uses of IPDIs

6.62   In drafting wills, especially in the context of the transferable nil-rate band under *IHTA 1984, s 8A*, a gift to a surviving spouse/civil partner by way of IPDI has the same IHT impact as an outright gift. Of course, an IPDI can also be left to any other beneficiary rather than an outright gift, though this will be a chargeable transfer and will take one into the relevant property regime.

An outright gift structure has the obvious advantages of simplicity. However, among some advantages of an IPDI, apart obviously from providing some form of security for the capital, are the following:

(1)   The most obvious use for an IPDI is in the case of a second (or subsequent) marriage where the first to die wishes the capital to go after the second death to the children of the first marriage. If this is achieved by the trustees terminating the IPDI during the survivor's lifetime with a view to the PET becoming exempt on survival for seven years but she does not (so making the gift chargeable), the survivor's stepchildren will have first call on her nil-rate band at the expense perhaps of her own children by the first marriage. The point needs to be appreciated and covered perhaps by a discretionary legacy to make adjustments as between the two sets of stepchildren in terms of the burden of IHT.

(2)   If following the first death the survivor is no longer in a position (eg through age) to decide on making an absolute gift by way of a PET, it would turn out to be convenient to give the discretion to the trustees by way of termination of an IPDI, no doubt in conjunction with a letter of wishes.

(3)   In the context of the transferable nil-rate band, an IPDI structure avoids the risk of the surviving spouse distributing chattels (and perhaps other property) within two years after the death in pursuance of a letter of wishes, so triggering a chargeable transfer by the deceased, following *IHTA 1984, s 143*. The trustees of an IPDI can transfer the chattels etc to the intended individuals, so terminating the IPDI and constituting a PET by the surviving spouse to that extent.

(4)   With an IPDI it is much easier to control the level of income for purposes of means-tested benefits, and with protection in the context of care home fees.

(5)   An IPDI might afford protection for the survivor from begging by the children (in appropriate circumstances).

(6)   At least to the extent of the trust fund, an IPDI avoids the need for a lasting power of attorney for free assets or indeed issues (notoriously complex and time-consuming and delaying) over application to the Court of Protection in appropriate circumstances.

(7)   An IPDI might be preferable where there is a real risk of the survivor's insolvency.

Chapter 7

Running a trust: stamp duties

BUYING UK SHARES OR LAND – THE BASICS

7.1 Stamp duties have been with us since 1694. Following the introduction of stamp duty reserve tax (SDRT) in 1996, a major reform in 2003 means that stamp duties may be divided into three categories:

- stamp duty charged at 0.5% on the acquisition for value of shares and marketable securities (see Example 7.1);

- SDRT on agreements to acquire chargeable securities for value (largely through The Stock Exchange); and

- stamp duty land tax (SDLT) on the acquisition of UK land and buildings (see Example 7.2).

Trustees are a purchaser of shares of land like anyone else and must therefore understand both the liability to pay the tax and the compliance obligations necessary. Broadly speaking, stamp duty on shares at 0.5% and SDLT on land and buildings (at rates in the range of 0%–4%) must be paid within 30 days after the relevant transaction.

Transfers between funds

7.2 A point has been cleared up by *FA 2006* and by assurance from HMRC Stamp Taxes. This concerns the case where, say, within a settlement there are two funds and there is either an exchange of land as between funds or acquisition of land by one fund from another. While there is a land transaction, is there chargeable consideration? In the case where the beneficiary has to give consent, *FA 2006, s 165* confirms that there is no chargeable consideration and HMRC have now said that in all other cases there never was chargeable consideration, going back to 1 December 2003.

Example 7.1—Share purchase

Trustees buy shares in the private company of one of the beneficiaries for full market value of £50,000. Stamp duty at 0.5% of £250 will be payable within 30 days. Note that there is no general market value rule. Prior to FA 2008, there was no *de minimis* provision either (as in SDLT). However, for transfers after 12 March 2008 (which are not stamped before 19 March 2008) there is no stamp duty on transfers of shares or marketable securities if the sale proceeds are £1,000 and the transfer document is certified at £1,000 (*FA 1999, Sch 13 para 3A*).

Example 7.2—Land purchase

The trustees buy a flat in London for £300,000 for one of the beneficiaries to occupy. They borrow £150,000 and pay the balance in cash. The existence of the mortgage does not affect the SDLT liability. SDLT at 3% (the purchase price being within the band £250,001 to £500,000) will be payable within the 30 days after the transaction, amounting to £9,000.

Example 7.3—Inter-fund exchange of land

Within the Chet settlement there are two funds 'Langley' and 'Loddon'. There is an exchange of real property within the funds (without any beneficiary involvement), with any balance of market value made up by cash. The exchange has no implications for either CGT or SDLT purposes.

SDLT ISSUES FOR TRUSTEES

7.3 On transfer of land to a trust, the trustees are treated as the purchaser of a chargeable interest in land (*FA 2003, s 47(4), (5)* and *Sch 16, para 4*). The responsible trustees have all the responsibilities of a purchaser, viz for payment of any tax and submission of a land transaction return or self certificate.

Who are the responsible trustees?

7.4 The 'responsible trustees' in relation to a land transaction are defined as the persons who are trustees at the effective date of the transaction and any person who subsequently becomes a trustee (*FA 2003, Sch 16, para 5*).

Where the trustees are liable to pay the tax, interest on unpaid tax, a penalty or interest on the penalty (or to make a payment because of an excessive repayment of tax) monies can be recovered from any one or more of the responsible trustees. No penalty or interest on the penalty can be recovered from a person who does not become a responsible trustee until after the date of the transaction.

Filling in the land transaction return: the 'relevant trustees'

7.5 A land transaction return may be delivered to the Land Registry by any one or more of the trustees who are responsible trustees in relation to the transaction. The trustees who make the return are defined as the 'relevant trustees'. The declaration confirming that the land transaction return is complete and true must be signed by all the relevant trustees.

That is, the trustees between them can appoint one or more of their number to deal with the compliance aspects of the acquisition of land or buildings.

Example 7.4—Compliance

The trustees of Albert's settlement buy Blackacre on 1 July 2009 for £500,000. The SDLT liability at 3% is £15,000. The trustees appoint two of their number to deal with compliance, ie submission of a land transaction return and payment of the tax within 30 days.

However, if those two trustees do not fulfil their obligations, the tax, interest on unpaid tax (currently running at 2.5%) and a penalty or interest on the penalty can be recovered from any one or more of the responsible trustees. The fixed penalty is £100 for submission of a return after the 30 days, which rises to £200 if the return is three months late or, if more than 12 months late, becomes tax geared (*FA 2003, Sch 10, para 3*). In addition, there may be a liability under the new *FA 2007* penalty regime applied to stamp taxes by *FA 2008, Sch 40* (see **4.15**). Moreover, if, let us say, Raymond is appointed as a trustee of the settlement on 1 August 2009, Raymond is personally liable for the tax and interest on tax: only in respect of a penalty or interest on the penalty can HMRC Stamp Taxes not recover that from him. An incoming trustee needs to be aware of this.

Chapter 8

Charitable trusts

GIFT AID RELIEF

8.1   The predecessor to the present gift aid scheme was deeds of covenant, which as long as they ran for more than three years would generate a tax recovery for the charity.

Gift aid was introduced from 1 October 1990 for one-off cash gifts of £600 or more (now in *ITA 2007, ss 413–446*). The upper limit was gradually reduced to £400 and then £250, before being removed altogether from 6 April 2000. The present gift aid declaration covers all cash gifts by an individual to a charity and simply acknowledges that the donor has sufficient liability to income tax or CGT to frank the gifts.

Generally, gift aid has made the deposited deed of covenant redundant. The donor is treated as having deducted basic rate tax, which the charity recovers. The gift is also relieved against the donor's higher rate liability.

The reduction in the basic rate from 22% to 20% with effect from 2008/09 has spelled bad news for charities (subject to the temporary relief mentioned in the next paragraph). Up to and including 2007/08, for every £100 cash given under gift aid the charity can recover £28.20 (22% of a gross gift of £128.20). However, as from 2008/09 the recovery falls by £3.20 to £25 (20% of a gross gift of £125). The donor's higher rate relief rises correspondingly (from 18% of the gross to 20% of the gross).

The income arising to charities from gift aid recovery falls by 11% in 2008/09 as a result of a reduction in the basic rate explained above. However, temporary relief is given by *FA 2008 Sch 19* for tax years 2008/09, 2009/10 and 2010/11. A charity is entitled to claim a 'gift aid supplement' which, with a basic rate of 20%, amounts to the missing £3.20 on a net gift of £100. From 2011/12, the loss of income will become permanent (subject to any further change in the legislation). It is possible for a higher rate taxpaying donor to direct all or any part of his higher rate credit to any charity, whether or not one to which he makes a payment. The self-assessment literature for 2008/09 highlights this, achieved by a simple tick in the box and entries on the tax form. And charities need to be alive to the possibilities, which could conceivably result in an unseemly scramble among charities for extra funds, since charity X would be able to get the benefit of the higher rate recovery on donations made to charities Y and Z as well as to itself. See Example 8.1 at **8.4** below: Zebedee would be able to redirect to any charity the tax saving of £300.

Deeds of covenant made before 2000/01

8.2   What is their status? Payments under a deed of covenant, which began before 6 April 2000, can continue without the gift aid declaration. While there is no tax reason for making a deed of covenant now, such deeds would be welcomed by charities as ensuring some continuity in giving. If a deed of covenant is made on or after 6 April 2000, the donor must still complete the relative gift aid declaration to enable recovery of tax by the charity.

The gift aid declaration

8.3   The declaration simply gives the name and address of the donor and acknowledges that the donor has sufficient tax liability to frank the gifts. No national insurance number is needed and the form need not even be signed. The original will go to the charity, with a copy kept by the donor to support any claim to higher rate relief.

Other methods of charitable giving

8.4

- Payroll giving, under which an employer deducts from an employee's salary, amounts to go to charity. *FA 2000* removed the previous limit of £1,200 per donor. *FA 2000* also increased the benefit of certain payroll giving schemes with a 10% supplement paid by the Treasury.

- Gift aid is also available to companies supporting charity.

- Income tax relief on non-cash gifts: for relief for gifts of listed shares etc and of UK property, see **3.30**.

Example 8.1—The benefit of gift aid

Zebedee has an annual earned income of £50,000. His wife has income of £5,000. Zebedee made a new four-year covenant with a charity on 1 January 2001 to make monthly payments of £100 net. His wife makes occasional gifts to the charity, having signed a gift aid declaration on 10 April 2005. For 2008/09, the total of her gifts was £500.

Zebedee's deed of covenant ran out on 1 December 2005. Following that date, whether or not he makes a new deed of covenant, he will have had to make a gift aid declaration to enable recovery of tax by the charity: this he did.

Meanwhile, for 2008/09 he has made gifts of £1,200 net, ie after deduction of tax at 20%. This equates to £1,500 gross and the charity may therefore recover £300 from HMRC. Zebedee's basic rate band is extended by the gross figure of £1,500, thus saving him higher rate tax of £1,500 × 20%, viz £300.

His wife has made gifts totalling £500, which equate to £625 gross and the charity may, therefore, on application to HMRC recover £125. She is not a higher rate taxpayer, so has no personal tax benefit.

The charity can apply to HMRC for the gift aid supplement for 2008/09, of 3.20% of each net gift, viz £38 for Zebedee's gift and £16 for his wife's gift.

Specimen gift aid declaration

8.5

THE RUSSIAN ORPHANAGE TRUST

[ADDRESS]

GIFT AID DECLARATION

I would like the Russian Orphanage Trust to treat the payment of £xxx I am making today and all further payments I make from the date of this declaration (unless I notify to the contrary) as gift aid.

Signature . . . .

Date . . . .

[Name and Address of Donor]

Trustees: . . . .

Registered Charity No: . . . .

INCOME TAX

8.6　　The general rule is this: income arising to a charity will be exempt from tax providing that it is spent or accumulated for charitable purposes. The income does not have to be spent in the year of receipt, nor indeed does the spending have to be for income-type purposes. It would, therefore, be quite reasonable for governors of a school to save up for a few years to fund extra classrooms; the income they receive ultimately to be spent on the classrooms is exempt (as indeed is the income arising from investment of that income).

The tax exemptions cover:

- rent and other income of a property business;
- interest and dividend income;
- certain trading income, as detailed at **8.7**;
- gift aid donations and covenanted payments;
- donations from another charity; or
- single gifts by companies from which tax has been deducted.

Trading income

8.7　　Traditionally, trustees wanting to trade would establish their own subsidiary company to carry on such a trade, and the company would covenant its income back to the charity. However, *FA 2000* removed the need for small charities to set up a subsidiary company to run their fund-raising trade. There is now a tax exemption (*ITA 2007, s 528*) for all 'trading incoming resources and miscellaneous incoming resources' which do not exceed the 'requisite limit' for the tax year (or where the trustees had a reasonable expectation at the beginning of the tax year that they would not do so). The 'requisite limit' is defined as 25% of the trust's total incoming resources for the tax year, though must not be less than £5,000 or more than £50,000.

Otherwise, trading income will be exempt:

- if the trade constitutes a primary purpose of the charity or if the work is wholly or mainly carried out by beneficiaries of the charity (*ITA 2007, ss 524–525*);
- if the trade is a fund-raising event (*ITA 2007, s 529*); or
- if the trade is a lottery (*ITA 2007, s 530*).

Example 8.2—Tax exemptions for charity

Since it was set up, the Russian Orphanage Trust has benefited from considerable capital gifts from members of Zebedee's family and from his friends. It is now quite a substantial trust.

The trustees have bought some commercial property and also have a portfolio of quoted shares and cash deposits.

More recently, Zebedee's wife has set up a trading side to sell goods and cards made by the children in the orphanages. Turnover is £10,000, generating net income of £6,000. The total income of the charity is £45,000.

The charity benefits from tax exemptions on:

• rent from the commercial property;

• interest; and

• trading income from the business. This does not attract the *ITA 2007, s 524* exemption, because the work in connection with the trade is not wholly or mainly carried out by beneficiaries of the trust, viz only production of the goods to be sold. However, it does attract *s 528* exemption; the turnover does not exceed £50,000 and is less than 25% of the charity's total income.

Dividend tax credit recovery

8.8   The abolition of the ability to get repayment of the tax credit from 1999/2000 was a serious blow to charities. Compensation was given for the first five years on a sliding scale. However, as from 6 April 2004, the tax credit is completely irrecoverable (as it is now for other taxpayers).

CAPITAL GAINS TAX

8.9   We have seen already that a gain that arises on disposing of an asset to a charity is tax free (see **3.30**). Similarly, there is a complete exemption from CGT for all chargeable gains made by the charity, provided that the proceeds are spent or accumulated for charitable purposes (*TCGA 1992, s 256*).

The exemption from CGT for a charity's gains means that, if a person is charitably minded and wishes to give out of his portfolio of investments some shares to a charity, he would be well advised to give those that carry a greater gain as opposed to those that carry a lesser gain. No CGT is payable on the gift, and the shares can be sold by the charity using the whole of the proceeds including the gain for charitable purposes.

If the shares carrying the greater gain are given to the charity, the shares left in the taxpayer's estate will be those that carry a lesser rather than a greater gain, so may, therefore, be realised by him with less adverse CGT consequences.

By contrast, if the shares had been sold by the individual, perhaps realising a liability over and above his annual exemption, and he had then given the net proceeds of the sale there would have been less for the charity to enjoy.

Example 8.3—Optimising tax efficiency for charitable gifts

The Zebedee Russian Orphanage Trust is now up and running. Zebedee now wishes to give to the trust unquoted shares worth £20,000, with an inbuilt gain of £12,000. Compare these two scenarios:

- Zebedee sells the shares himself.

Proceeds of sale	£20,000
Less cost	(£8,000)
Gain	£12,000
Less annual exemption for 2009/10	(£10,100)
	£1,900
Tax @ 18%	£342

Given that Zebedee pays the tax out of the sale proceeds before making his charitable gift, he can give away just £19,658 (£20,000 less £342).

- Zebedee gives the shares to the charity, which then sells them for £20,000 free of tax and has £20,000 to use.

At first sight, the second scenario might seem better. However, the equation is not quite so simple. Assume the first alternative, ie Zebedee makes a net gift of £19,658. This could itself be a payment made under gift aid. Grossed up at 20%, it becomes £24,572, ie the charity can recover £4,914 giving it in total £24,572. Furthermore, under *FA 2008, Sch 19*, the charity can claim the gift aid supplement amounting to £630. So, the charity ends up with funds of £25,202 (£24,572 plus £630). Moreover, Zebedee, having income charged at

40% of at least this amount, can recover 20% of the gross by way of higher rate tax relief. This amounts to £4,914. Thus the 'cost' to Zebedee of putting the charity in funds worth £25,201 is £19,658 less £4,914 = £14,744. (Furthermore, under the gift aid scenario Zebedee could also elect to give the charity his higher rate benefit of £4,914 – though this would not alter the balance of advantage between the two alternatives.)

In these circumstances, at least, the first alternative can be shown to have been preferable from everybody's point of view (except perhaps that of HMRC).

Note that income tax relief on a gift of shares to a charity is not available on unquoted shares (see **3.30**).

INHERITANCE TAX

8.10   Gifts to a charity, whether made during lifetime or on death, are completely free from IHT (*IHTA 1984, s 23*). Exemption does depend upon the charity existing permanently for charitable purposes (ie a 'time charity'), that is, one where the charitable status might come to an end after, say, ten years, does not have the same blanket exemption (*IHTA 1984, s 69*). Similarly, if there is a possibility of a benefit to the settlor, anti-avoidance provisions come into play.

A transfer out of a discretionary settlement to a charity is exempt, ie the normal 'exit' charge (see **6.34–6.36**) is precluded.

To get the exemption, therefore, a gift must be an outright gift. Provided that a person is prepared to 'do without' the income and other benefits of a gift of cash (not shares or other assets in kind), he would therefore be better off doing this in his lifetime as there would then be the benefit of gift aid relief for both the charity and the donor.

Post death variations and gift aid relief

8.11   An interesting question arises where a person who has inherited money under a deceased estate varies his entitlement within two years after the death in favour of charity (see **13.1–13.4**). Provided that the statutory requirements are met, then so far as the deceased estate is concerned the benefit of the charities exemption from IHT is available.

However, for income tax purposes the gift is treated as having been made by the individual beneficiary. Why should he not get the benefit of gift aid relief?

8.11 *Charitable trusts*

In *St Dunstans v Major* [1997] STC (SCD) 212, a case decided by the Special Commissioners in 1997, it was held broadly speaking that one could not get both IHT exemption and gift aid relief. This was on the footing that the IHT saving was a 'benefit', which denied gift aid relief. However, if the IHT saving goes not to the original beneficiary but to some other person or charity, the decision in *St Dunstans v Major* should not apply.

Example 8.4—Post death gift aid double dip precluded – albeit with limitations

The deceased left an estate of £500,000 to his wife in 2009/10. This is all spouse exempt. One year after he died, his widow varied the will by making a gift of £150,000 to the daughter and £150,000 to the son. This used the nil rate band of the deceased, the appropriate procedures were followed and no IHT was chargeable on the gift treated as made by the deceased.

The son then made a gift of £10,000 net to the Red Cross. This is treated as a gross gift of £12,500, ie enabling the Red Cross to recover tax of £2,500, plus the transitional supplement of £320. Is the son, being a higher rate taxpayer, able to get higher rate relief on the gross payment? *St Dunstans v Major* seems to present no problem because there is no IHT saving to anybody, whether to the son or anybody else. Assuming no further variation is made, what turns out to have been the case, is that, of the £300,000 passed away by the widow, only £290,000 was retained by the children with £10,000 applied for charitable purposes. In this case, however, no IHT saving is made, other than the usual one that the gift by the son would not be a chargeable transfer for IHT if he were to die within seven years.

The same would apply if the husband's will had left express legacies of £150,000 to each of his children, ie there had been no variation by the widow and the son simply varied £10,000 of his entitlement in favour of the Red Cross. This is because the whole gift is within the nil rate band and there is therefore no room for the charities exemption to apply. If by contrast, the gift to the son had been £175,000 (out of a total chargeable transfer of £350,000), the question would depend on where the IHT saving went; if under the terms of the will, the son had to bear any tax chargeable on his gift, he would have benefited and *St Dunstans v Major* would apply, denying gift aid relief.

If on the other hand, as is more usual, the IHT liability was borne by residue, the beneficiary of the charitable gift would have been the mother and not the son and therefore *St Dunstans v Major* would not apply and gift aid would be available.

VALUE ADDED TAX

8.12 There is no automatic exemption for charities from VAT. VAT is a tax on goods and services supplied by a taxable person. Subject to the turnover level (£68,000 from 1 May 2009), a charity whose taxable supplies exceed this must register, assuming that the taxable supplies are standard-rated. Examples might be:

- first aid classes where fees are taken;
- food provided to employees in a canteen;
- sales of second-hand goods.

Transactions in property will not necessarily be exempt and can result in a VAT liability.

A taxable person must account to HMRC for tax on their 'outputs', that is, supplies of goods and services, if VAT registered. The person can offset against that liability the input tax that is on goods and services bought in for the business, referable to the business. Very often, the problem for a charity is that there is a shortage of input tax, which can be related to the taxable activity.

Charities do benefit to some extent from reliefs, in that a number of different supplies to them are zero-rated. To the extent that charities are concerned with listed buildings there are concessions in respect of building works.

A number of beneficial VAT changes were made by *FA 2000*, viz:

- an extension and alignment of the income tax and VAT exemptions for charity fundraising events;
- a significant extension to the VAT zero-rating of advertisements bought by charities;
- raising from £250 to £1,000 the *de minimis* limit to which charities and other businesses do not have to account for VAT when they de-register.

Example 8.5—Watch the VAT registration threshold

The small trading operation set up as a charity by Zebedee's wife has an annual turnover of only £10,000, ie well below the VAT registration limit. Not having to add VAT to goods sold makes them more marketable, and therefore Zebedee's wife decides not to apply for registration. The corresponding 'down side' is that she cannot offset the input tax on goods supplied for purposes of the business.

More generally, the VAT applicable to any services supplied to the charity, eg by solicitors and accountants, must be borne by the charity with no prospect of recovery.

STAMP DUTIES

Shares

8.13   The acquisition of shares by a charity (ie 'a body of persons established for charitable purposes only') is expressly exempt from stamp duty (*FA 1982, s 129*). This exemption depends on a compliance process known as 'adjudication', ie the document of transfer must be submitted to HMRC Stamp Taxes for confirmation. Note that this exemption for tax covers only transfers to a charity and not transfers by a charity. However, it is likely that in the latter case no stamp duty will be charged because where shares are transferred to a beneficiary a transfer may be certified as exempt under Category L of *The Stamp Duty (Exempt Instruments) Regulations 1987*.

If, on the other hand, the charity sells shares as part of the normal management of its portfolio, stamp duty at 0.5% will be payable on the purchaser.

Land or buildings

8.14   The purchase of land by a charity is expressly exempt from SDLT, subject to satisfying certain conditions (*FA 2003, Sch 8*):

- the acquiring charity must intend to hold the land for qualifying charitable purposes (QCP);

- the transaction must not be entered into for the purpose of avoiding SDLT whether by the purchaser or by any other person; and

- the relief must be claimed in a land transaction return.

Charities relief will be withdrawn where either the purchaser ceases to be a charity, or the land is used otherwise for certain charitable purposes within three years of the transaction or in pursuance of or in connection with arrangements made within that period.

This was the original clawback regime. A charity could qualify for relief from SDLT only if, when acquiring the land, it intended to hold all the property for qualifying charitable purposes. If having obtained the relief a charity decided to dispose of some or all of the property it could do so without clawback. That is, the eligibility of the relief was based purely on intention at the time of purchase.

Now, since 22 July 2004 a charity that intends to hold the majority of the acquisition for a QCP is eligible for partial charities relief. This works by granting full relief initially and then clawing back relief in proportion to the disposals made. However, there is no relief if the charity intends to hold the minority of the acquisition for a QCP.

Note that this deals only with disposals made within three years of acquisition. In other words, there is no clawback if the charity continues to hold the property but uses it for a non-QCP.

Example 8.6—SDLT relief for charities

A charitable trust buys land that it intends to develop for its own charitable purposes. No SDLT needs to be paid. The relief has to be claimed within the land transaction return submitted within 30 days after the effective date (although in practice, if the claim is accepted, no interest will be charged; however, there will be the fixed penalty of £100 if the return is between more than one and less than three months late: see Example 7.4 at **7.5** for SDLT penalties).

Provided that the whole of the land was initially to be held for qualifying charitable purposes, the sale of part within the following three years will not attract a clawback of the relief. A purchaser (not being a charity) will have to pay SDLT in the normal way.

ADMINISTRATION AND ANTI-AVOIDANCE

8.15   Two offices within HMRC have been designated to deal with the income tax affairs of charities. These are now called 'HMRC Charities', operating within the Financial Intermediaries and Claims Offices (FICO) at Bootle and Edinburgh. They used to be known as Claims Branches. District inspectors are involved only to a very limited extent, because the district would be involved only if a charity ceased to be charitable or carried on a non-exempt activity. Where a district inspector receives a claim that a charitable trust or disaster fund has been set up, he will refer the matter to HMRC Charities.

Charities used to send their accounts to FICO by way of routine, so that HMRC could confirm that their income was being used for charitable purposes. However, this ceased to be necessary from 4 March 1998 and HMRC Charities will request to see the accounts only when they want to check them.

Anti-avoidance

Non-charitable expenditure

8.16   Legislation followed *IRC v Helen Slater Charitable Trust* [1982] Ch 49, which was decided against HMRC in 1981. The circumstances of that case involved a donation made by one family charity to another family charity, which was an application of income by the first charity to charitable purposes. It was then open to the second charity to invest the donation in some non-charitable family venture. The legislation withdraws the tax exemptions from any amount of 'non-charitable expenditure' or, if less, the amount of 'attributable income and gains', ie those that would be taxable. Non-charitable expenditure does not include investments or loans (*ICTA 1988, s 506(3)–(5); ITA 2007, ss 539–448*). Even if a charity is outside the legislation, it cannot simply do as it pleases and must devote income and gains to charitable purposes. Grants made by one charity to another would come within the provisions unless used for charitable purposes. This legislation should prevent exempt income being used to fund family trading ventures and the like.

'Substantial donors'

8.17   Transactions which take place between a charity and its 'substantial donors' may lead to a restriction of the charity's tax relief. An individual or a company will be a 'substantial donor' if they give to the charity £25,000 or more in any twelve month period or £100,000 or more over a six-year period. The six-year threshold has been raised to £150,000 following Budget 2009. The donor will be a substantial donor for the chargeable period in which they exceed these limits and the following five chargeable periods. The rule (introduced in 2006) applies to certain specified transactions unless the transaction is otherwise exempt, viz those in which HMRC are satisfied that a charity engages for genuine commercial reasons, on terms which are no less beneficial to the charity than those that might be expected on an identical arms-length transaction, so long as the transaction is not part of an arrangement for the avoidance of tax. (*ICTA 1988 ss 506A, 506B; ITA 2007, ss 549–557*).

The IHT related property rules

8.18   Under the 'related property' rules (in *IHTA 1984, s 161*), assets of husbands and wives are generally aggregated in valuation terms. For example, suppose that the husband owns three chairs of a set of 12 and the wife owns nine. On the husband's death, his three chairs are valued not in isolation, but as one-quarter of a complete set of 12 chairs, a greater value. Assets transferred to a charity are within these related property provisions. (*IHTA*

1984, s 161(2)(b)(i)). While the rule does not affect the trustees, it does affect the estate planning of the donor, who is treated as continuing to own the assets for five years after sale by the trustees.

Example 8.7—Related property

Zebedee's father dies leaving Zebedee 51% of the family investment company (if not attracting business property from IHT) and 49% to Zebedee's sister. Assume Zebedee transfers to the Russian Orphanage Trust 2% of the company. This is free from both IHT and CGT.

However, for IHT purposes on Zebedee's death, his 49% shareholding would be valued as if it formed part of a 51% holding, ie valued at 49/51 of the value of a 51% holding. This assumes that the charity has not sold its 2% at least five years before Zebedee dies.

Administration responsibilities

8.19 Following the end of each year, every registered charity must complete and return to the Charity Commission:

- A database update form. This is used to keep the public register of charities up to date. The trustees have a legal duty to tell the Commission about any changes to their entry. The database update form includes a summary of financial information.

- An annual return. Only charities with gross income or expenditure of £10,000 or more must complete this form as well as the database update form. The deadline is ten months after the end of the accounting period.

- A trustees' annual report, accounts and an accounts scrutiny report. Only charities with gross income or total expenditure exceeding £10,000 need to send these documents.

Chapter 9

Ending a trust

THE PERPETUITY PERIOD

Capital distribution compared with termination

9.1   Under English law, at least, a non-charitable trust cannot continue for ever. There is a 'rule against perpetuities'. The most common so called 'perpetuity period' is 80 years from the date of the settlement, although there are other possible periods. A well drafted trust document will prescribe what happens to any property left in the trust at the end of the perpetuity period (commonly called the 'vesting date'). Note that following enactment of the *Perpetuities and Accumulations Bill 2009* there will be a single perpetuity of 125 years. Trustees of a settlement made before the new Act takes effect will be able by deed to opt for the 125-year rule in place of an existing perpetuity period in the trust deed.

The beneficiaries could, for example, be the named children of the settlor in existence at the date of the trust deed. If by the vesting date any of them had died, their share would pass according to the provisions of their will or intestacy.

Sometimes, one comes across a trust deed that has not been drafted so completely, which leaves it open as to what happens in such circumstances. Typically, there will be a 'resulting trust' to the settlor or to his estate. This carries the adverse effect of bringing into play the anti-avoidance rules for income tax (see **4.26–4.29**) and for IHT (see **6.16–6.21**). In any case, it is possible for the future, though not for the past, to remedy this situation by having the settlor or spouse as the case may be, irrevocably assigning any rights under the settlement to, for example, their named children.

Trustee responsibilities

9.2   For so long as the trust continues, the legal, though not the beneficial, ownership of the trust fund remains vested in the trustees. They have the responsibility for managing the property and they must deal with any income tax, CGT or IHT compliance duties. Once property leaves the trust, either through exercise by the trustees of a discretion, or because that is what the trust deed provides (eg on the 25th birthday of beneficiary X), the capital concerned is freed from the trust subject only to any necessary 'lien' for expenses or perhaps tax (in other words, the trustees may resort to that capital for paying such expenses or tax). Whether there is such a lien or not will depend on the terms of the trust deed. Once that capital belongs absolutely to a particular beneficiary, it will be his responsibility for dealing with compliance as well as deciding what to do with the capital.

Capital distribution

9.3   There may be a distribution of capital out of the settlement, in which case the remaining trust fund continues subject to the trusts of the settlement. In either case, the trustees need to have regard to any compliance aspects, as well as to the possibility that even if future tax implications are down to the beneficiary, there could be some recourse against them if he defaults; typically, if any gain on leaving the settlement is held over – see **9.6–9.7**.

Example 9.1—The 'life or lives' of an old A&M settlement

The Adrian and Belinda A&M Settlement (see Example 2.2 at **2.8**) may perhaps be regarded as having four or five beneficial stages or 'lives':

- an A&M trust for their children, Caroline, David and any future children, which will come to an end in each presumptive share as the child reaches the age of 25, or lower 'specified age';

- a life interest for Caroline, David and any future children;

- a successive A&M settlement for the grandchildren of Adrian and Belinda, which again may translate into a life interest settlement insofar as the specified age for any of the grandchildren is lower than 25;

- a life interest for the grandchildren between the specified age, typically 18, and age 25, followed by;

- absolute entitlement to capital on the part of the grandchildren at age 25.

It is likely that each of the shares, whether at child or at grandchild level, can be varied. Assuming that they are not varied, however, and let us say that there are nine grandchildren, as each reaches the age of 25, each will become absolutely entitled to income and capital underlying his share (if *per capita* see below). When the youngest of the grandchildren reaches the age of 25, the whole of the settlement will come to an end. This is likely to be within 80 years after the settlement commenced. Even so, all that is necessary to happen within the perpetuity period is that the interest vests 'in interest' not in possession, ie it does not matter if there are still some grandchildren under the age of 25 on the vesting date. There is then simply an ongoing life interest in that share of capital until the age of 25 is reached.

It is likely that the trust deed will contain a default trust in favour of Caroline and David and their respective legal personal representatives. If the share of any child or grandchild fails, the settlement will probably provide that this be added pro rata to the other shares.

There is an important distinction, at grandchild level, between *per capita* and *per stirpes*. The former means that the capital is divided between the grandchildren according to their number, regardless of how many children, Caroline, David and any other children of Adrian and Belinda may have. *Per stirpes* means that the shares are to be divided according to each branch of the family. Thus, if Adrian and Belinda have four children, Caroline, David, Edward and Fiona, and Caroline has one child, David two, Edward three and Fiona none, Caroline's child will be entitled to one-third of the capital, each of David's children to one-sixth of the capital and each of Edward's children to one-ninth of the capital, all at age 25.

Note: The *FA 2006* rules for A&M settlements made before 22 March 2006 will mean generally that from 6 April 2008 the trust fund will enter the 'relevant property' regime, if not before that date to the extent that an interest in possession arises. This is subject to advantage not being taken before that date of the transitional rules. See **6.49–6.51**, and specifically Example **6.15** at **6.51** addressing the impact for the original Adrian and Belinda settlement example.

INCOME TAX

9.4   This chapter concerns capital, not income, leaving a trust. Question 13 of the trust and estate tax return (see **4.61**) seeks to establish what part of the trust income is subject to the trustees' discretion and what part is not, whether in each case charged at 10% or 20% (for 2008/09). Question 14 goes on to ask whether any discretionary payments of income have been made to beneficiaries. Question 15 asks whether the trustees have made any capital payments to, or for the benefit of, 'relevant' (ie minor unmarried and not in a civil partnership) children of the settlor during his lifetime; this is because such payments could have income tax consequences (see **4.26–4.29**). Question 15A asks whether there were capital transactions between the trustees and the settlors; this is intended to seek out situations covered by *ITTOIA 2005, ss 633–645* where, for example, a settlor has made a loan to the trustees which is repaid in whole or in part and, to the extent of any undistributed income in the trust, that income is assessed on the recipient settlor at higher rates for up to a maximum of ten years; see **4.28**. Although question 16 asks for details of capital payments or any benefits provided to the beneficiaries, this is only in a case where the settlement has been non-UK resident or has received any capital from another trust which has been non-UK resident; see **5.58**.

In other words, there is no general obligation on the trustees' part to notify HMRC of capital distributions made to the beneficiaries. The only requirement, if the trust comes to an end during the tax year, is that the date of termination must be given in Box 21.1. This will (or should) ensure that no further self-assessment returns are generated by HMRC in subsequent years. It is, coincidentally, important to ensure that if a self-assessment return is generated, it is returned, even on a nil basis, to avoid the automatic penalty of £100 if not delivered on or before 31 January following the end of the tax year. (It is hard to see that such a penalty would be levied if the trust had come to an end and HMRC had been told as much, but the point is made.)

In other words, all that will happen for income tax purposes as a result of the capital leaving the trust is that any income generated in future by that capital will cease to be income of the trust. There is no obligation either on the trustees or on the recipient of the capital to notify HMRC. What the absolute beneficiary must of course do for the future, is to ensure that he duly returns on his self-assessment return the income that is generated by the capital.

Example 9.2—Tax liability for income

Following the appointment of £20,000 by the trustees of the Albert settlement to Charles, which happened during the tax year, the income of the trustees for the year will of course reduce. Charles invests the income for his own benefit and receives dividends of £500 net per annum. He must ensure that in future he records this income on his self-assessment return.

CAPITAL GAINS TAX

9.5   We said at **9.4** that there are no particular obligations to notify, at least for income tax purposes, the event of capital leaving a trust. For CGT, however, when capital leaves a trust, whether or not the trust is terminated, the trustees are treated as having made a notional disposal and reacquisition of that capital at market value (*TCGA 1992, s 71(1)*). This means that if over the trustees' period of ownership there has been an increase in value, there will be a capital gain on the capital leaving the trust. To the extent that the gain (taken with other gains and losses during the year) exceeds the annual exemption, there will be a tax liability at 18% that must be paid by the trustees. If the trust is discretionary or the asset concerned is a qualifying business asset, the trustees can, jointly with the beneficiary, make a hold-over election whereby the beneficiary 'inherits' the in-built gain (see **3.5–3.7**).

Hold-over relief

9.6 If the asset advanced is sterling cash, there will be no CGT implications. If a gain does arise, it must be reported as such on the capital gains supplemental pages SA 905 and again on the main SA 900, with the tax paid by 31 January following the end of the tax year. However, the trustees may decide to hold over the gain. This could be advantageous in a case where, for example, they had already used their annual exemption, or the gain far exceeded their annual exemption and the gain could be realised over one or two tax years by the beneficiary or perhaps several beneficiaries taken together. A word of warning, given anti-avoidance principles it would be sensible not to be too 'blatant', ie if on day one, trustees of a discretionary settlement appointed shares carrying gains of £30,000 to three beneficiaries equally, and on day two, those beneficiaries each sold the shares within their annual exemptions of £10,100 for 2009/10, the circumstances may lead HMRC to argue that in reality the disposals had been made by the trustees. In such circumstances, no particular guidance can be given as to how long a period should safely be allowed to lapse. It is a good idea, for example, to have some income arising to the beneficiaries through dividends, for the beneficiaries to take independent advice and perhaps not all to act together. Having said that, it would be unlikely that an interval of a week or two could realistically be challenged, especially if the amounts of tax at stake are likely to be relatively small.

Clawback on emigration of beneficiary

9.7 However, there is one problem with a hold-over election. If within six years after the end of the tax year in which the appointment is made, the beneficiary becomes non-UK resident, the held-over gain immediately crystallises (*TCGA 1992, s 168*). If the beneficiary fails to pay the tax within 12 months after the due date, there is a right for HMRC to pursue the trustees for the tax, in either case at 18% (in 2008/09 or 2009/10) though at an uncertain rate before 2008/09. Accordingly, it is very important for trustees to protect themselves in such cases. They may consider that indemnities from the beneficiary's parents are sufficient. However, the only safe way would be for them to retain the legal ownership of the assets concerned, or at least sufficient of the assets concerned to cover the tax until the danger period had expired.

Losses

9.8   If the deemed disposal and reacquisition of the assets leaving the trust produces a loss, it is set first of all against other trust gains. However, to the extent that a loss remains unused in the trust, it may be 'inherited' by the beneficiary. Until June 1999, that loss could be used by the beneficiary against his general gains. Now, however, it can be offset only against a gain arising on the asset advanced to him out of trust or, if the asset was land, against some other interest in land deriving its value from that land (*TCGA 1992, s 71(2)–(2D)*).

Private residences: anti-avoidance rule

9.9   The rules effective from 10 December 2003 on putting a property into a discretionary trust and electing to hold over the gain, with a view to sheltering the gain by main residence relief on sale by the trustees, apply equally to restrict the relief on property coming out of trust: see **5.27** and Example 5.9. There are various permutations. Broadly speaking, however, if the trustees elect to hold over a gain on a property on leaving the trust (whether or not it has been occupied by a beneficiary), the beneficiary receiving the property cannot use main residence relief himself to shelter the gain on ultimate disposal (*TCGA 1992, s 225A*). Problems may arise because the beneficiary and the trustees will have to join together in the hold-over election in these circumstances and it may not be in the beneficiary's interests, with long-term appreciation in property values (notwithstanding falls generally since Autumn 2007), to take a proportionately larger CGT 'hit' in the future than the trustees, but the balance of advantage will depend on the specific circumstances.

Death of the life tenant

9.10   The general CGT rule on death is that there is no charge, but that the beneficiary under the will is treated as becoming entitled at market value at the date of death. That is, any inherent gain in the assets is 'washed'; equally, any inherent loss simply disappears. A similar rule operates within qualifying interest in possession trusts so that, whether the trust continues or comes to an end on the life tenant's death, there is a deemed uplift to market value of the assets within the trust but with no CGT charge. The only two exceptions are:

●   where the capital on the life tenant's death 'reverts' to the settlor absolutely. In this case there is no uplift to market value and the assets are inherited at their original cost (*TCGA 1992, s 73(1)(b)*); and

●   where property went into the trust with the benefit of a hold-over election. In this case, the held-over gain is crystallised (*TCGA 1992, s 74(2)*). It may, however, be held over again, either as a chargeable transfer under *s 260*, eg the assets passed to the life tenant's children or under *s 165* where the assets concerned are qualifying business assets. A CGT charge will have to be paid therefore only where a surviving spouse inherits non-business assets.

Note that, under the new IHT regime for trusts introduced by *FA 2006* from 22 March 2006, the above treatment will apply on the death of the life tenant only where the trust does not then fall within the 'relevant property' regime (see **6.57**).

Revocable appointments

9.11   There will be CGT implications of property coming out of trust if some other person becomes 'absolutely entitled' against the trustees (*TCGA 1992, s 71*). It may be that the property passes not to a beneficiary outright, but to the trustees of some other settlement. If the trustees of the second settlement are 'absolutely entitled' against the trustees of the first, there will be a CGT charge in the usual way. It may be possible, however, for the appointment of capital to be made in such a way that it is revocable, or that reference has to be made back to the original settlement for some administrative or beneficial powers, or, eg for the default trust (see HMRC Statement of Practice 7/84). In this case, it cannot be said that the trustees of the second settlement have become absolutely entitled and there will be no CGT event. It will mean, however, that any inherent gains in the assets concerned will be taken on board by the trustees of the second settlement, which they should bear in mind.

INHERITANCE TAX

Discretionary trust: the exit charge

9.12   The mechanics of the exit charge were explained in **6.34–6.36**. The thinking behind the IHT regime for discretionary trusts, which has been with us since 1975, is that such trusts should be treated as a separate taxpayer. Therefore, when capital leaves the trust to go into the estate of say, a beneficiary, there is an 'exit charge', the calculation of which varies according to whether it occurs during the first ten years, or after the first ten-year anniversary.

Even if there is no charge to IHT (because the value concerned is within the nil rate band), subject only to the *de minimis* provisions (as revised from 2007/08: (*Inheritance Tax (Delivery of Accounts) (Excepted Settlements) Regulations 2008, SI 2008/ 606*)) the trustees still have an obligation to return the event to HMRC Inheritance Tax on form IHT 100 within 12 months after the end of the month in which the exit occurs. Note that the liability to pay any tax due falls six months after the end of the month in which the chargeable transfer was made, except in the case of one made after 5 April and before 1 October (otherwise than on death), when the tax falls due on 30 April in the following year (*IHTA 1984, s 226(1)*).

Example 9.3—IHT on appointments out of trust

The trustees of the Albert Settlement have made the following recent appointments of capital:

- 1 June 2008: £20,000 cash to Charles.

- 1 June 2009: £25,000 of shares to Debbie.

The trustees were aware of the first ten-year anniversary on 1 January 2008, and have both submitted form IHT 100 and paid the tax due. Thinking that they can now 'rest on their laurels', and need not do anything more on the compliance front until 1 January 2018, they are rather taken by surprise when the family's new solicitor does a 'financial health check' and advises them of the following:

- In respect of the distribution of capital to Charles, form IHT 100 should have been submitted on or before 30 June 2009. Tax fell due on 30 April 2009 (though happily interest on unpaid tax since then is, at the date of going to press, 0%).

- In respect of the distribution of shares to Debbie, they have a bit more time, as form IHT 100 is not due until 30 June 2010, the tax to be paid by 30 April 2010.

A&M trusts

9.13   Although in the heading to this page (and elsewhere in this book), the expression 'A&M' trusts is used, it is preferable for reasons already given (see **6.45**) to refer to 'the A&M regime'.

The position before 6 April 2008

9.14   This page presupposes that capital leaving the trust, whether as a partial distribution or as a termination of the whole trust, does so at a time when it is subject to the A&M regime.

9.15 *Ending a trust*

A distinction should be drawn between the A&M regime coming to an end:

- though the trust continues, with an ongoing life interest; and
- the case where capital is advanced outright to any of the beneficiaries, whether this is at a particular age prescribed in the trust deed, or because the trustees exercise their discretion to advance capital earlier.

In the former case, there will be no IHT (or indeed CGT) implications of the A&M regime turning into an interest in possession regime. The trust simply continues. The difference for IHT will be that capital that was not hitherto treated as part of anyone's estate will now be treated as if it belonged to the relevant beneficiaries.

The same is of course true of the second eventuality, though in addition there would be a CGT event because someone, viz the beneficiaries, would be treated as absolutely entitled to the capital as against the trustees.

The position after 5 April 2008

9.15 If, following the *FA 2006* changes (see **6.49–6.51**), a pre-22 March 2006 A&M trust has if necessary had its terms changed so that capital vests absolutely at 18, the above treatment will apply.

If, before 6 April 2008, the trusts have been changed (if necessary) to provide that capital entitlement arises after age 18 but on or before age 25, there will be an exit charge (of no more than 4.2%) upon that entitlement, based on the number of completed quarters during which the property has remained in the trust since the beneficiary attained 18 or, if later, 6 April 2008.

In any other case, the trust will enter the 'relevant property' regime on 6 April 2008 and will become subject to the system of ten-year and exit charges (see **6.30–6.36**).

CGT on advance of capital

9.16 One advantage of a pre-22 March 2006 A&M trust, which as at 6 April 2008 fell into the 'relevant property' regime is that, where capital vests outright following (and not at the same time as) an entitlement to income, hold-over relief will now generally be available to shelter gains on non-business assets under *TCGA 1992, s 260*, whereas it would not have been before. The only exception is the case where capital leaves the trust during a quarter beginning with the date of commencement of the settlement or with a ten-year anniversary (*IHTA 1984, s 65(4)*).

Example 9.4—Decisions on trust capital

Consider the Adrian and Belinda Settlement. It is now towards the end of 2017 and (curiously) the general tax regime has remained the same, apart from the *FA 2006* changes. The settlement has become very valuable, largely through expert and perhaps fortunate investment in some high performing stock exchange securities. None of the children has yet become entitled to income, though Caroline will soon do so on reaching the age of 25. David is 22, Edward is 18 and Fiona is 16. The 21-year accumulation period has not yet ended. Of course, the terms of the settlement not having been changed before 6 April 2008, the trust fund entered the 'relevant property' regime on that date and so the first ten-year anniversary charge arose on 1 January 2009 (see Example 6.15 at **6.51**).

It would be open to the trustees to exercise powers in the settlement to advance to each of the four children the capital of their respective presumptive shares, although they also have power, if they want, to vary the shares; this they do not want to do.

Each of the children, therefore, ends up owning a considerable value of shares with large inherent gains. Those held-over gains would 'come home to roost' in respect of each share, if the relevant child were to become non-UK resident within six years after the end of the relevant tax year (*TCGA 1992, s 168*). That is the gains cannot be 'washed' simply by the children emigrating and becoming genuinely non-UK resident (which they now have to do for a period of at least five consecutive tax years), except after the six year risk period has expired.

What Adrian and Belinda might have in mind is that, to protect the underlying capital, each of the children might resettle at least some of the capital. The basic trust issue is that of course this should not happen simply because 'Mum and Dad wanted me to' as there would be issues of undue influence, ie each of the children should get their own independent professional advice. The other problem is that such a settlement would trigger a disposal for CGT purposes. Any such settlement would be within the 'relevant property' regime, therefore attracting hold-over relief for CGT. However, to the extent that the value exceeds the nil rate band there would be an automatic charge to IHT at 20%. Meanwhile, it is unlikely that any of Caroline, David, Edward or Fiona would really want to make a trust under which they could not benefit. Caroline, though not her siblings, has become married. Subject to general anti-avoidance principles, it might be open to her to give to her husband, say £325,000 of investments, and for him, having retained the investments for a period of time and perhaps with independent advice to make his own discretionary settlement. The wife to husband transfer would be 'no gain, no loss' so that the gain would be inherited by the husband, who would therefore be able to make his own nil rate band discretionary settlement.

Interest in possession trusts in (or deemed as in) being at 22 March 2006

9.17   Following *FA 2006*, this paragraph sets out the rules only for those interests in possession, which were in being at 22 March 2006 or, which by virtue of being a TSI were treated as such (see **6.58**).

An interest in possession trust may come to an end before the death of the life tenant in circumstances where:

- The capital has been advanced to the life tenant, in whole or in part. To that extent he is treated as receiving capital that he is already treated as owning and there is a 'non-event' for IHT purposes (*IHTA 1984, s 53(3)*).

- An advance of capital pursuant to powers in the deed to the spouse of the life tenant. This will be spouse exempt and therefore not a chargeable transfer for IHT purposes. The only qualification here is if the life tenant is actually, or deemed to be, domiciled in the UK for IHT purposes and the spouse is neither actually nor deemed UK domiciled. Here, the unlimited spouse exemption does not apply and the exemption is limited to £55,000 on a cumulative lifetime basis, ie with no seven year limitation (*IHTA 1984, s 18(2)*).

- An advance of capital to someone other than the life tenant or his spouse, which constitutes a PET by the life tenant, ie assumed to be exempt except and unless the life tenant dies within seven years. Even then, the gift will have 'first call' on the life tenant's nil rate band, subject to any chargeable transfers he might have made in the seven years before the capital left the trust (and therefore may attract tax at the nil rate, even though it would have the effect of denying the nil rate band to that extent to the deceased estate).

Similarly, if the life interest continues until the death of the life tenant, it would be treated as part of his estate. The trustees will have to complete Inheritance Tax Account form IHT 100 and they will be liable for their share of the tax at the estate rate on the trust assets (see **3.20** and Example 6.18 at **6.53**). If, however, under the trust the surviving spouse becomes entitled on the life tenant's death, there will be no liability to tax because of the spouse exemption.

There is one rather curious type of life interest settlement called an interest '*pur autre vie*'. There is a life interest insofar as the beneficiary is entitled to income from the trust property. However, the person by whose life the interest is measured is not the beneficiary but someone else – that is the *'autre vie'*. When, typically, the *autre vie* dies, the interest will come to an end and the beneficiary will cease to be entitled to the income. What happens as a matter of trust law will depend on the terms of the trust. And an interest *'pur autre vie'* may for IHT purposes either be a qualifying interest in possession or fall within the relevant property regime. We assume the former here. Let us say, the children of the *autre vie* then become entitled. So long as the beneficiary survives the death for at least seven years, he will be treated as having made a PET, which becomes exempt and there will be no implications. If not, he will be treated as having made a chargeable transfer on the death of the *autre vie*.

Example 9.5—Capital leaving a qualifying interest in possession trust

The trustees of Alistair's settlement (which has a qualifying interest in possession) decide to advance to Alistair £100,000. This has no IHT implications as Alistair was treated as entitled to the underlying capital anyway. There will be no IHT compliance obligations either then, or indeed if Alistair were to die within seven years after the advance. On that death, the trustees will complete form IHT 100, recording the assets then in the trust.

Insofar as they are chargeable assets (ie not business or agricultural property), there will be a chargeable transfer because the beneficial entitlement passes to his children, subject to them reaching the age of 25. The tax payable will depend on Alistair's free estate, with the estate rate applied to the trust fund and the liability to tax, due six months after the end of the month in which Alistair died, falling on the trustees.

Assuming that at his death all Alistair's children have attained the age of 25, the trustees would want to ensure that:

- they have paid the IHT due;

- the executors have obtained a clearance certificate in the estate from HMRC Inheritance Tax (so that the trustees know that there are no further IHT liabilities in the estate that might impact on the estate rate for the settlement); and

- all costs and other liabilities of the trust are paid before capital is advanced to Alistair's children.

Lifetime termination: use of annual (or marriage/civil partnership) exemption

9.18 If, while the life tenant is alive, there is an exit of capital to someone other than the life tenant or his spouse, and the life tenant has not otherwise used his annual exemption for the tax year in question (and perhaps the previous tax year, which can be carried forward for one year only), the annual exemptions of £3,000 (or £6,000), or part, may be set against the transfer of value on exit. However, this is subject to notice being given by the life tenant to the trustees within six months of the exit (*IHTA 1984, s 57*). Once the six-month period has passed, no relief can be given.

The same point applies to use by the life tenant of his marriage/civil partnership exemption.

TAX PLANNING POINTS

Termination under the trust deed

9.19 This could be because:

- with an A&M settlement, capital vests outright, say, at age 18; or

- with an interest in possession trust, the life tenant has died and the trust deed provides that the children of the life tenant become absolutely entitled in equal shares, whether or not on attaining a particular age.

Under an A&M settlement where capital has not vested absolutely by 6 April 2008 and the vesting age is over 18, the 'relevant property' regime will apply until it does vest (or, under an age 18-to-25 trust, an exit charge will accrue from age 18). The same point will apply to an interest in possession arising on or after 22 March 2006 which is not a 'transitional serial interest' (see **6.58**).

On the face of it, there is not much that can be done about either eventuality, except that in the A&M case 'one can see the event coming'. The usual tax which comes to mind on the ending of a trust is CGT (rather than IHT). However, if, as in the life interest case, the trust comes to an end on death, there will not be a CGT issue (because of the tax-free uplift to market value on death). Nonetheless, remember that any gain previously held over on transfer to the trustees may crystallise (see **9.10**). By contrast, there will be an IHT bill, except to the extent that any value falls within the nil rate band or perhaps that the value is protected by reliefs for agricultural or business property.

In the A&M case, there will be no IHT to pay. Equally, following 6 April 2008, there should be no immediate CGT issue given the facility to hold over any gains because, under *TCGA 1992, s 260*, capital vests at age 18 without an intervening right to income. One advantage of a pre-22 March 2006 A&M trust which as at 6 April 2008 falls into the 'relevant property' regime is that, where capital vests outright following (and not at the same time as) the date of an entitlement to income, hold-over relief will now generally be available under *TCGA 1992, s 260*, whereas it would not have been before. However, see the last sentence of **9.16** for the one qualification to this principle.

In the case where capital vested before 6 April 2008 under an A&M settlement see the final paragraph of **9.19** in the 2008/09 edition of this book.

Trustees exercise discretion to pay out capital

9.20   Here the assumption is that the trustees are exercising powers in the settlement to advance capital. Well-advised trustees will always take into account the possible tax implications. For example:

- IHT with a discretionary trust. What are the exit implications? The trustees of every discretionary trust should carefully review the situation, say, nine years after commencement. This is because if there has been rapid growth in the settlement it may be possible to exit the funds, perhaps into some other type of trust. But so long as an exit is made out of the discretionary regime within the first ten years, there will be no IHT to pay if, on entering the trust, the property was within the nil rate band and the exit is made before the first ten-year anniversary (subject to a caveat with agricultural or business property (see **6.35**)).

- For CGT, it may be possible to hold over any gain out of a discretionary trust (though bear in mind the danger of the beneficiary emigrating within six years and subject to what is written elsewhere about private residences occupied by beneficiaries – see **9.7** and **9.9**). With qualifying interest in possession trusts, by contrast, there may be a CGT problem, unless the assets concerned are qualifying business assets and attract hold-over relief under *s 165*.

In every case, it is important to review the tax implications and ensure that all necessary returns are made to HMRC.

However the termination occurs

9.21   If capital leaves an interest in possession trust by appointment to a person other than the life tenant or spouse, bear in mind the possibility of using the life tenant's annual exemption for the current tax year, and perhaps the previous tax year, or his exemption for gifts on marriage/civil partnership.

However, this requires notice by the life tenant to the trustees within six months – see **9.18**.

STAMP DUTIES

9.22   Shares or land may cease to be owned by trustees, whether because they are sold and the proceeds of sale are held as part of the trust fund instead or where they are advanced out to a beneficiary, (either because he becomes absolutely entitled under the terms of the trust or because the trustees exercise a discretion whereby he becomes so entitled).

In the former case of sale, any stamp duty or SDLT is payable by the purchaser.

In the latter case of distribution to a beneficiary, there will be an exemption from either stamp duty or SDLT:

- In the case of shares, the transfer document escapes the normal £5 charge by being certified by Category J of *The Stamp Duty (Exempt Instruments) Regulations 1987*. The £5 charge has been removed by *FA 2008, s 99* and *Sch 22* from instruments transferring stocks and shares on or after 13 March 2008 which were previously chargeable with that amount of stamp duty, whether fixed or *ad valorem*.

- In the case of land, the transfer to the beneficiary is self-certified under *FA 2003, Sch 3, para 1*. For land transactions made before 12 March 2008, this self-certificate (form SDLT 60) was then delivered to one of HM Land Registries in support of an application for re-registration of the beneficiary as the registered owner. The requirement to complete form SDLT 60 has been removed from 12 March 2008 by *FA 2008, s 94* and *Sch 30*: the re-registration is now secured by delivery of Land Registry Transfer TP1.

Note a trap in particular in the latter case. If the land is subject to a mortgage and the beneficiary takes over liability for the mortgage, the amount of the liability counts as chargeable consideration. In the case of residential land, the SDLT charge will be at 0% if the amount does not exceed £125,000 (£175,000 for transfers after 2 September 2008 and before 1 January 2010) and in the case of non-residential land £150,000. Otherwise, SDLT will be charged at 1% if the consideration does not exceed £250,000, 3% if the consideration does not exceed £500,000 and otherwise 4%. However, if there is consideration payable of £40,000 or more the transaction cannot be self-certified and must be the subject of a land transaction return, which should be submitted to HMRC Stamp Taxes at Netherton within 30 days (see the last sentence of Example 9.6 below).

Example 9.6—Appointments of shares and land to beneficiaries

The trustees of a family settlement resolve to appoint £100,000 worth of shares and £300,000 of land to Jack and Jill respectively, beneficiaries in favour of whom they may exercise their discretion. This they do on 1 January 2010.

The transfer documents of the shares delivered by the trustees to Jack each carry the certification Category J under the 1987 Regulations. Jack produces the transfers to the registrars of the relevant companies so that he may be registered as the new owner.

The land is subject to a mortgage of £50,000 for which Jill agrees to assume future responsibility. This land transaction cannot be self-certified and must be the subject of a land transaction return delivered by the trustees to the HMRC Stamp Taxes within 30 days after their appointment. HMRC Stamp Taxes will deliver Inland Revenue certificate SDLT 5 to Jill with which she may procure registration of the land. Being within the £125,000 threshold for residential property, no SDLT is payable. (Had the mortgage been less than £40,000, no land transaction return would have been necessary, following an extension to the *de minimis* regime by *FA 2008, s 94(1),(2)* with effect from 12 March 2008: see *FA 2003, s 77A*).

Chapter 10

Deceased estates: introduction

DUTIES OF PERSONAL REPRESENTATIVES

10.1   The expression 'personal representatives' (PRs) comprises both executors (in the event of a will) and administrators (in the event of an intestacy). The duty of the PRs is to gather in the assets of the estate, to pay off any liabilities (including personal debts of the deceased, and IHT) and to distribute those assets, or their proceeds of sale, among the beneficiaries, according to the provisions of the will or intestacy.

In doing so, eg exercising any discretions or deciding whether to sell, when and at what price, the PRs should take into account, though they will not be bound by, the wishes of the beneficiaries.

It is surprising how many people die without having made a will. In this case, rules are found in the *Administration of Estates Act 1925* (with different provisions applying to Scotland), which lay down who is entitled to what. The rules are set out below.

The Inheritance Act 1975

10.2   Generally speaking, a person can leave his assets to whosoever he wishes (unlike the rules in most other European countries – the so-called 'community of property' regime – see **11.23**). That said, there is the ability under the *Inheritance (Provision for Family and Dependants) Act 1975* for certain individuals who feel that the terms of a will or the intestacy rules do not make reasonable financial provision for them, to apply to the court for such provision. Typically, these will be a surviving spouse, who can apply for what provision it would be reasonable in all the circumstances of the case for them to receive, ie capital as well as income. Other beneficiaries such as an ex-spouse who has not remarried, a child, or anyone else treated as a child of the deceased, or someone being maintained by the deceased may receive what is reasonable for them to get by way of maintenance, ie just income. Applications have to be made within six months of the grant of probate.

It is possible for one or more beneficiaries to vary their entitlement within two years after the death. This variation can be done in an intestacy, just as much as with a will. This is discussed in more detail at **13.1–13.4**.

Intestacy rules – a summary (under English law) and proposals for change in Scotland

10.3

- A surviving spouse will take the whole estate if they survive for 28 days and the deceased left no children, parents, brothers or sisters or their issue.

- If there are children surviving: the spouse gets personal chattels, the statutory legacy of £250,000 (increased from £125,000 on 1 February 2009) and a life interest in half of residue. The other half of residue goes to the children on the 'statutory trust', which means that they become entitled in equal shares at age 18.

- If there are no children, but one or more of parents, brothers and sisters and their issue survives: the statutory legacy is increased to £450,000 (increased from £200,000 on 1 February 2009), and the interest in half of residue becomes absolute, the other half of residue goes to first, the parents, or if none, brothers and sisters, or if none, their issue.

Proposals have been made by the Scottish Law Commission to make significant reform of the laws of Scotland governing inheritance, wills and intestacy (ie the *Succession (Scotland) Act 1964*). The principal changes proposed are:

- a surviving spouse or civil partner to inherit the first £300,000 of the estate on intestacy, the remainder to be shared equally with the deceased's children and grandchildren;

- where a survivor takes the deceased's share of the couple's home by survivorship, the value of the property will be taken into account when calculating the survivor's entitlement;

- unmarried cohabitees will have the right to apply to the court for an amount not to exceed the first £300,000 of the estate;

- disinherited spouses or civil partners will receive a quarter of what they would have inherited on intestacy; and

- the six-month deadline for a claim under the *Inheritance (Provision for Family and Dependants) Act 1975* is to be abolished.

10.4 *Deceased estates: introduction*

In relation to children there are alternative proposals:

(a) disinherited children, dependent or otherwise, to receive a quarter of what they would have inherited on intestacy (moveable or otherwise); or

(b) dependent children to have right to apply for a capital sum, but other children to have no entitlement and no right of challenge.

Procedure

10.4

- The PRs first obtain probate from the court, which depends upon prior submission of the Inheritance Tax Account form IHT 400 and payment of IHT immediately due. Probate is the authority of the court for the PRs to deal with the assets of the deceased. Under a new procedure operating from 5 November 2007, an IHT reference and a payslip must be obtained using form IHT 422 before form IHT 400 is submitted. Payment with the payslip is sent to HMRC's cashiers in Nottingham and the form IHT 400 is sent either to Nottingham or, if a grant of confirmation is required in Scotland, to Edinburgh.

- There then follows the period of administration of the estate, during which the PRs gather in the assets, pay off any debts, taxes or other liabilities and establish the entitlements of the beneficiaries. This would include paying off any legacies, leaving them with something to pass on to those entitled to 'the residue'.

- It is not always easy to determine when the administration comes to an end, though this will be once the residue has been 'ascertained', and typically the estate accounts are signed by the residuary beneficiaries. It might also follow the submission of a final corrective account to HMRC Inheritance Tax and the issue of a clearance certificate by HMRC, though in any particular case not all of these things may happen.

- Once the estate administration has come to an end, the PRs are relieved of their duties as such. If the will, or the intestacy rules, prescribe a continuing trust, eg for the children of the deceased, and the same persons are to be trustees, their 'hats' change and different tax rules apply to trustees from those that apply to PRs. The distinction is important and it is vital in any case to know at what stage the administration comes to an end and in what capacity the individuals are acting, ie whether as executors or as trustees (see **2.14**).

- There can be interim distributions of assets from an estate, ie once the PRs are satisfied that those assets are not required to pay debts or other liabilities they may be released to the beneficiaries.

COMPLIANCE OBLIGATIONS

Inheritance tax

10.5   PRs must deliver 'an account' of the assets of the deceased (*IHTA 1984, s 216*). The time limit is the expiry of 12 months after the end of the month in which death occurred. Any IHT must be paid on or before delivery of the account (not including instalment property or cases where PRs are not primarily liable, eg failed PETs). Typically, a provisional account may be delivered to the extent that property cannot yet be properly valued.

If no UK grant has been taken up within the time limit, there is a duty on certain other people to deliver an account.

There is a *de minimis* provision in the case of 'excepted estates', where no account need be delivered. See **10.8** to **10.10** below.

In the case of a PET that has become chargeable, or a gift with reservation, there is an obligation to report on the part of the transferee.

PRs now also have a statutory obligation to report chargeable transfers made by the deceased within seven years before his death.

The main form IHT 400 and the supplementary forms constituting the Inland Revenue Account are discussed in detail; see **11.1** onwards.

Income tax and capital gains tax

10.6   The income and gains of the estate must be distinguished from those of the deceased. The tax liabilities of the deceased must be computed and paid by the PRs and these will rank as a deduction in calculating his estate for inheritance tax purposes. The income and gains of the estate must be returned in form SA 900 and supplementary pages. These are discussed in more detail: see **12.1** onwards.

Clearance application

10.7   It is customary, once the estate administration has run its course, for the PRs to submit a clearance application to HMRC Inheritance Tax (*IHTA 1984, s 239*). Generally speaking, this will confirm that the PRs have satisfied their liabilities in respect of the assets disclosed. The PRs may have some concern that having completed the estate, a PET made within seven years before the death, may subsequently come to light. HMRC Inheritance Tax have said that, provided the PRs have made the fullest enquiries as are reasonably practicable to discover the existence of such PETs, and have done all in their power to make disclosure to HMRC Inheritance Tax, HMRC will not hold them liable if they have obtained a certificate of discharge and distributed the estate before a chargeable lifetime transfer comes to light (IHTM 30044). The above said, HMRC announced in their IHT Newsletter of April 2007 that, although formal application for clearance certificates could still be made, they would urge agents and taxpayers to rely on the assurance provided by HMRC's closure letter instead. In practice solicitors and others dealing with deceased estates will continue to apply for clearance certificates, given the measure of protection which it affords the personal representatives.

Excepted estates

UK domiciled deceaseds

10.8   The limits are as follows

(a)   The gross value of the estate plus chargeable lifetime transfers does not exceed the nil-rate threshold (£312,000 for 2008/09 and £325,000 for 2009/10); or

(b)   the gross value of the estate does not exceed £1 million, which is IHT exempt because of (only) the spouse/civil partner or charity exemption.

● Any trust assets in which the deceased had an interest in possession were held in a single trust and do not exceed £150,000 (unless spouse or charities exempt).

● Non-UK property does not exceed £100,000.

● Any chargeable lifetime gifts made within seven years before death were only of cash, quoted shares or securities or land and buildings (and contents given at the same time) and do not exceed £150,000 in total.

● The deceased had not at any time made a gift with reservation of benefit.

There is no charge under the alternatively secured pensions provisions.

Non-UK domiciled deceaseds

10.9

● The deceased had never been domiciled or treated as domiciled in the UK.

● The value of UK assets does not in total exceed £150,000 and consists only of cash or quoted shares or securities.

10.10   The control document is form IHT 205 (or C5 in Scotland).

The changes made on 1 November 2004 have brought excepted estates within reach of the penalty regime. The intention is that this will deter the misuse of the excepted estates process to facilitate applications for grant of probate in cases where an IHT account is properly required at the time of the grant application.

THE INTEREST AND PENALTY REGIME

Interest

10.11   Tax on death is due six months after the end of the month in which the death occurred. It is not uncommon for IHT to be paid later than that and this will trigger a liability to interest.

The same rule applies to tax on the chargeable lifetime transfer, eg a PET that has become chargeable made between 1 October and 5 April in any year. Tax due on a chargeable lifetime transfer between 6 April and 30 September becomes due at the end of April in the following year.

Recent rates of interest on unpaid IHT are set out in **6.14**.

Penalties

10.12   A new penalty regime is in place for deaths occurring on or after 1 April 2009: see **6.13** and **4.17**. For deaths occurring before that date see **10.12** of the 2008/09 edition of this book. Statute sets out various penalty regimes for failure to deliver accounts (*IHTA 1984, s 245*), failure to provide information, etc (*IHTA 1984, s 245A*) and provision of incorrect information (*IHTA 1984, s 247*). For example, under *s 247*, the delivery of incorrect accounts by the person liable for the IHT carries a maximum penalty of 100% of the additional tax liability. Delivery by a person not liable for the tax carries a maximum penalty of £3,000. For the statutory reductions of the maximum penalties see **4.17**. A February 2002 Special Commissioner's case (*Robertson v IRC* [2002] STC (SCD) 182) illustrates how HMRC Inheritance Tax are keen to apply penalties where they consider that a PR has not been sufficiently careful to ascertain market values at death, even where an urgent grant of probate is required. Happily, the Special Commissioner in this case found for the solicitor PR and overturned the penalty.

Chapter 11

Deceased estates: IHT compliance

INHERITANCE TAX ACCOUNT FORM IHT 400 AND THE SCHEDULES

11.1   Form IHT 400 is the 'control' document for dealing with a person's inheritance tax liability following death. Replacing the IHT 200, use of the IHT 400 has been obligatory since 9 June 2009. The form will not be required in every case, for example:

- where the 'excepted estates' rules apply, which is a *de minimis* protection for small estates – see **10.8–10.10**; or
- where the only property owned by the deceased was held jointly with his spouse and himself as 'joint tenants' which passes by survivorship to the surviving spouse.

IHT 400

11.2   Form IHT 400 is divided into the following parts, listed below.

Deceased's details.

If the deceased was domiciled in Scotland at the date of death.

Contact details of the person dealing with the estate.

Deceased's will.

Items referred to in the will but not included in the estate.

What makes up the Inheritance Tax account – Schedules.

Estate in the UK.

Deductions from the estate in the UK incurred up to the date of death.

Exemptions and reliefs.

Other assets taken into account to calculate the tax.

Working out the Inheritance Tax.

Simple Inheritance Tax calculation.

Direct Payment Scheme.

Declaration.

Checklist.

Additional information.

The pack also includes: the IHT 400 calculation, nil rate bands, limits and rates and the help sheet.

11.3   Within the pack, the most commonly used schedules are provided as follows:

IHT 402 Claim to transfer unused Inheritance Tax nil rate band.

IHT 403 Gifts and other transfers of value.

IHT 404 Jointly owned assets.

IHT 405 Houses, land, buildings and interests in land.

IHT 406 Bank and building society accounts.

IHT 407 Household and personal goods.

IHT 408 Household and personal goods given to charity.

IHT 409 Pensions.

IHT 410 Life assurance and annuities.

IHT 411 Listed stocks and shares.

IHT 421 Probate summary.

IHT 422 Application for an Inheritance Tax reference.

IHT 423 Direct payment scheme, bank or building society account.

The balance of forms is as follows:

IHT 401 Domicile outside the UK.

IHT 412 Unlisted stocks and shares, and control holdings.

IHT 413 Business and partnership interests and assets.

IHT 414 Agricultural relief.

IHT 415 Interest in another estate.

IHT 416 Debts to the estate.

IHT 417 Foreign assets.

IHT 418 Assets held in trust.

IHT 419 Debts owed by the deceased.

IHT 420 National Heritage assets Conditional exemption and offers in lieu of tax.

Finally there are the IHT 400 Notes 'Guide to completing your Inheritance Tax Account'.

The various schedules are referred to at boxes 29 to 48 of the IHT 400, with the instruction (familiar from self-assessment for income tax) to fill in any applicable schedules before proceeding to box 49.

UK-domiciled deceased

11.4   In circumstances where the estate is taxable (even within the nil rate band), form IHT 400 and any supplementary pages, a copy of the will and form IHT 421 (the probate summary) should be sent to HMRC Inheritance Tax, whether in Nottingham or Edinburgh, in a single envelope. Prior to 5 November 2007, a cheque for the tax due was also enclosed, though this is now sent separately with the payslip to HMRC's cashiers in Nottingham (see **10.4**, first bullet point). In the absence of any complications, HMRC Inheritance Tax will endorse form IHT 421 and return it to the sender to enable an application to be made to the Probate Registry for the grant of probate. It is this grant which authorises the executors to deal with the assets of the deceased.

If any IHT is payable on the estate, form IHT 422 should be used to obtain an IHT reference number to be sent to HMRC Inheritance Tax in either Nottingham or Edinburgh. If there is no tax payable, form IHT 421 does not require endorsement and can be sent direct to the Probate Registry (having completed Box 6 with 'nil' before signing the form). At the same time, the Inheritance Tax Account, supporting papers and a copy of the will are sent to HMRC Inheritance Tax.

Non-UK domiciliaries

11.5   If, on the other hand, it is claimed the deceased was neither actually, nor deemed domiciled in the UK, HMRC Inheritance Tax should be sent the Inheritance Tax Account, supporting papers, a copy of the will and form IHT 421. The estate is assessed and HMRC Inheritance Tax send out a calculation showing the tax due. Once the tax is paid, form IHT 421 is endorsed and returned.

Scotland

11.6   Form C1 takes the place of form IHT 421 and the Sheriff Court performs the functions of the Probate Registry.

Corrective accounts

11.7   It would be unusual for PRs to 'get it right first time' when delivering the Inheritance Tax Account. Provided that all proper care is taken, and reasonable estimates of valuations are made, the Inheritance Tax Account will be accepted, so long as any estimated values are clearly marked as such. The way in which revisions to the estimated accounts, or if further assets come to light, are dealt with is by means of a 'corrective' account. HMRC Inheritance Tax have emphasised that, where £1,000 or more of tax, ie £2,500 of value, is at stake, they wish to know about corrections or errors, including newly discovered assets:

●   in information or documents, within 30 days of discovery; and

●   in accounts, within six months of discovery.

In cases where errors arise as a result of carelessness (previously, negligence) or fraud, penalties might apply and HMRC Inheritance Tax expect to be told immediately when such errors are discovered (see **10.12**).

REDUCED ACCOUNT FOR EXEMPT ESTATES

11.8   An initiative launched in September 2000 enables the delivery of a 'reduced' Inheritance Tax Account, where because of exemptions, some or all of an estate is exempt.

The qualification and procedure for reduced accounts can be found on pages 4 and 5 of the 'Guide to Completing your Inheritance Tax Account'. In brief, the estate qualifies if:

●   the deceased was UK domiciled;

●   some, or all of the property passing by will or intestacy, passes to an 'exempt beneficiary', viz either absolutely or for an interest in possession trust for a surviving spouse, or to become the property of an exempt body (eg the National Trust) or of a charity; and

●   the gross value of property passing by will or intestacy to chargeable beneficiaries, together with other property chargeable on death and any chargeable lifetime transfers, does not in total exceed the inheritance tax threshold. This will include the deceased's share of any jointly owned assets, any assets chargeable under the reservation of benefit regime and any assets outside the UK which do not pass under the UK will or intestacy.

Where the reduced account procedure applies, only certain parts of IHT 400, as listed on pages 5 and 6 of HMRC's guide, have to be completed, together with any schedules which apply to the assets for which the grant is required.

Note in this connection that the gross value of an asset is the value before deducting liabilities, reliefs or exemptions.

11.9

Example 11.1—Qualification for reduced estate procedure

Gabriel died on 1 September 2009, domiciled in England and Wales. His estate consisted of:

- a half-share in a house, which he held as tenant in common in equal shares with his wife, Harriet. The gross value of their house is £400,000, subject to a mortgage of £150,000;

- a sole proprietor business, £150,000;

- stocks and shares worth £75,000;

- cash at bank, £10,000; and

- personal chattels, £5,000.

Three years before he died, Gabriel had made gifts of £20,000 to each of his three children. His will leaves legacies to the children of £50,000 in total.

He also leaves the business (attracting 100% business property relief) to his eldest son. Apart from the gifts to the children, Gabriel's will leaves all his property absolutely to Harriet, subject to surviving him for 30 days (which she did).

The gross value of property passing by will to chargeable beneficiaries, together with chargeable lifetime transfers is as follows:

Lifetime gifts (net of two £3,000 annual exemptions)	£54,000
Gross value of business	£150,000
Legacies under will	£50,000
	£254,000

The total of these assets does not exceed the IHT threshold of £325,000 (for 2009/10); the balance of his property passing to his wife is spouse exempt. The reduced account procedure may be followed.

Valuations

11.10   Where property goes to an exempt beneficiary, the PRs may estimate the open market value of the property without the need for a professional valuation. It may be that an open market value at the date of death is required for capital gains tax purposes.

Corrective accounts

11.11   It may be that after submitting a reduced account, it is found that the estate does not meet the conditions, or perhaps, as a result of a post-death deed of variation, exempt assets become chargeable. In such a case, a corrective account is required in the usual way. It may then be appropriate to obtain professional valuations.

INHERITANCE TAX ACCOUNT FORM IHT 400: DETAILS

11.12   The various parts of the form are scheduled at **11.2** above. Much of this is fairly routine detail although this section of the book picks up one or two particular questions. The first point to note is that whereas under IHT 200 there was a separate supplementary form D1 governing the will, questions 24 to 28 of the IHT 400 now cover this ground.

Deceased's address

11.13   Question 25 asks whether the address for the deceased shown in the will is the same as the one shown at box 11 of form IHT 400. Very often, a person will have moved house after executing his last will and testament. All that HMRC Inheritance Tax need to know is that the property mentioned in the will has been replaced by that shown on the form IHT 400.

If, by contrast, no residential property is included as part of the estate, HMRC Inheritance Tax will want to know what happened to the property mentioned in the will and, if sold, whether the sale proceeds are included as part of the estate (box 26). It might happen, for example, that where a will made by one spouse shows them as resident at an address, that spouse does not in fact have a beneficial interest in the property, which belongs in entirety to the other – this would have to be explained.

Specific gifts in the will

11.14 Question 27 seeks to ensure that any particular items, eg personal possessions, stocks and shares, etc which are referred to as given in the will are included in form IHT 400. The point might extend to the writing-off of a loan still outstanding at death, or there might be reference in the will to gifts made during the deceased's lifetime, but within seven years before death. Alternatively, the asset concerned might have been sold, in which case, again, HMRC Inheritance Tax need to know which assets on form IHT 400 represent the sale proceeds (assuming that they have not been spent). If the answers to these questions are not clearly positive, HMRC Inheritance Tax need to know why any items are not included in IHT 400.

Example 11.2—Where the will mentions assets not owned at death

Joe died on 1 September 2009, having made his last will on 1 January 1984 'in contemplation' of his forthcoming marriage. Marriage normally revokes the will unless it is expressed to be in contemplation of a particular marriage. He was then living at 'Hollyhocks', which was sold after the marriage, the proceeds being reinvested in 'Town End House', which at the date of his death he owned as joint tenant with his wife.

Among the specific gifts mentioned in the will are three watercolours by a minor Norwich School artist, one left to each or his three children. In the year before he died, one of the pictures was stolen and a second was sold to meet grandchildren's school fees.

Joe's half-share in the house is left to his wife, with the residue of the estate (within the nil rate band) passing to the three children in equal shares.

Boxes 25 to 27 are answered as follows:

- The address shown in the will is not the same as the address on page 2 of form IHT 400. This is because 'Hollyhocks' shown in the will was sold and the proceeds were reinvested in 'Town End House', which at the date of his death was owned equally by the deceased and his wife.

- Two of the items mentioned in the will, viz two watercolours, are not included in form IHT 400. The one because it was stolen in the year before the deceased died and the insurance proceeds were included in the figure for cash. The second was sold (in order to meet grandchildren's school fees). Both legacies to two of the three children therefore fail.

The chargeable estate

11.15 Pages 6 and 7 of the IHT 400 (boxes 49 to 79) detail the component parts of the estate in the UK. This is followed on pages 8, 9 and 10 by deductions from the estate (eg mortgages) at boxes 80 to 91. Exemptions and reliefs form boxes 92 to 96 (including the spouse and charities exemption), before boxes 97 to 108 on page 10 require details of other assets taken into account to compute the tax, eg foreign assets and gifts with reservation of benefit. Page 11 (boxes 109 to 117) deal with the calculation of inheritance tax, the option to pay by instalments and a simple calculation in an appropriate case. The top of page 12 (box 118) asks whether the direct payment scheme is to be used under which participating banks and building societies will release funds from the deceased's accounts directly to HMRC to pay inheritance tax. And the form concludes at pages 12 and 13 with the declaration at box 119 before a final checklist on page 14 and the white space on pages 15 and 16.

SCHEDULE IHT 401: DOMICILE OUTSIDE THE UNITED KINGDOM

11.16 The UK continues to be one of the most attractive tax havens in the Western world. A person who has his domicile (broadly, the country in which he intends to make his permanent home, or morbidly, to die) outside the UK is liable to IHT on, broadly, only property situated within the UK at death. There are further possible benefits for income tax and CGT during his lifetime, known as the 'remittance basis'. The above said, note the current HMRC and Treasury review of residence and domicile (see **4.3**), together with the new statutory rules for both residence and the remittance basis for non-UK domiciliaries from 2008/09.

Information required

11.17 Deceased's domicile: has it been agreed for other HMRC purposes?

● Deceased's residency for tax purposes: was the deceased UK resident for income tax purposes during the four years up to the date of death? If so, dates of UK residence are required for the 20 years before death.

- Deceased's history: to get a full picture of the deceased's life, specific information is required under various questions.

- Deceased's estate: who will benefit from the deceased's estate under the law or will that applies in the claimed country of domicile. Are you deducting surviving spouse/civil partner exemption? If 'Yes', brief details of property that the surviving spouse will receive are required. Did the deceased leave assets outside the UK? If so, give their approximate value. (Answering this question should be resisted, although HMRC Inheritance Tax have affirmed its importance. The intention is obviously to enable HMRC Inheritance Tax to see the advantage of claiming non-UK domicile, though the values should not be relevant to the issue of principle). Does a double tax treaty apply to any of the foreign assets owned by the deceased? Is any foreign tax to be paid on UK-situated assets following the deceased's death?

Establishing domicile

11.18   Questions 7 to 18 ask for specific information to provide a full picture of the life of the deceased. This will help to establish the validity of a claim to a non-UK domicile. There was a particular complication for a woman married before 1 January 1974, in which case she automatically acquired the domicile of her husband. Since then, however, a wife has been able to establish her own independent domicile.

Importantly, for IHT though not for income tax or CGT, there is a special deemed domicile rule under which a person is treated as being domiciled in the UK (*IHTA 1984, s 257*) if either:

- he has been domiciled in the UK during the previous three calendar years (not tax years), ie it takes at least three years effectively to 'shake off' a UK domicile; or

- he was resident in the UK for income tax purposes for at least 17 out of the last 20 tax years (not calendar years), remembering to include part years (ie under this rule, a person may become deemed UK domiciled at the beginning of the 15th calendar year of residence, starting with 6 April).

A person who was not actually, but was deemed domiciled, in the UK is subject to IHT on worldwide assets, subject only to any relief under a double tax treaty.

Although it is likely that the issue of domicile will have been tested for income tax purposes during lifetime, possibly on a five-year rolling basis, nonetheless, one can understand why HMRC Inheritance Tax will be especially interested in any claim to non-UK domicile on death, to ensure that the claim is a proper one.

SCHEDULE IHT 402: CLAIM TO TRANSFER UNUSED NIL RATE BAND

The principle

11.19   Where the death occurred on or after 9 October 2007 and follows the prior death of a former spouse/civil partner, it is possible to enhance the nil rate band on the second death by the proportion of any unused nil rate band on the first death (*IHTA 1984, s 8A*). A claim is required. Schedule IHT 402 seeks to ascertain the extent to which the nil rate band available on the first death was not used and therefore the percentage by which the nil rate band on the present death may be enhanced.

Section 8A will apply where the IHT nil rate band of the first deceased spouse or civil partner was not fully used in calculating the IHT liability of their estate, whenever the first death occurred. When the surviving spouse or civil partner dies, the unused amount may be added to their own nil rate band.

Where a person dies having survived more than one spouse or civil partner (or dies having been married to, or the registered civil partner of, someone who had themselves survived one or more spouses or civil partners), the amount of additional nil rate band which can be accumulated by any one survivor will be limited to the nil rate band in force at the second death.

The claim mechanism operates at the second death only, to be made by (usually) the PRs of the second spouse or civil partner to die. But of course evidence will be required of the unused nil rate band on the first death, which could have been very many years before – and may present difficulties in digging out the paperwork.

The balance of advantage

11.20   On the assumption that the nil rate band will generally increase over time (though note one proposal to link it, in part at least, to house prices – so what happens if they fall dramatically?), it should prove sensible to minimise chargeable transfers on the first death, so maximising the nil rate band on the second. Indeed, if a Conservative government is elected in 2010 and they honour their pledge to increase the nil rate band to £1million, *s 8A* would provide a dramatic benefit in the case where the first spouse died before the increase and the second died after; this is of course assuming that *s 8A* is not repealed (which the Conservative opposition have confirmed they would not do). Note that chargeable gifts made in the seven years before death or caught by the reservation of benefit regime will in effect eat into the nil rate band on the first death.

The spouse/civil partner exemption under *IHTA 1984, s 18* can be achieved by an IPDI as much as by an outright gift. As soon as reasonably (and decently) possible after the first death, the survivor should make such gifts as he/she can reasonably afford to do without, keeping outside the gifts with reservation of benefit regime; however, gifts which exceed the survivor's nil rate band will need to be absolute rather than in trust, to avoid an immediate 20% IHT charge. Under an IPDI the trustees would terminate the life interest to that extent (and, being an IPDI, there would be no reading back into the will under *s 144*). CGT should be considered, but should not be a problem insofar as no growth in value since death.

Clearly, the new *s 8A* should not be regarded as providing the best structure in all circumstances. Consider for example:

- protection of the home from liability for care fees;

- cases where the capital appreciation in the nil rate band will trust is anticipated to outstrip future increases in the nil rate band; and

- cases where it is desired, perhaps for non-tax reasons, to have two relevant property nil rate band trusts for children/grandchildren going forward, the one established under the will of the first to die and the other set up *inter vivos* by the survivor.

Some practical points

11.21   As well as generally maximising the benefit of the zero rate of IHT in the two estates, the new regime will prove especially beneficial in dealing with the family home, not having to worry about the debt/charge scheme etc or nil rate band discretionary trusts (viz, do they in substance give an interest in possession to the survivor and what about CGT main residence relief in the light of *TLATA 1996, s 12,* etc)?

Where on the first death there is property which clearly attracts APR or BPR at 100%, advantage should be taken of this, perhaps by a gift into a discretionary trust.

Beware the scope of *IHTA 1984, s 143* with chattels or other property. For example, a gift by the surviving spouse of a painting to a child within two years after the death (even if the wish of the deceased was expressed informally) will take effect as a chargeable transfer by the deceased.

In applying the *s 8A* rule, it matters not that the estate of the first to die was below the nil rate band threshold.

How does s 8A work if the first death occurred during capital transfer tax or estate duty? HMRC advice

11.22 The same basic principles apply, subject however, to some modifications to reflect the differences between inheritance tax and capital transfer tax/estate duty. Inheritance tax was introduced on 18 March 1986, so points to bear in mind for deaths before that date are:

- Where the first spouse died between 13 March 1975 and 18 March 1986 then the estate would have been subject to capital transfer tax. Any transfers to the spouse would have been exempt from tax in the same way as for inheritance tax and the transfer of nil rate band provisions will operate in exactly the same way as it works for inheritance tax.

- Before 13 March 1975 estate duty applied. Under estate duty there was no tax-free transfer permitted between spouses until 21 March 1972 when a tax-free transfer between spouses of up to £15,000 was introduced. This limit was removed for deaths after 12 November 1974.

- Where the first spouse died between 21 March 1972 and 13 March 1975 a claim to transfer the nil rate band to the surviving spouse will be based on the proportion of the tax-free band that was unused on the death of the first spouse. For example, if a husband died in 1973 and left an estate valued at £10,000 that was all transferred to his wife, then as this is all within the spouse's exemption the husband's tax-free band is unused. So if his widow dies in December 2008, her nil rate band can be increased by 100% to £624,000. Where any part of the first spouse's individual tax-free band was used then there will be a proportionate reduction in the amount by which the surviving spouse's IHT nil rate band may be increased.

- Before 21 March 1972, there was no relief from estate duty for transfers between spouses so the amount by which the surviving spouse's IHT nil rate band may be increased will be based on the proportion of the individual tax-free band that was unused on the death of the first spouse.

The above adopts an HMRC publication from November 2007. Of course, in practice where the first death occurred under estate duty and certainly before 21 March 1972, it is going to be only in the comparatively rare case that the gross estate was below the threshold that any benefit is going to be obtained from *s 8A* – except in the situation where there was complete exemption under the so-called 'killed in war' provisions of what is now *IHTA 1984, s 154* (see **11.97** to **11.98**).

Example 11.3—(from HMRC's October 2007 pre-Budget Report Notes)

(i)   On the first death none of the then nil rate band was used because the entire estate was left to the surviving spouse. If the nil rate band on the second death is £350,000, that would be increased by 100% to £700,000.

(ii)   If on the first death the chargeable estate is £150,000 and the nil rate band £300,000, 50% of the original nil rate band would be unused. If the nil rate band on the second death is £350,000, that would be increased by 50% to £525,000.

'Community of property'

11.23   If the surviving spouse/civil partner exemption is claimed, it must be confirmed whether or not in the country of domicile, there was a 'community of property' and whether that jurisdiction recognised civil partnerships or something equivalent. This might have arisen simply because of the deceased's marriage, or because he signed a marriage contract. The rules vary from country to country, but broadly speaking fetter the ability of a party to the community to dispose of his property (and of course this is especially relevant to any property under the community that might have been situated in the UK at the date of death). For example, the rules might provide that the estate should be divided into three parts, one of which must go to the spouse (or civil partner), one to the children and the third of which the deceased would have a discretion.

SCHEDULE IHT 403: GIFTS AND OTHER TRANSFERS OF VALUE

11.24   IHT works by adding to the total chargeable estate on death, the chargeable value (ie after any exemptions) of all gifts made in the seven years before death. It has always been necessary for PRs to know the total of such gifts, because in particular, they would not otherwise be able to confirm the amount of the nil rate band left unused (if any) at the date of death – lifetime gifts have first call on the nil rate band according to the order in which they are made. However, *FA 1999* imposed a statutory obligation on PRs to give this information to the best of their knowledge and belief. Ascertaining the existence of such transfers can be quite an onerous task.

Schedule IHT 403 is divided into four parts.

Gifts made within the seven years before death

11.25 The question is whether the deceased in that period:

- made any gift or transferred assets to or for the benefit of another person;

- created any trust or settlement;

- transferred additional assets into an existing trust or settlement;

- paid any premium on a life policy for someone other than his spouse/civil partner;

- ceased to benefit from any assets held in trust; or

- made any gifts claimed to be exempt as regular gifts out of income.

In the event that the answer to any of these questions is affirmative, full details are requested.

Each of these events would be a transfer of value, which, subject to an exemption, would be a chargeable transfer. The exemptions, of which details are requested by the schedule, are set out below. Only outright gifts between individuals that are covered by an exemption need not be listed.

Gifts with reservation

11.26 If, on or after 18 March 1986, the deceased made a gift from which he enjoyed some benefit (other than a minimal one), and he enjoyed that benefit at his death, he is treated for IHT purposes as still being entitled to the property given away, ie at its then value. If the benefits ceased in the preceding seven years, he is treated as having made a potentially exempt transfer of the asset at its then value at the date of cessation of benefit (see **6.16–6.21**). Details must be given at boxes 8 to 12. The rules also apply if the recipient of the gift failed to enter into 'possession and enjoyment' of it.

Pre-owned assets

11.27 Questions 13 to 16 ask for details of any gifts made where the pre-owned assets regime (see **4.44** to **4.54**) would apply but for an election out of that regime into the gifts with reservation of benefit regime, so obviating the income tax charge but treating the assets concerned as continuing to be owned by the donor for IHT purposes.

Earlier transfers

11.28 The normal 'danger period' for recapture of gifts for IHT is seven years. However, there is a trap, which can make gifts within 14 years before death relevant. This is where there was a gift in the seven years before death, and within seven years before that gift, there had been a chargeable transfer (or itself made more than seven years before death). That earlier transfer can have an effect on the IHT implications of the later gift. This is the point behind questions 18 and 19.

The lifetime exemptions

11.29 The spouse/civil partner exemption (*IHTA 1984, s 18*). This is unlimited except where the transferor is actually or deemed UK domiciled and the transferee is not, in which case the exemption is limited to £55,000.

- The annual exemption of £3,000 per donor per tax year. Where in any tax year more than £3,000 is given, any unused balance of the £3,000 annual exemption of the previous year may be carried forward (though for one year only): *IHTA 1984, s 19*.

- The small gifts exemption of £250 per donee (*IHTA 1984, s 20*).

- The 'normal expenditure out of income' exemption. A transfer is exempt to the extent that it is made out of the income of the year, having taken account of all normal 'revenue' type expenditure. A pattern of giving must be established over at least three years, or it must be shown that the deceased had made a commitment to a series of gifts (*IHTA 1984, s 21*). Information on such gifts is provided on Schedule IHT 403 at boxes 20 to 22.

- The marriage exemption, which is £5,000 for a gift to a child, £2,500 to a grandchild or £1,000 to anyone else (*IHTA 1984, s 22*).

Note that the above prevent a transfer of value from being a chargeable transfer. There is a rule in *IHTA 1984, s 11* which prevents a lifetime disposition from being a transfer of value at all (dispositions for maintenance of family). This is one made by one spouse or civil partner for the maintenance of the other or for the maintenance, education or training of a child while under the age of 18 or in full-time education or training. *Sections 10* and *12 to 17* list other types of disposition which are not transfers of value.

Example 11.4—Implications of lifetime gifts

Frank died on 1 September 2009. He had made the following gifts in the seven years before he died:

- On 1 January 2005, £50,000 to his son.

- On 1 January 2007, £50,000 to his daughter.

- On 1 January 2008, a gift of £10,000 to his grandson on his marriage.

- On 1 January 2008 and 1 January 2009, premiums of £5,000 on a new life insurance policy written on the joint lives of his wife and himself, written on wide discretionary trusts (excluding settlor and spouse).

The IHT implications are as follows:

Date	Transfer of value	Exemption	Chargeable transfer
1.1.05	£50,000	Two annual exemptions	£44,000
1.1.07	£50,000	Two annual exemptions	£44,000
1.1.08	£10,000	£3,000 annual + £2,500 marriage	£5,500
1.1.09	£5,000	? normal expenditure	? Nil
1.1.10	£5,000	? normal expenditure	? Nil
Total	£93,500		

Accordingly, as at his death in 2009/10, when the nil rate band was £325,000, Frank had used £93,500 (probably) of his nil rate band, leaving £231,500 available for use against chargeable gifts under the will.

SCHEDULE IHT 404: JOINTLY OWNED ASSETS

The law

11.30   English law distinguishes between a joint tenancy and a tenancy in common. An interest under a joint tenancy passes on death of one joint tenant automatically by operation of law (or 'survivorship') to the surviving joint tenant(s), *pro rata* if more than one. By contrast, an interest under a tenancy in common is an asset of which the owner can dispose, whether by his will or otherwise, and will be in a particular percentage or proportion of the asset, ie not necessarily 50/50 where there are two tenants in common. The law presumes joint ownership to be a joint tenancy, unless there is evidence to the contrary, in particular where one joint tenant has served notice on the other(s) of the intention to 'sever' the joint tenancy.

For IHT purposes, each type of interest must be valued and, subject to the spouse exemption, will be charged to tax on death according to the share in the asset owned by the deceased. If the other joint owner was the surviving spouse, the percentage taken is simply the proportion owned. For example, where the matrimonial home was owned as tenants in common in equal shares, the deceased's share will be one half of the whole. To the extent that the joint owners are not husband and wife, a discount of certainly 10% and arguably up to 15% (or even more) may be applied from the proportionate share of the deceased. This discount is intended to reflect the difficulty in realising a part share in property. In appropriate cases it may be as well to take specialist valuation advice. This discount is not applicable to cash.

The required information

11.31 Schedule IHT 404 deals separately with joint interests in houses, buildings and land and a controlling holding of shares and securities (box 1) on the one hand and other jointly owned assets (eg bank accounts, household and personal goods) at box 6 on the other. For each category of jointly owned assets values must be shown, with applicable liabilities and exemptions and reliefs.

Survivorship assets

11.32 Applying the principle set out at **11.31**, box 11 requires details of assets which pass by survivorship and hence while included in the deceased's estate for IHT purposes, are not included in the value of the estate for probate or (in Scotland) confirmation purposes. Brief explanations are given of the position under English and Scottish law respectively.

Example 11.5—'Things may not always be what they seem'

This example is based on a Special Commissioner's case in 1998 (*O'Neill v IRC* [1998] STC (SCD) 110). Father opened a bank account in the Isle of Man in his sole name. Later in 1980, the balance was transferred to a new account in the joint name of the father and daughter. Father added to the account. Interest was rolled up until June 1992. Thereafter, interest was paid to an account in father's name.

In 1984, father opened a second account in his name jointly with daughter, and added to it. Interest was rolled up. Daughter did not know of the accounts during father's lifetime. She received from him an envelope just before his death to take to the bank manager. This disclosed the existence of the accounts. HMRC determined that all of the money formed part of father's estate.

Daughter and father's executors appealed, arguing that only half of each account belonged to father, and that IHT should, therefore, be charged, only on half of each account.

The Special Commissioner asked whether daughter had a present interest in the accounts during father's lifetime. HMRC had argued that a gift of a joint bank account might be an immediate gift of a fluctuating and defeasible asset, and that daughter's interest was defeasible by father's. The Commissioner agreed that father had a general power over the whole account, which meant that he should be treated as beneficially entitled to all of it. Father's motives looked obvious. He took the money offshore, which was suspicious. The interest was never returned for tax purposes, which turned the suspicion into a virtual certainty. But for daughter's honesty, HMRC might never have known of the account. Father had been estranged from his wife and in matrimonial proceedings he had denied the existence of the fund. It was not until the divorce was over that any interest came back to father. Father intended some benefit to daughter, but that was not his only motive.

Daughter was of full age seven years before father died, yet daughter was not informed of the account. Only father could operate the accounts because daughter was never asked to sign. Father had made provision for daughter in his will, which suggested that he had intended the earlier provision by way of joint accounts to operate as a 'legacy only', through survivorship. The normal presumption of 'advancement' whereby daughter would be treated as entitled to a half share in each account, was rebutted by all these factors.

The Commissioner concluded that father enjoyed the entire beneficial interest in the accounts during his lifetime and the appeal was dismissed.

SCHEDULE IHT 405: HOUSES, LAND, BUILDINGS AND INTERESTS IN LAND

11.33   In very many cases this schedule will be completed simply to reflect an interest in the family home. There may of course be other buildings or interests in land to include on this form. It is a good idea in every case to get a professional valuation as at the date of death. Such land or buildings may be:

- the main family home;
- a second family home (whether or not in the UK);
- a house or flat owned for investment purposes;
- an interest in land owned for a business;
- farmland or buildings.

The two latter categories may attract business property relief or agricultural property relief (see **11.51–11.66**).

IHT 405 is divided into five sections:

- Details of the person HMRC should contact about the valuation of houses or land: the name and address of the valuation adviser to be contacted by the Valuation Office is to be given, along with reference and telephone number. Where the client's valuers have not already been instructed, this section need not be completed and HMRC will refer to the practitioner, with whom any minor problems can be sorted out without reference to a specialist valuer.

- Deceased's residence: this asks for the full address or description, the tenure (ie freehold or leasehold), details of any leases, the element of agricultural, timber or heritage value, and the open market value.

- Other land, buildings and rights over land: this asks for similar details as for the deceased's residence, in relation to such as fishing or mineral rights.

- Special factors that may affect the value: any of the properties listed might have been subject to major damage, which would affect their value; this must be detailed. If the damage is covered by buildings insurance, HMRC Inheritance Tax need to know details of the policy. For example, a loss in value of £75,000, of which £60,000 will be covered by insurance, should result in a deduction of only £15,000 from the open market value of the property, although this is likely to be reflected in the open market value given at G in box 7 or 8.

- Property sale within 12 months after death: the sale price received on sale within 12 months after death will usually be a good indication of value at the date of death, though not conclusively, ie circumstances, namely the market, or perhaps planning considerations, might have changed since death. It is the value at the date of death that is required for IHT purposes. Note that selling costs may not be deducted. If the sale was for a preferential price to a relative, arm's-length value will have to be substituted. Any apportionment of value to fixtures and fittings, carpets, curtains etc must be given. You are given the option of using the sale price as the value at the date of death.

Relief for loss on sale within four years after death

11.34   If having agreed a market value at death of, say, £200,000, the land is subsequently sold for say, £180,000, it is possible by election to have that lower value substituted by any consequential repayment of IHT (*IHTA 1984, ss 190–198*). The claim is made on form IHT 38.

For this to apply:

- the reduction in value must be greater than the lesser of £1,000 and 5% of the value at death;

- all sales must be aggregated for computing the relief, ie including sales at a gain within three years after death and sales at a loss within four years after death;

- the relief is restricted *pro rata* to the extent that the seller, viz typically, the PRs (though it could be the beneficiary) reinvests in replacement land within four months after the last sale within three years after death;

- the relief will apply only if a value has to be 'ascertained' at death, ie it cannot apply if the land passes to a spouse, or is covered by 100% agricultural and business property relief, or is entirely within the nil rate band;

- the relief is given only if the sale is made by the 'appropriate person', viz the person who pays the tax. The person who pays the tax *must be* the person who makes the sale;

- the sale must be to a person *other than* the beneficiary, the spouse of the beneficiary, a direct descendant of the beneficiary or trustees of a settlement in which the beneficiary has a life interest. The beneficiary means the person to whom the property is bequeathed, either under the will, or to whom it passes under the intestacy, or (remember this trap) to whom the property is redirected under a post-death deed of variation (see **13.1–13.4**);

- the revised IHT value at death will be used as the beneficiary's base cost in computing any gain on a future sale.

Gains on sales within three years after death

11.35   The form IHT 38 procedure may also be used, somewhat paradoxically, where the gross proceeds on a sale within three years after death exceed the market value at death. The reason for initiating the revaluation procedure in such a case, which requires there to be some IHT issue at stake, would be that the CGT advantage outweighs the IHT downside.

How soon can a claim be made after sale?

11.36   The rules for making a claim on form IHT 38 provide that the claim cannot be submitted within four months after the date of sale. If all the qualifying property has not been sold, relief will not be final until four years from the date of death. Form IHT 38 has been revised, allowing the claimant to say whether or not the relief claimed is final. If final, HMRC Inheritance Tax will be able to deal with the claim before the four-month period has elapsed (and will be able to issue clearance as soon as all other matters on the estate have been agreed).

SCHEDULE IHT 406: BANK AND BUILDING SOCIETY ACCOUNTS AND NATIONAL SAVINGS AND INVESTMENTS

11.37 The five boxes on this Schedule ask for:

- details of bank and building society accounts in the deceased's sole name;

- National Savings accounts, including the account numbers;

- Premium Bonds, including the bond numbers and the value of any unclaimed or uncashed prizes;

- other national savings and investment products; and

- total of National Savings and Investments.

SCHEDULE IHT 407: HOUSEHOLD AND PERSONAL GOODS

11.38 This Schedule asks about what are formally known as 'personal chattels'. It is important not to be too cavalier, ie simply to put in a 'broad-brush figure' of say £1,000. Clearly, things like clothes are likely to be of no realistic value, except in particular circumstances. However, it may be rather different with household furniture, especially anything which ranks as antiques, paintings, silverware, etc and indeed personal possessions of any particular value.

'Personal chattels': the statutory definition

11.39

'Carriages, horses, stable furniture and effects (not used for business purposes), motor cars and accessories (not used for business purposes), garden effects, domestic animals, plate, plated articles, linen, china, glass, books, pictures, prints, furniture, jewellery, articles of household or personal use or ornament, musical and scientific instruments and apparatus, wines, liqueurs and consumable stores, but do not include any chattels used at the death of the intestate for business purposes, no money or securities for money.'

The definition is found in the *Administration of Estates Act 1925, s 55(1)(x)*. The fact that this Act was passed over 80 years ago might explain some of the terminology in the definition. The definition is expressly to be used in the case of intestacies, though is of general application.

Various categories of goods

11.40   The four sections of IHT 407 deal separately with: (a) jewellery; (b) vehicles, boats and aircraft; (c) antiques, works of art or collections; and (d) other household and personal goods, in each case distinguishing between goods which have not and goods which have been sold (in which case the relationship between the purchaser and the deceased must be stated). Individual items of jewellery valued at £500 or more must be detailed, together with a professional valuation if obtained.

Sales

11.41   It may be that at the time of completing the Inheritance Tax Account any goods have already been sold, in which case the gross sale proceeds must be completed. The gross sale proceeds are presumed to be the value at death. Note that no deduction is allowed for professional costs of sale. It may be that a sale is intended but has not yet taken place. Generally speaking, a sale which takes place a reasonable time after death will fix the value at death.

Basis of valuation

11.42   HMRC Inheritance Tax emphasise that the basis of valuation of all property owned at death, including household and personal goods, is open market on the basis of a hypothetical sale (*IHTA 1984, s 160*). Note, for example, as emphasising this rule, detailed articles in the December 2004, April 2005 and April 2006 editions of the IHT Newsletter (www.hmrc.gov.uk/cto/newsletter.htm).

Note also that insurance value is not market value. It has been traditionally thought that 'probate value' means a value (acceptable to HMRC Inheritance Tax) which represents a discount of up to one-third on market value. That is not the case. In the author's view, it is important not to use the expression 'probate value', as this might suggest to HMRC that a discounted value has been adopted. The legislation requires all the assets of the deceased to be valued on an open market basis, 'willing buyer willing seller', and this extends to personal chattels. In the absence of a formal valuation, brief details of the items and their value must be given.

Where professional valuations are not obtained

11.43 The most straightforward method of dealing with this subject is to get a professional valuation of everything owned by the deceased. Note that, say, a half share as joint tenant of property owned by the deceased with his spouse (albeit such value will be subject to the spouse exemption) will be recorded not on IHT 407 but on Schedule 404 Jointly Owned Assets.

The value of any items included in 'other household and personal goods' may have been individually listed on the deceased's household insurance policy; if so, a copy of the policy at schedule if appropriate should be supplied.

SCHEDULE IHT 408: HOUSEHOLD AND PERSONAL GOODS DONATED TO CHARITY

11.44 This is used to record details of gifts to be made to charity by the original beneficiary, so enabling the application of the provisions of *IHTA 1984, s 142* (deeds of variation within two years after death) and therefore the charities exemption from IHT.

SCHEDULE IHT 409: PENSIONS

11.45 Schedule IHT 409 comprises seven parts:

- Did any pension payments continue after the deceased's death? If so, details must be given in part 2. The deceased may on retirement have taken out a pension with a minimum period guarantee. The value of future guaranteed instalments must be discounted back to the date of death.

- Details are requested of the pension scheme or policy, including the right to receive payments falling due after death.

- Was a lump sum payable as a result of death? Here, a distinction (drawn out by the various questions) should be drawn between:

  - cases where the lump sum is payable to the PRs, or where the deceased could have made a 'nomination', which bound the pension scheme trustees to make the payment to the deceased's nominee. In this case, the lump sum forms part of the deceased estate. The lump sum will be treated as forming part of the deceased's estate if the deceased could have bound the trustees of the pension scheme to make a particular payment. In other words, it is not enough simply to ascertain that the death benefit has been transferred into trust. The personal pension scheme rules of the pension provider must be reviewed to see what rules apply to the distribution of the lump sum death benefit and a copy of any letter of wishes, direction or nomination made by the deceased must be obtained.

–   cases where the death benefit was held under trust, whether or not made by the individual when he took out the policy. In this case, the lump sum does not form part of the taxable estate.

However, HMRC Inheritance Tax like to know about both cases, with the production of evidence to substantiate the second.

●   Did the deceased, within two years of the death, dispose of any of the benefits payable, or make any changes to the benefit to which he was entitled under a scheme? Here HMRC Inheritance Tax want to know whether the deceased had within two years before death:

–   nominated or appointed the death benefits to another person;

–   assigned the death benefits into a trust; or

–   made changes to the pension benefits intended to be taken when there may have been a liability to IHT.

●   Did the deceased (or his/her employer) make any contributions to a pension scheme for the deceased, within two years of the death? Here HMRC Inheritance Tax want to know whether the deceased or their employer make any contributions to a pension scheme within two years of the death. This could encompass payments made by the employer of the deceased, presumably which benefits another person? See **11.46**.

●   Did the deceased benefit from an alternatively secured pension at the date of death and, if so, how did it arise.

●   Had the deceased been entitled (as a 'relevant dependant') to an unsecured benefit arising under a registered pension scheme established by a person who had died aged 75 or over? If so, various details are requested.

Changes in benefit

11.46   Up to some 18 years ago, the then Inland Revenue argued that if a person could take a pension, but exercised his right not to do so, eg having attained the age of 50 under a personal pension scheme (and being under age 75 at death), he might be charged under rules which provide that a person makes a transfer of value if he omits to exercise a right (*IHTA 1984, s 3(3)*). Although strenuous opposition from the Association of British Insurers at the time led the Revenue to back down in 1991, the point still exists in principle. HMRC say, for example, that if the deceased was in very poor health and then took out a new policy and assigned the death benefit into trust, or assigned a death benefit of an existing policy into trust, or paid further contributions to a policy where the death benefit had previously been assigned into trust, or deferred the date for taking his retirement benefit, the point might apply unless, perhaps, the death benefit were paid to the spouse or dependants, or where the member survived two years or more after making such arrangements. This is the background to part 4 of Schedule IHT 409.

Under the 'income drawdown' option, a person elects to convert part of the fund to provide an annuity, with the remaining fund left to build up in the normal tax preferred pension regime.

Two examples (among others) of change in benefit are given on page 28 of the Guide, viz:

- the deceased reaches pension age and decides not to take the payment of pension at the time, or chooses to take 'income drawdown'; and

- where the deceased, having got to pension age and having chosen to take 'income drawdown', decides at a later date (and whilst in ill health) to reduce the level of income taken.

New pension regime from 6 April 2006

11.47 It is beyond the scope of this book to go into the new regime in any detail. The existence of the regime is merely noted. The broad principles applying to pension benefit trusts up to 5 April 2006 continue thereafter, however, subject to some specific changes, and the concessionary practice noted at **11.46** now has legislative authority (*IHTA 1984, s 12*). Specifically, the last two questions noted at **11.45** have been introduced following the new regime.

SCHEDULE IHT 410: LIFE INSURANCE AND ANNUITIES

11.48 This form is required if the deceased was paying regular monthly or lump sum premiums on any:

- life assurance policies, or if any sums are payable by insurance companies to the estate as a result of the deceased's death. (It does not matter if the policies were on the deceased's life or someone else's life or whether the policies were for the deceased's benefit);

- unit-linked investment bonds with insurance companies or other financial service providers that pay 101% of the value of the units to the estate;

- investment or reinvestment plans, bonds or contracts with financial service providers that pay out to the estate on death;

- insurance policies and unit-linked investment bonds that are payable to the beneficiaries under a trust and do not form part of the estate; or

- joint life assurance policies under which the deceased was one of the lives assured but which remain in force after the date of death.

Life assurance policies

11.49   Question 1 simply asks whether, as a result of the death, sums were payable by insurance companies to the estate. This would cover a case where the deceased had taken out a life policy, whether endowment or whole of life, and the proceeds had not been written under trust. Box 2 asks for details of sums paid.

Question 3 is aimed at continuing life policies, eg a joint lives and survivor policy where the other life assured has not died. Question 4 asks whether the deceased is a beneficiary of another life policy on the life of someone else who remains alive. Such a policy might have been purchased second-hand. The value of any such policy, as provided by the insurance company, should be included, together with a copy of the insurance policy. Box 5 requires details of all relevant life policies, with copies to be provided and the total value to be given at box 6.

Other questions

11.50

- Was the deceased at his death receiving annuity payments, which are guaranteed to continue after his death (Boxes 7 and 8)? The right to receive the remaining payments will be an asset of the estate and must be discounted back to the date of death.

- Was a lump sum payable under a purchase life annuity as a result of the death (Boxes 10 and 11)?

- Was the deceased paying premiums on policies for someone else's benefit, other than a spouse/civil partner (Box 12)? The payment of such premiums will rank as a gift (subject to the lifetime exemptions).

- Did the deceased, within seven years of his death, pay any premium on a life insurance policy for the benefit of someone else, other than the deceased's spouse/civil partner? Was an annuity purchased at any time

(Box 13)? If so please provide a copy of the policy schedule and provisions.

● Did the deceased have a right to benefit on a life policy written on another's life and held in trust for the benefit of the deceased – and others (Box 14)?

Example 11.6—Various life policies

George died unexpectedly aged 55. Some 20 years before, he had taken out a with-profits policy on his own life, which he had written in trust for his two children. In the seven years before he died, he was making annual premium payments of £3,000 per annum (and was not otherwise using his annual exemption). Question 12 must be answered affirmatively. These premium payments will constitute transfers of value, protected by the £3,000 annual exemption to be reported on IHT 403.

George's wife had already died. When George died, there were five years outstanding on an endowment policy, which he and his late wife had previously taken out on a joint lives and survivor basis to pay off the mortgage when George was age 60. The endowment policy proceeds fell into George's estate and must be reported in Box 1. The policy had not been written in trust for the lender under the mortgage, though the lender had retained possession of the policy document. The outstanding liability under the mortgage will be deductible in George's estate, with the policy proceeds chargeable as an asset.

Finally, George had been in partnership with two others in a business that made widgets. They had, some years ago, taken out cross life policies, written in trust for the surviving partners, with a view to enabling the survivors to buy out the estate of the deceased under options (not constituting 'binding contracts for sale', which would have denied the availability of business property relief). Annual premiums were charged against the partnership profits each year, though these were not deductible for income tax purposes. While the policy payable on George's death crystallised the benefit of his two surviving partners, he also had a right to benefit from their life policies. Accordingly, question 14 must be answered in the affirmative. Although the point must be put to HMRC Inheritance Tax, the argument would be that the value at George's death of his rights under the other policies should not have been brought into his estate because the arrangements were made as part of an arm's-length transaction, under which any rights he had were balanced by the rights of the others under the policy on George's life.

SCHEDULE IHT 411: LISTED STOCKS AND SHARES

UK government and municipal securities

11.51   Included here are:

● any government securities;

● any municipal securities, mortgages, debentures and stock held in countries, cities and towns, docks, harbours and water boards.

The basis of valuation is the CGT one, viz either:

● one-quarter up from the lower to the higher limit of the prices quoted; or

● halfway between the highest and lowest bargains recorded for the day, but excluding bargains at special prices (*TCGA 1992, s 272*).

Any dividend or interest due, but unpaid at the date of death must also be valued as an asset (ie not included in the valuation).

Listed stocks, shares and investments that did *not* give the deceased control of the company

11.52   This will include:

● Personal Equity Plans (PEPs), including a figure for any uninvested cash;

● shares held in an Individual Savings Account (ISA), including a figure for any uninvested cash but not for any other cash or insurance policies;

● unit trusts (give the full name, for example, AXA Equity and Law Unit Trust Managers, Pacific Basin Trust Accumulation Units);

● investment trusts;

● holdings in Open-Ended Investment Companies (OEICs);

● foreign shares, but only if they are listed on the London Stock Exchange.

Example 11.7—Adapting a former HMRC example

Fred died on 1 August 2009, owning 1250 10p Ordinary shares in XYZ plc. The Stock Exchange list provides that the closing quotation on the date of death was 'p1091–11 xd' and the dividend was 2.3p.

To calculate the value of the shares, the number of shares should be multiplied by the 'quarter-up' price. The 'quarter-up' price is the lower price (1091) plus one-quarter of the difference between the two prices (one-quarter of 10p or 2.5p). The 'quarter-up' price is, therefore, 1091 + 2.5 = 1093.5p. Therefore, the value of the shareholding will be 1250 × 1093.5 = £13,668.75.

The shares are marked xd. Let us say that the dividend per share was 2.3p. The value of the dividend will then be 1250 × 2.3p = £28.75.

Alternatively, the dividend may be given as a percentage, say, 2.6%. In such case, the amount of the dividend can be calculated by finding out the percentage of the nominal value of the stock. If the deceased had owned £400 of loan stock, the dividend would be 2.6% of £400 or £10.40.

If the death occurred when The Stock Exchange was closed, the price for either the following day or the last day when The Stock Exchange was open may be taken. Therefore, if the death occurred on a Sunday, the price for either the Monday after or the Friday before may be taken. Whichever day gives the lower valuation may be used.

SCHEDULE IHT 412: UNLISTED STOCKS AND SHARES, AND CONTROL HOLDINGS

11.53   The supplementary form 7 to the previous IHT 200 covered both listed and unlisted stocks and shares. The two categories have been split out under two schedules to IHT 400. IHT 412 deals with stocks and shares:

- listed on the Alternative Investment Market (AIM) or traded on OFEX;

- held in a private limited company, Business Expansion Scheme (BES) or Business Start-up Scheme (BSS); or

- listed on a recognised stock exchange where the deceased had control of the company.

Five categories of stocks and shares are given as follows:

- traded unlisted stocks and shares that did *not* give the deceased control of the company;

- unlisted stocks, shares and investments that did *not* give the deceased control of the company;

- unlisted stocks, shares and investments that *gave* the deceased control of the company;

- traded unlisted stocks, shares and investments that gave the deceased control of the company; and

- listed stocks, shares and investments that gave the deceased control of the company.

In each case the following information is required:

- name of the company and type of shares or stock;

- number of shares or amount of stock held;

- market price per share/stock at date of death;

- total value of shares/stock at date of death;

- dividend due to date of death;

- owned for two years (Yes or No);

- amount of business relief (BR) due; and

- rate of BR, 100% or 50%.

The valuation, whether estimated or final proposed, will be referred by HMRC Inheritance Tax to their Shares and Assets Valuation (SAV) division.

SCHEDULE IHT 413: BUSINESS AND PARTNERSHIP INTERESTS AND ASSETS

11.54   Again, this is a complex subject (*IHTA 1984, ss 103–114*). In outline, however, see below.

Relevant business property

11.55   The property must be (*IHTA 1984, s 105(1)*):

- a business, or an interest in a business, which must be carried on with a view to profit;

- unquoted shares or securities;

- a controlling holding of quoted shares;

- land or buildings, machinery or plant used in a business by a company controlled by the deceased, or by a partnership of which he was a partner; and

- land or buildings, machinery or plant owned by trustees and used in a business where the deceased had a life interest.

Period of ownership

11.56   The relevant business property must have been owned for at least two years by the deceased subject to provisions for replacement of property (*IHTA 1984, s 106*).

Rate of relief

11.57   100% relief will be given for the first two categories above, otherwise 50% (*IHTA 1984, s 104*). Shares in AIM companies are treated as unquoted companies.

Type of business

11.58   The business must not be an investment or a dealing business. Generally speaking (*IHTA 1984, s 105(3)*), BPR is given only to trading businesses. Accordingly, a business of owning property that is let residentially or commercially will generally not attract BPR. Many businesses will be 'mixed', comprising of a number of different factors. Here regard must be had to the whole, to see whether the trading or the investment side predominates.

Excepted assets

11.59   Even if the business as a whole qualifies, there may be some assets in the business regarded as 'excepted assets' (*IHTA 1984, s 112*). These will be excluded from relief where broadly not used for the business for future business use, that is, a business cannot simply 'park' spare cash, surplus to business requirements, with the proprietors expecting to get BPR on all the cash.

Details of IHT 413

11.60   Here there are four main parts, with the last one relating only to gifts made within seven years before death where BPR is claimed.

- Ownership, contract for sale and business interests. This seeks to ensure that the period of ownership condition is met (**11.56** above) and that relief is not prejudiced because the property was at the date of death subject to a binding contract for sale which denies BPR under *IHTA 1984, s113.*

- Business or interest in a partnership. Boxes 7 to 17 request various details, including questions designed to clarify the proper valuation of the net value of the business on which relief is claimed. Box 8 asks for the main activity of the business or partnership, to ensure that it is not disqualified as wholly or mainly dealing or investment (see **11.58** above).

- Asset(s) owned by the deceased and used by a company controlled by the deceased or a partnership of which they were a member. This asks for details of the assets listed at bullet point 4 of **11.55** which attract 50% relief.

- Business relief on lifetime gifts. This is the 'clawback' question, as with APR. If a lifetime gift of business property had been made within seven years before death, BPR will be denied retrospectively unless, broadly speaking:

    − the original donee had retained either the original asset given away or qualifying replacement property throughout the period from the date of the gift to the date of death; and

    − the original or qualifying replacement property continued to attract relief in the hands of the donee at the date of the donor's death.

SCHEDULE IHT 414: AGRICULTURAL RELIEF

11.61 Agricultural relief (or rather agricultural property relief or APR) together with its sister relief business property relief (BPR) (see **11.54–11.59**)), is very complex (*IHTA 1984, ss 115–124C*). See further *Agricultural and Business Property Relief*, 6th ed, by Toby Harris, published by Tottel Publishing. What follows is only a summary.

Agricultural property

11.62 This is defined as: (1) agricultural land or pasture; (2) woodland and buildings used for intensive rearing of livestock or fish, if the occupation of the woodland or building is ancillary to agricultural land or pasture; and (3) cottages, farm buildings and farm houses together with their land as are of a character appropriate to the property (*IHTA 1984, s 115(2)*). The agricultural property must be situated within the European Economic Area (or, in cases where inheritance tax was paid or was due before 23 April 2003, in the United Kingdom, the Channel Islands or the Isle of Man): *IHTA 1984, s 115(5)* as amended by *FA 2009, s 122*. A controlling interest in a farming company will also attract APR (*IHTA 1984, s 122*).

The ownership or occupation test

11.63   The deceased must have occupied the agricultural property for agricultural purposes for at least two years, or must have owned the agricultural property for at least seven years, with continuous occupation by someone for agriculture (*IHTA 1984, s 117*). There are reliefs for replacement of property (*IHTA 1984, s 118*).

Rate of relief

11.64   The rate is (*IHTA 1984, s 116*) 100% if:

- the deceased has vacant possession, or the right to obtain it within 12 (24 by concession F17) months of his death;

- the deceased had owned his interest in the land since before 10 March 1981 and would have been entitled to the old 'working farmer' relief, with no right to vacant possession since then; and

- the deceased was the landlord of a tenancy commencing on or after 1 September 1995.

Otherwise, he will get only 50% relief, typically where he is the landlord of property let under a tenancy under which he does not have the right to get possession within 24 months.

Agricultural value

11.65   APR is given not on the market value of the property (like BPR), but on the 'agricultural value' only; this presumes that the property is subject to a perpetual covenant prohibiting non-agricultural use (*IHTA 1984, s 115(3)*). District valuers have been using this to argue for a discount of up to one-third on the market value of the farmhouse. This (or, rather, 30%) was the discount applied by the Lands Tribunal in the case of *Lloyds TSB Private Banking plc (Personal Representative of Antrobus (Deceased)) v Twiddy* [2006] 1 EGLR 157. Claims to APR on the farmhouse have been the subject of a number of recent decided cases. The property must be a farmhouse on the facts before any question of relief arises. Revised Chapter 24 in HMRC's Inheritance Tax Manual confirms that, contrary to the analysis of the Lands Tribunal in the so-called *Antrobus No 2* case, a farmhouse can be the place from which management operations are conducted (under for example a contract farming agreement) as well as the residence of the day-to-day farmer.

Details required by IHT 414

11.66   The six parts of the schedule are broken down as follows:

- Agricultural property. The address and a full description of the holding must be given. In addition Schedule IHT 405 Houses, Land, Buildings and Interests in Land must be completed to give details of the property concerned.

- Use of agricultural land. Here a detailed description of the day-to-day farming activities carried out on the land throughout the seven years or two years in question must be given, together with details of the extent of the deceased's involvement in these activities. As an example, the actual tasks carried out by the deceased and the number of hours spent on those tasks should be given.

- Let land. Here the details of any lease, licence or tenancy to which the land was subject should be given.

- Farmhouses and cottages. This part of the schedule addresses limb 3 of the definition of 'agricultural property' in *IHTA 1984, s 115(2)*: see **11.62** above. There is room for details of two properties, with further properties to be given on an additional sheet. Details are required of address, occupation, whether the deceased lived there (if not, the details of the occupant and the extent of their involvement in the farming activities) and details of any letting

- Farm buildings. Full details of use must be given, noting that phrases such as 'general storage' or 'agricultural purposes' are unacceptable.

- Agricultural relief and lifetime transfers. These questions are intended to address the matter of the clawback of relief in *IHTA 1984, s 124A* and *B* – and to confirm that the property was not subject to a binding contract for sale. Broadly, to retain APR, it must be shown that the donee of the property given away occupied it for agricultural purposes throughout the period from the gift to the date of death and that he continued to own that property at the donor's death, with provision for replacement.

- There is then the white space for 'any other information'

SCHEDULE IHT 415: INTEREST IN ANOTHER ESTATE

11.67   This form is for use where the deceased had a right to a legacy or share in an estate of someone who died before them but which they had not received before they died. A separate form should be completed for each estate in which the deceased had a right to a legacy or share. Clearly, if someone is entitled to a gift of, say, £50,000 under the unadministered estate and this has been paid over by the executors, and the beneficiary then dies, the £50,000 (or such of it as remains unspent), will be a chargeable asset in the beneficiary's estate, attracting IHT (subject to the rules for quick succession relief: see **11.85–11.88**). If, on the other hand, the executors have not yet paid out the legacy when the beneficiary dies, it cannot be said that the beneficiary has an entitlement to £50,000. For example, all or part of the money may be required to pay IHT on the earlier death or perhaps debts owed by the deceased or his estate. In other words, until such time as an entitlement is paid over, all that a beneficiary under an estate has is what is called a 'chose in action', that is a right to have the estate property administered and, in the course of time, his entitlement (whatever it may turn out to be) paid over to him by the executors. Even in a case where there is a legacy of a specific chattel, eg a grandfather clock, it may have to be sold, and the proceeds used to pay tax or other liabilities. All that said, the beneficiary does have a valuable right in the unadministered estate, which will be an asset of his. This is the purpose of IHT 415.

Example 11.8—Interest in unadministered estates

Jim died on 1 January 2006, leaving half the residue of his estate to his brother, Kenneth. Kenneth died on 1 August 2008. Jim's estate was complex and is still in the course of administration.

In Kenneth's form IHT 400, Schedule IHT 415 must be completed, giving:

- Jim's name;
- the date of Jim's death;
- the HMRC Inheritance Tax reference of Jim's estate;
- Kenneth's entitlement from Jim's estate, viz a one-half share in residue;
- whether Kenneth had received any part of his entitlement before he died; answer 'No'; and
- details of the entitlement that Kenneth had still to receive.

This question may well be difficult and indeed not possible to answer when submitting the details of Kenneth's estate to HMRC Inheritance Tax. The solicitors acting in Jim's estate should be asked for an estimate, perhaps subsequently to be confirmed, of the extent of Kenneth's entitlement, subject obviously to any legacies, taxes or liabilities.

There will be an entitlement to quick succession relief, as Kenneth died at least three, but less than four years, after Jim (see **11.85–11.88**).

SCHEDULE IHT 416: DEBTS DUE TO THE ESTATE

11.68 The deceased might have had an involvement with a debt, not as a sum of money that he owed, but as a sum that was owed to him. This is an asset that forms part of his chargeable estate, except perhaps to the extent that it can be shown clearly that the debt was irrecoverable. A separate form should be used for each debt. Questions 1 to 5 ask various details of the debt, including the original value of the loan and the amount of the loan including interest outstanding at the date of death. Question 9 envisages that a figure for the loan might be different from the total amount outstanding at Box 3: if so, an explanation is required.

Alternatively, the debt might have been written off. This would take effect as a gift and, if written off within seven years before the date of death, should again be included in the list of chargeable lifetime transfers. In the normal case, a debt should be written off by deed, ie not orally or by a letter that is not executed as a deed. This is because those methods of writing off are not generally enforceable and, whatever the intention as between the parties, the creditor (who has now died) should have a legal claim for the debt against the debtor if a deduction is to be obtained. (However, note that there is an argument to the contrary, based on the *Bills of Exchange Act 1882*.) Hence, HMRC Inheritance Tax will need to be satisfied as to the circumstances of writing off.

Irrecoverable debts

11.69 Many of the debts due to the estate will have been between members of the family and it may not always be easy to determine the precise terms. A debt will be irrecoverable at law if it has become 'statute barred'. Where a loan is made orally, or under simple writing (ie not a deed) and the debt was not for a fixed term, the limitation period is normally six years. This means that, if no acknowledgement is made of the debt, eg by payment of interest, and a period of more than six years has run since the loan or the last acknowledgement was made, the debt becomes irrecoverable. If the loan was made by deed, the period becomes 12 years. This is one of the reasons why question 8 asks for evidence of the existence of a loan, question 6 for payment of interest and question 7 repayment of capital.

Insurance schemes

11.70 There is a further point on question 8. A number of insurance-based IHT mitigation products include a loan made by the taxpayer (in this case the deceased) to the trustees of a settlement or of a life policy. It may be that under the arrangement any outstanding part of the loan (that had not been repaid during the lifetime) must be repaid on the death of the taxpayer. The effectiveness of the scheme will often depend upon the independence of the loan from the policy and, therefore, HMRC Inheritance Tax will wish to have copies of all relevant documentation.

Example 11.9—Writing off loans

In 1996, Fred made a loan to his son of £100,000 interest-free to help the son meet some heavy trading losses. The loan was made by a simple letter, with no interest payable, expressed to be repayable on demand. Father and son had informally agreed between them that the son would repay 'as and when' he could.

As time went by, Fred realised that it would be more IHT efficient to turn the loan into a gift and annually as from 2003/2004 has purported to write off £3,000 of the loan within his annual exemption. This was done by simple letter. The letter serves as acknowledgement of the loan, ie it cannot be argued that it has become statute-barred. However, after Fred's death on 1 August 2009, a claim for use of his annual exemptions is likely to be resisted by HMRC Inheritance Tax because the annual writings off were not effected by deed. It could be worth challenging the refusal of the exemptions, on the grounds of the *Bills of Exchange Act 1882* argument (see **11.68** above).

SCHEDULE IHT 417: FOREIGN ASSETS

11.71 Assuming that the deceased was domiciled or deemed domiciled in the UK at death, the worldwide estate will be subject to IHT. It may of course be that foreign tax is paid on the foreign assets, typically where these consist of real property. There may be a double tax treaty, which expressly gives relief for the foreign tax paid against the UK liability, eg Ireland, The Netherlands, South Africa, Sweden or the US. Otherwise, 'unilateral relief' may be given by deducting the foreign tax against the UK liability (*IHTA 1984, s 159*). In no circumstances will there be a repayment of the foreign tax; ie if the UK liability is 50 but the foreign tax, 60, there will simply be no UK IHT to pay.

If by contrast the deceased was not actually domiciled outside the UK (nor deemed domiciled within the UK) IHT 417 should not be used; instead HMRC Inheritance Tax request an approximate value for all the non-UK assets owned by the deceased in answer to question 22 on Schedule IHT 401 (though there is no obligation to provide this): see **11.17** above.

The Schedule asks first for details of houses, land and buildings; businesses or interest in businesses; and controlling holdings of shares and securities. In each case there must be given a description of the assets, the value in foreign currency at the date of death, the exchange rate at the date of death and the pounds sterling value of the assets at the date of death. There follow boxes for details of deductible liabilities and exemptions and reliefs in each case, concluding with a net total of those types of assets. Next, in boxes 6 to 10, such details must be given of any other assets owned by the deceased outside the UK eg bank accounts.

Foreign liabilities

11.72 Subject to satisfying the general rules about deductibility (viz in particular the deceased must have given value for the debt, see **11.78–11.79**) a foreign liability may be deducted for IHT purposes just as a UK liability. However, where the debt is to be discharged outside the UK and is not secured on UK property, it is so far as possible, taken to reduce the value of the non-UK property (*IHTA 1984, s 162(5)*).

Expenses of administration

11.73 The legislation recognises that there may be extra expenses of administering foreign property. However, the executors are not given 'carte blanche' and there is a limitation to 5% of the value of the property at death (*IHTA 1984, s 173*). If, therefore, the expenses amount to 3%, it is those actual expenses that are deductible. If they amount to 6%, only 5/6 of the expenses are deductible.

Example 11.10—Foreign assets

John died UK domiciled owning the following non-UK assets:

- shares quoted on the New York Stock Exchange worth £5,000;

- a bank account in Greece, with a balance at date of death of £1,000; and

- a holiday home in Greece, worth £200,000.

His PRs will complete:

- The first part of the form with the holiday home. On such assets tax may be paid by instalments, the family intend to keep the property and wish to pay the tax by instalments, less Greek death duties. The resultant IHT will be payable by ten equal annual instalments, the first falling due six months after the end of the month in which death occurred and the remaining nine on the annual anniversaries. Any interest due will be added to the unpaid instalments. Here the value of the Greek property will be shown, less the costs of administering the property (interestingly, this would not be allowed in the UK) of say, £2,000, net value £198,000.

- The second part of the form by listing the US shares and the Greek bank account, showing a total value of £6,000 from which there are no liabilities or exemptions and reliefs, other than the management costs of the Greek letting agents outstanding at date of death of £200, total net value £5,800.

SCHEDULE IHT 418: ASSETS HELD IN TRUST

11.74   With trusts or settlements, the basic distinction has been explained (see **3.12**) between:

- a trust made before 22 March 2006 in which a person has a right to receive the income, or enjoy the trust fund (eg a right to occupy a property) – called a life interest or an interest in possession; and

- a trust where the trustees have a discretion over income, called a discretionary trust, or any other non-charitable trust (other than a qualifying disabled trust) made on or after 22 March 2006.

The rule with life interest trusts is that the income beneficiary is treated for IHT purposes as owning the assets that underlie his interest: if, for example, he has a right to half the income, then he is treated as owning half the capital.

The trustees of a life interest trust have a 'stand alone' obligation to return the chargeable transfer, which occurs on the life tenant's death (subject, of course, to the spouse exemption). However, IHT 418 exists to enable the personal representatives to return details of the trust in order that they can correctly compute the total tax payable. The notes emphasise that the primary compliance liability rests on the trustees not on the PRs. The way in which IHT is calculated and shared between the trustees and the PRs is explained in **6.53** and Example 6.18.

What types of qualifying life interest trust are potentially subject to IHT?

11.75

- Settled property situated outside the UK, held by trustees of a settlement made by a settlor who was UK domiciled when the trust was made.

- Settled property in the UK held in a trust made by anyone, ie regardless of domicile when the trust was established.

- Settled property over which the deceased had a general power of appointment (ie he could determine who, including himself, would benefit from the property *and* the deceased exercised that power in the will).

What types of trust are not caught?

11.76   If the settled property was situated outside the UK, and the settlor was domiciled outside the UK when the trust was made, this is an 'excluded property settlement' and is outside the scope of IHT (*IHTA 1984, s 48(3)*). The reference to domicile includes the deemed domicile rule (see **6.6**). Even here, however, the notes say that the details of such a trust should be included in questions 2 to 5. This gives HMRC Inheritance Tax the opportunity to check the facts.

11.77   Schedule IHT 418 is divided into six parts:

- Deceased's interest in possession. Here there must be distinguished an interest in possession which commenced before 22 March 2006 and remained in existence until death; an immediate post-death interest; a disabled person's interest; and a transitional serial interest. With all of these the deceased will be treated as having owned the underlying capital, for which the details must be given in the remainder of the form.

- About the trust. Here details are required, including HMRC's unique taxpayer reference.

- Assets in the trust. Here are required details of houses land and buildings; businesses or interests in businesses; and controlling holdings of shares and securities. On these types of property instalment relief (see **11.92–11.95** below) may be claimed.

- Other assets in the trust. This is non-instalment property, for example bank accounts and quoted shares.

- Future rights to assets in a trust. This series of questions is intended to seek out reversionary interests, that is at the date of death some person other than the deceased was entitled to income. While generally such a future reversionary right will not be taxable in the deceased's estate, it may be in some circumstances eg where the deceased or his spouse/civil partner was the settlor.

There is then a white space box for 'any other information'.

SCHEDULE IHT 419: DEBTS OWED BY THE DECEASED

11.78 The PRs will want to rank as a deduction any debts that were properly owed by the deceased, from the chargeable estate for IHT purposes. These will not extend to liabilities, eg money owed to local tradesmen or funeral expenses, but will rather cover debts which are claimed to be owed to members of the family, other more substantial loans, debts covered by a guarantee and debts which may be subject to anti-avoidance rules.

11.79 The five sections on the form ask the following details:

- Money spent on the deceased's behalf, eg the payment of domestic bills during the deceased's lifetime.

- Loans and liabilities. Details of the loans, including written evidence, must be provided whether they were from financial institutions or from close friends and relatives.

- Liabilities related to an insurance policy, whether a policy or an investment bond where the value of the policy or bond is not fully reflected elsewhere in the IHT 400.

- Guaranteed debts. If the deceased had guaranteed to pay someone else's borrowing, the deceased would get a deduction only if the guarantee had been, or was likely to be, called. If there was only a contingent possibility of the guarantee being called, any deduction is likely to be merely nominal.

- Gifts to and loans from the same person. This is designed to catch situations where the deceased made a gift to someone before or after 18 March 1986 and at any time after that gift borrowed money from that same person. These represent complicated anti-avoidance rules, which are on the 'other side of the coin' of the reservation of benefit regime (*FA 1986, s 103*). It would be quite easy to get round the reservation of benefit rules; see for example, the scenario described in Example 11.11 at **11.80**. Broadly, a deduction is denied (*IHTA 1984, s 103*) if:

  - the deceased had borrowed money from a person on or after 18 March 1986; and

  - if the deceased had at any time (whether or not after 18 March 1986 and whether or not connected with the loan) made a gift to the creditor; or

  - the liability is in any way related to a policy of life assurance and the sum assured is not fully reflected in the estate of the deceased.

If the creditor was a close friend or relative of the deceased, details of the loan may already have been given in Box 2.

11.80

Example 11.11—Anti-avoidance rules (FA 1986, s 103)

Without these rules it might be quite easy to get around the reservation of benefit regime by using, for example, the following arrangement.

Father gives to his daughter shares worth £200,000. Daughter sells the shares and buys a house. Father then buys from the daughter the house for £225,000 (its market value), but cannot afford to pay for it, so leaves the purchase price outstanding as an interest-free, repayable on demand loan. Father dies five years later, when the house is worth £300,000. In the absence of these rules, father's IHT 400 would show a house worth £300,000 less a liability owed to the daughter £225,000, net equity £75,000. However, these rules prevent a deduction and therefore the £300,000 is charged in father's estate in full.

The thinking behind the rules is that father has enjoyed a benefit from a gift that he made to the lender and therefore, to the extent of the gift, is denied a deduction. Interestingly, the rules would be applied even if father had paid interest at market rate on the loan. By contrast, if the money had been borrowed at interest from a clearing bank or building society, a deduction would have been applied.

In the author's view, the rules are applied by HMRC Inheritance Tax more widely than is justified by the legislation, which to his mind implies (by the use of the word 'consideration') some necessary connection between the gift and the loan.

There is no *de minimis* let-out. The only limitation afforded is that the rules cannot apply to a disposition which is not a transfer of value. Hence if at outset, father had sold the shares to his daughter and later bought the house leaving the price outstanding, there would be a deduction for the debt.

Spouse/civil partner exempt gifts are not excluded from the operation of the rules. This was the basis of the decision of the Special Commissioner in the case *Phizackerley v HMRC* [2007] STC (SCD) 328. Dr Phizackerley had given to his wife a half share in the house. On her death, her share in the house was assented to Dr Phizackerley on his giving an IOU for its then value to the trustees of her nil rate band trust. On Dr Phizackerley's death a deduction for the IOU was denied because of the prior gift of the half share in the house.

SCHEDULE IHT 420: NATIONAL HERITAGE ASSETS – CONDITIONAL EXEMPTION AND OFFERS IN LIEU OF TAX

11.81 Conditional exemption from IHT is available for objects, land and buildings if they are important to the national heritage *(IHTA 1984, ss 30–35)*. In return new owners must agree to look after the assets and provide public access. This form is used:

- to claim conditional exemption for any assets in the estate;

- if heritage exemption was allowed on any of the assets in the estate in the past; or

- if the PRs wish to offer any assets in lieu of IHT.

OTHER HMRC INHERITANCE TAX FORMS

Further Schedules to account form IHT 400

11.82 Schedules IHT 401 to IHT 420 have been discussed in **11.16–11.81**. There are three further Schedules:

- IHT 421 (or in Scotland C1): this is the form which is sent to the Probate Registry (or in Scotland Sheriff Court), in either case endorsed in taxable estates by HMRC Inheritance Tax: see **11.4**.

- IHT 422 is the application for an IHT reference (see **10.4**, first bullet point).

- IHT 423 is an application to transfer funds from any of the deceased's bank or building society accounts to pay IHT (the direct payment scheme).

Other forms

11.83

- IHT 35 (claim for relief: loss on sale of shares): see **11.84**.

- IHT 38 (claim for relief: loss on sale of land): see **11.34–11.36**.

- IHT 100 (account of a transfer of value). This would be used where, for example, a person makes a discretionary settlement, whether within or outside the nil rate band, subject to the *de minimis* limits (see **3.19– 3.20**). From April 2003, this form is used also to report chargeable events within relevant property trusts.

Relief for loss on shares

11.84 The relief for sales of quoted shares or units or authorised unit trusts for a price less than their market value on death (*IHTA 1984, ss 178–189*) is similar to the relief for land (see **11.34–36**), except that:

- the shares must be sold, or become valueless, within 12 months after death;

- it does not matter to whom they are sold;

- the repurchase restriction applies if shares are bought within two months after the last sale in the 12-month period; and

- there is no *de minimis* restriction.

Example 11.12—Shares sold at a loss

Don's estate included four parcels of quoted shares each worth £5,000 at death. In the following 12 months the PRs sold three parcels at £3,000, £4,000 and £6,000 respectively.

The aggregate loss on sale is: £15,000 × £13,000 = £2,000 and, on a claim on form IHT 35, the chargeable value of the shares will be reduced to £18,000.

QUICK SUCCESSION RELIEF

11.85 Where, within a period of five years, there are two chargeable transfers of which the second is (if not both are) on death, relief is given against the IHT liability on the second event (*IHTA 1984, s 141*). There is no requirement that the person given the asset under the first transfer retained the actual asset. What is required is that the value charged on the second transfer reflected the increase in value made by the first.

Measure of relief

11.86 The relief is a prescribed proportion of the tax charged on the value transferred by the previous transfer as is attributable to the donee's estate. The table is set out below.

Donee predeceasing donor

11.87   Suppose that at the date of the donee's death, the donor is still alive, ie having made a PET. If the donor dies within seven years of the gift, the PET will become chargeable. Quick succession relief will become available on the donee's estate.

Rates of quick succession relief

11.88

Period between transfer and death	Percentage relief
Less than 1 year	100%
1–2 years	80%
2–3 years	60%
3–4 years	40%
4–5 years	20%

THE ESTATE DUTY SURVIVING SPOUSE EXEMPTION

The estate duty regime

11.89   Tax was charged on the whole estate of the first spouse to die (subject to the threshold, to any spouse exemption and to reliefs for business property). Provided that under the will of the first to die, the surviving spouse was left a life interest, under which there was no power to draw on capital, the value of the assets subject to the life interest on the second death were exempt from estate duty.

Transitional provisions

11.90   Transitional provisions under both CGT and IHT ensure that, where the first spouse died before 13 November 1974, ie under estate duty, and tax was paid, or would have been paid, but for the threshold or any relief, the estate duty exemption that would have applied on the second death is carried over (*IHTA 1984, Sch 6, para 2*). Accordingly, one has what is known as an 'estate duty protected life interest'. Cases benefiting from this exemption still exist, although they will reduce in number as the years go by. This means in effect that the life interest is a capital tax-free fund, exempt on death from both CGT and IHT.

Lifetime assignments

11.91   The life interest could come to an end during the lifetime of the surviving spouse, eg if she (let us assume it is the widow) assigns the right to receive income to say, her children, who will become entitled to capital on her death. This creates an 'interest *pur autre vie*'. On the face of it, that is bad news, in the sense that the usual CGT-free uplift to market value will not be available on the second death. However, in cases where CGT is not such an issue, such a course of action might be appropriate. This is because although the estate duty protected life interest does not itself come into charge on the second death, it is nonetheless taken into account in valuing other property in the surviving spouse's free estate. The legislation provides that in such a case if the surviving spouse dies within seven years after the assignment of the life interest, no IHT is payable, ie it is not treated as a PET that becomes chargeable.

Example 11.13—First spouse's death under estate duty

Leonard died on 1 October 1973. Estate duty was paid on his estate. His will left a life interest to his widow Gladys. Gladys had a long widowhood and died only on 1 June 2009, having made no chargeable gifts in the seven years before she died. She had a free estate of £300,000 and an estate settled under the will of her late husband worth £1 million. No capital taxation (IHT or CGT) is payable on her death. Her own estate is covered by the nil rate band of £325,000 and the £1 million is covered by the 'estate duty protected life interest' exemption. As time progresses this type of case will arise less and less.

INSTALMENT PAYMENT

11.92   The legislation recognises that it might be unfair to require executors to pay tax within (broadly) six months after death if the property concerned is land or, perhaps, business or private company shares which are not going to be sold and there is no spare cash in the estate to pay the tax. Accordingly, under the instalment payment rules, provided that the property concerned falls within certain prescribed categories (whether the property is within or outside the UK), an election to pay the tax by instalments may be made (*IHTA 1984, s 227*): see **11.95** below.

The first instalment falls due on the date on which the tax would otherwise have to be paid and the remaining nine instalments on anniversaries of this date, so that, broadly speaking, the whole tax has been paid nine and a half years or so after death. If at any time during the instalment period, the property is sold, the whole of the outstanding instalments become immediately due and payable.

Interest

11.93 If the qualifying property is an interest in a business, shares or securities which attract BPR, land used in a business or timber, no interest is payable on outstanding instalments, providing that they are all paid on the due dates. Otherwise, for example, in the case of the main family home or a holiday home, any interest due is payable on outstanding instalments. In this case, an assessment made by HMRC Inheritance Tax for each instalment of the tax will have added to it a request for interest due.

Elect with care

11.94 There was an unfortunate Special Commissioner's case in 1997 called *Howarth's executors v IRC* [1997] STC (SCD) 162. The two executors were the son of the deceased, and a solicitor (not a partner) in the firm which acted in the estate. An election was made for instalment payment, following which the property was transferred into the name of the son as the residuary beneficiary. The son then became bankrupt and the instalment property was sold. The Special Commissioner upheld a determination made by HMRC against the solicitor who had retired on account of ill health: 'In trusting the beneficiary, he took a risk'.

This decision emphasises that IHT is a personal liability of each personal representative and is not a responsibility that can easily be shed. A personal representative in such a case needs to ensure, eg by retaining legal ownership of the assets concerned, that the instalments of tax can be met.

Qualifying property (IHTA 1984, ss 227(2) and 228)

11.95

- Land or buildings, wherever situated.
- Quoted or unquoted shares or securities, which gave control.
- Other unquoted shares or securities where:
    - there would be undue hardship if the tax were to be paid in one sum; or
    - the transfer was on death and at least 20% of the tax due is attributable to unquoted shares or securities, or to other property qualifying for instalment relief.

- Unquoted shares worth more than £20,000 where either:

  - the shares constitute at least 10% of the issued share capital of the company; or

  - the shares are ordinary shares, and their nominal value is at least 10% of all the ordinary shares in issue.

- The net value of the business or an interest in a business carried on for gain.

- Timber.

See pages 6 and 7 of the IHT 400 and pages 53 and 54 of the Notes.

PAGE 11: CALCULATING THE TAX LIABILITY

11.96 HMRC Inheritance Tax expect a solicitor or other agent acting on behalf of the PRs to work out the tax due before submitting form IHT 400. If lay PRs are applying for a grant without the help of a solicitor or other agent, there is a choice, either to work out the tax themselves or to let HMRC Inheritance Tax do the work.

The exercise may be quite straightforward – or (especially where grossing up applies (see **11.99–11.102**)) it may be extremely complicated.

In any event, the figures shown on form IHT 400, which brings in the amounts from the supplementary pages, are carried over onto the IHT worksheet.

There is also a checklist on page 14 of the IHT 400 to ensure that all the appropriate forms are sent to HMRC Inheritance Tax. An example of how the tax calculation works is shown below.

Example 11.14—Tax on instalment and non-instalment property respectively

Alfred died on 1 September 2009 owning a UK estate worth £500,000, including his home worth £200,000. He had an interest in a trust fund set up by his late father, which passes on his death to his children, worth £150,000.

He had, in 1999, made a gift to his son of a cottage in Brighton, worth then £25,000 but worth at his death £175,000 in which his use had amounted to a reservation of benefit. In the seven years before he died, Alfred had made net chargeable gifts of £40,000. Just under three years before he died, he had received a legacy from his brother's estate of £50,000 after tax of £30,000 paid by his brother's estate.

Tax on both the home and the Brighton cottage is payable by instalments.

Alfred is a widower. After charitable legacies of £5,000 and chargeable legacies (net of tax of £10,000) he leaves his estate equally between his two adult children. The calculation works as follows:

Assets where tax may not be paid by instalments	
UK estate (less charities exemption)	£495,000
Settled property	£150,000
Assets where tax may be paid by instalments	£200,000
Other property taken into account to calculate the total tax	
Gifts with reservation	£175,000
Chargeable estate	£820,000
Cumulative total of lifetime transfers	£40,000
Aggregate chargeable transfer	£860,000
Working out the total tax that is payable	
Aggregate chargeable transfer	£860,000
Tax threshold	(£325,000)
Value chargeable to tax	£535,000
Tax due (at 40%)	£214,000
Tax on lifetime transfers	Nil
Relief for successive charges (see **11.85–11.88**)	£18,000
Tax payable on chargeable estate	£196,000
Tax which may not be paid by instalments (620/820)	£148,195
Tax which may be paid by instalments (200/820)	£47,805

DEATH FROM ACTIVE MILITARY SERVICE

11.97 It has long been a very reasonable principle of the death duties regime that the estate of a person who gave their life for their country should be free from death duties (*IHTA 1984, s 154*).

The condition is that the death arose from:

- a wound inflicted, accident occurring or disease contracted at a time when he was a member of any of the Armed Forces of the Crown or, not being such a member, was subject to the law governing any of those forces (by reason of association, whether accompanying any body of those forces) and was either on active service against an enemy or on other service of a war-like nature, which in the opinion of the Treasury involved the same risks as service of a war-like nature;

- a disease contracted at some previous time, the death being due to, or hastened by, the aggravation of the disease during a period when the above conditions were satisfied.

The main point is that the wound, accident or disease need not be the only or even the main cause of death, just 'a' cause of death. That is, it may well be possible even now over 50 years later, to claim the exemption in respect of a wound inflicted, etc during the Second World War, not of course to mention conflicts since, most recently in Iraq and Afghanistan.

There are, of course, 'grey areas' although the author's understanding is that the exemption is applied relatively benignly.

Procedure

11.98 The procedure is relatively straightforward. When form IHT 400 is submitted, it should be accompanied by a letter or report by a physician who knew the deceased, in support of the application, the exemption being claimed by the person who sends in the account. HMRC Inheritance Tax will then pass the letter or report to the Ministry of Defence who may ask further questions and then will simply respond affirmatively or negatively.

The exemption is a complete exemption, and therefore well worth having. Note, however, that it will be given only if the death actually resulted from the wound, accident or disease. That is, if a person who had been wounded in active conflict, and who would certainly have qualified for the exemption, is in fact killed in a car crash, no relief will of course, be due. In other words, it is only following the death that one can be sure that the exemption is given.

Example 11.15—The 'killed in war' exemption

Joe has recently died (in 2008/09) at the age of 86. He had been wounded in the Battle of Arnhem in 1944 and had been retired from the Army on medical grounds. He had never been able to hold down a job since, and had worked from time to time on his own account. The death certificate (helpfully) refers to the war wound as having been a contributing cause of death.

On application, subject to the appropriate medical evidence, the exemption should be given.

Joe's estate amounted to £400,000. Under his will he left the whole of this to his wife. It would be open to his wife, within two years after Joe's death, to vary his will (see **13.1–13.4**), whereby the whole estate is held on discretionary trust for the beneficiaries to include her, children and grandchildren, etc.

However, HMRC Inheritance Tax will not consider the exemption unless there is at least £10,000 of IHT at stake. It may, therefore, be necessary in the first place for the widow to vary Joe's will as to say, £340,000 accepting that if the exemption is not given, then there would have been a chargeable transfer of £28,000 with tax due of £11,200. This, however, is thought to be a risk worth taking. Having got the exemption, she could then make a second deed, within the two-year period, varying the balance of the estate into the same discretionary trust.

THE GROSSING UP RULES

11.99 Grossing up is an issue that can crop up, although (happily) not all that frequently. However, it is necessary to have some understanding of what grossing up is, and in what circumstances it might happen.

Taxable and/or exempt transfers

11.100 When someone dies, they are treated as making, for IHT purposes, a single gift of the whole estate, which may be:

- wholly taxable, eg passing just to the children;

- partly taxable and partly exempt, eg passing partly to a surviving spouse and partly to the children; or

- wholly exempt, eg passing entirely to the surviving spouse or to charity.

There are rules to ensure that where there are both exempt and chargeable gifts, exemptions are properly attributed among the various gifts (*IHTA 1984, s 38*).

Residue and specific gifts

11.101 There is a distinction between:

- gifts of residue, which may or may not be exempt, but where they are chargeable always bear their own tax; and

- specific gifts, which may or may not be exempt and where they are non-exempt, may or may not, bear their own tax depending on the terms of the will.

The main difficulty for IHT purposes lies in calculating the value of non-exempt specific gifts where there may or may not be the need to gross up and where any grossing up may be on a single or on a double basis. The situation in any particular case is dependent on:

- whether any non-exempt specific gift does, or does not, bear its own tax; and

- the nature of any gift or gifts, which there may be in addition to any specific non-exempt gift.

The purpose of the grossing up rules therefore (not described in any detail here), is to ensure the proper attribution of, in particular, the nil rate band.

Example 11.16—No grossing up

Fred died on 1 April 2009, leaving an estate of £700,000, having made no lifetime chargeable transfers. His will gives a legacy to his son of £100,000, subject to tax, and divided residue between his widow and daughter equally. Residue is therefore £600,000 and a half share, £300,000. Tax is accordingly due on £400,000 at death, viz £35,200.

The son will pay:	(£100,000 ÷ £400,000) × £35,200	=	£8,800
The daughter will pay:	(£300,000 ÷ £400,000) × £35,200	=	£26,400
			£35,200

No grossing up is required because the only non-exempt specific gifts bear their own tax. Where on the other hand, the only non-exempt gifts are specific gifts not bearing their own tax, there must be grossing up (on a single basis). This has the result that the amount attributable to the specific gifts is the total of the sum of their value, and the amount of tax chargeable is the value transferred equal to that total.

Example 11.17—Single grossing up

Having made no prior lifetime chargeable transfers, Jim died on 1 April 2009 with an estate of £800,000. His will leaves a legacy of £412,000, free of tax to his son, with residue to his widow.

Jim is treated as having made a net transfer on death of £100,000 on top of the net nil rate band of £312,000. IHT on £100,000 net is £66,667 (ie £166,667 less tax @ 40% is £100,000). The grossed up legacy is therefore £478,667 and the exempt residue is £321,333.

Double grossing up

11.102 This gets rather more complicated. It arises where there is both a specific gift, which is free of tax and residue, which is partly exempt and partly chargeable. In other words, in the above example, had residue been divided between Jim's widow and Jim's son, there would have been the need to gross up on a double basis, to ensure that both the son and the daughter have fair call on the nil rate band. Such an example is, however, not illustrated.

THE BENHAM ISSUE AND THE RATCLIFFE RATIO

11.103 The words 'Benham' and 'Ratcliffe', refer to two cases decided in the courts, *Re Benham's Will Trust* [1995] STC 210, and *Re Ratcliffe (deceased)* [1999] STC 262.

The decision *Re Benham* rather 'put the cat among the pigeons' in apparently expressly disregarding a statutory rule. The statutory rule in question (*IHTA 1984, s 41(b)*) provides that a share in residue that is exempt, (eg as passing to a surviving spouse) shall not bear the tax on a chargeable share of residue, eg as passing to the daughter.

The tax issues in *Re Benham* were rather complicated but may be illustrated simply as shown below.

The judge in *Re Benham* ruled that because (in our example) the testator had indicated that he wanted the widow and the daughter to receive the same amount in terms of cash (notwithstanding the effect of the spouse exemption), the daughter's share of residue had to be grossed up so as to produce an amount, which after tax, would equal the same as the widow's share. This had the unfortunate result of increasing the amount of tax payable.

Re Benham caused some concern as, in a not atypical situation, one would always expect in a case where the chargeable gifts exceed the nil rate band, the widow to be better off than the daughter because of the spouse exemption. Happily, the decision was not generally applied by HMRC Inheritance Tax, and therefore for most probate practitioners and indeed wills draftsmen, life continued as usual. *Re Benham* did, however, do everybody a service in focusing the mind on the problem as to whether or not in making a will, with residue divided between the surviving spouse and one or more children, the testator did in effect want the benefit of the spouse exemption to be shared among all members of the family. The presumption in *s 41(b)* is that it should not be.

Even more happily, four years later in 1999, the decision in *Re Ratcliffe* effectively overruled *Re Benham*, which by then had generally been written off by the experts as wrong (though being too polite to say so, they used the expression that it had been decided '*per incuriam*'). Because, like *Re Benham, Re Ratcliffe* was decided in the High Court and not in the Court of Appeal, the decision did not expressly overrule *Re Benham*, but nonetheless, is generally thought to represent the law in upholding the effect of *s 41(b)*. The judge in *Re Ratcliffe* said 'If I had thought that *Re Benham's Will Trust* laid down some principle, then, unless convinced that it was wrong, I would have felt bound that I should follow it. I am not able to find that it does and, accordingly, I do not feel bound to follow it'.

Example 11.18—The *Re Benham* effect

A woman dies, leaving residue of £800,000 (having used her nil rate band in lifetime gifts). Under her will, residue is split equally between her husband and her son.

In the following two columns are set out, first the solution normally expected applying *s 41(b)* where, albeit there is pre-tax equality, the non-exempt beneficiary bears the tax; and second the situation following *Re Benham* where HMRC receive more tax, but the exempt and non-exempt beneficiaries receive the same after tax. To achieve this result, the will would have to provide, for example, that 'the rule in *Re Benham* shall apply'.

	Section 41(b)	*Re Benham*
HMRC	£160,000	£200,000
Exempt beneficiary	£400,000	£300,000
Chargeable beneficiary	£240,000	£300,000
	£800,000	£800,000

Chapter 12

Deceased estates: income tax and CGT

INCOME TAX COMPLIANCE

12.1 The income tax affairs of the deceased must be distinguished from those of the estate. The outstanding income tax liability of the deceased is worked out as usual, is paid by the PRs and ranks as a deduction for IHT purposes.

The PRs must pay income tax on the estate income during the period of administration. They are not entitled to personal reliefs and allowances, though the income they receive is taxed only at the 10% dividend or 20% basic rate (for 2008/09 and 2009/10). Administration expenses, even if properly chargeable to income, are not tax deductible. The only deductible expense is interest on a loan taken by the PRs obtained before they acquire the grant of probate to satisfy the IHT on personal property. Interest relief is given only for a period of one year from the making of the loan *(ITA 2007, ss 403–405)*.

PRs will be treated as UK resident (and therefore liable to tax on worldwide income) unless *(ITA 2007, s 834)*:

- they are all resident and ordinarily resident outside the UK; or
- there is at least one PR who is and at least one PR who is not resident and the deceased at his death was none of domiciled, resident or ordinarily resident in the UK.

Distributions to legatees

12.2

- Payment of a cash legacy or a personal chattel does not have an impact on estate income.

- Payment of a legacy that produces income, such as shares, will carry the relevant income since death. Any dividend for a period spanning death must be time apportioned and the period before death belongs to the capital of the estate.

- PRs are meant (subject to anything in the will) to pay legacies within the 'executor's year', ie a year after death. Interest on a legacy paid thereafter is paid gross (subject to income tax for the beneficiary).

- Payment of income to a residuary beneficiary will be made under deduction of tax, whether starting rate, lower rate or basic rate as the case may be. The beneficiary will be given form R185 (Estate Income), which takes into account dividend income at 10% as well as income tax at 20%. The applicable tax rate is that in the year of distribution (not in the year of receipt). The basis on which residuary beneficiaries are taxed is explained in **12.6–12.7**.

Administration expenses

12.3   PRs' expenses are treated as paid first out of dividend income and then out of income taxed at the basic 20% rate.

Interaction with IHT

12.4   There can be double taxation, where shares are valued at death cum-div, ie the capital reflects the fact that a dividend is about to be paid. IHT is due on that value. When the dividend is paid, it is received by PRs as estate income and subject again to tax in their hands, albeit satisfied by the tax credit. There has, therefore, been double taxation, for which a beneficiary with an absolute interest in residue (that is one entitled to both capital and income) receives credit. The average rate of IHT in the estate is applied to the income that has been taxed twice and he then receives a credit in his self-assessment against his higher rate liability *(ITTOIA 2005, s 669)*.

Identifying the type of income

12.5   Estate income derived from dividends is treated as dividend income in the hands of the beneficiary. Therefore, if the beneficiary is a basic rate taxpayer, he will be assessed on that income at 10% (treated as satisfied by the tax credit).

Where there are two or more beneficiaries of the estate they will each share the dividend income and other income in the proportion of their interests.

Payments made by the executors are treated first as made out of basic rate income, then income taxed at the lower rate and finally dividend income *(ITTOIA 2005, s 679)*.

Example 12.1—The beneficiary's income tax liability

An estate has gross dividend income of £4,000 and gross other income of £6,000. In 2008/09, the executors pay £3,000 to Fiona the residuary legatee (in the course of administration). Fiona will have taxable income of £3,750 (£3,000 × 100 ÷ 80) on which she will be assessed in 2008/09.

THE RECEIPTS BASIS

12.6   The rule (broadly) is that residuary beneficiaries are assessed as and when they receive the income (*ITTOIA 2005, ss 652, 654*). However, this can lead to a 'bunching' problem; see below. Although partial distributions may be made from an estate, indeed distributions of income may be made 'as things go along', this is probably the exception rather than the rule. What might well tend to happen is that apart from payment of legacies and perhaps limited distributions of capital to residuary beneficiaries, the administration ends after two or three years with a payment made to the beneficiaries, most of which comprises capital but some of which comprises income arising over the tax years covered by the administration.

There is a distinction between an absolute interest and a limited interest in residue. Under an absolute interest, the beneficiary is entitled to both income and capital, whereas under a limited interest he is entitled to income only (an interest in possession). For absolute interests, the basic amount of estate income (for years before the final tax year) is the lower of the total of all sums paid in the tax year and the beneficiary's assumed income entitlement. This effectively excludes surplus payments of income: the beneficiary may receive sums which comprise both capital and income, though only the income element is taxed. For the final tax year the beneficiary's assumed income entitlement for that year is taxed (*ITTOIA 2005, s 660*).

For a beneficiary with a limited interest in residue, the basic amount is the total of the amounts referred to in *ITTOIA 2005, s 654*, confirmed in *s 661*. Note, however, the point made in the second paragraph at **12.7**.

The 'bunching' effect

12.7   Under the receipts basis, all the income is taxed in the year of receipt. That could have the unfortunate consequence of pushing a beneficiary up from being a non-taxpayer to a basic rate taxpayer, if, for example, the income year by year would have been within the personal allowance or a basic rate taxpayer up to a higher rate taxpayer. It is always open to the PRs to avoid this result by distributing income as they go along, but to do so they need to have some awareness of the personal income tax circumstances of each of the beneficiaries and, except from within a closely knit family, this might be quite difficult.

There is a further problem: the payment of capital or (albeit unlikely) the release of a debt although capital in nature, might trigger an income tax liability on the beneficiary to the extent that there is during that tax year, or a previous tax year of the estate, undistributed income (*ITTOIA 2005, s 681*). Accordingly, a distribution of chattels to beneficiaries may trigger income tax liabilities: beware. There is an example below. The effect of *ITTOIA 2005, ss 649, 652, 681, 665, 660* and *656* (most helpfully, in that order) is that, assuming no distribution of income, the value of the chattel is grossed up at 'the applicable rate' for the year, as defined in *ITTOIA 2005, s 663*, which varies according to the rate of income tax borne by the various elements of income of the estate and therefore, in relation to a particular distribution of income, the income out of which the payment is made.

Example 12.2—A trap for the unwary

Susan's estate is worth £500,000. The residuary beneficiary is her daughter, Ursula. The residuary income for 2007/08 is £5,000 and for 2008/09 £6,000. In 2008/09, while the estate administration continues, the executors transfer to Ursula a collection of silver owned by her mother worth £15,000. No other distributions are made.

In 2008/09, Ursula is treated as having received income of £11,000 gross subject to deduction of tax of £2,200 (say at 20%, assuming that to be the applicable rate for the sake of simplicity, as confirmed by the PRs) which she should therefore record in her self-assessment. The executors are not paying out income and therefore need not deduct and account for it to HMRC. This is simply a consequence of the statutory rule.

As and when, say, in 2009/10, the executors do distribute income as such to Ursula, they will need to take into account on form R185 (Estate Income) the fact that £11,000 of the estate income has already been treated for tax purposes as gross income arising in her hands.

CGT COMPLIANCE

12.8   The CGT affairs of the deceased, as with income tax, must be put into order. Any liability paid by the PRs will be a deductible liability in the estate.

The general rule is that the PRs are treated as acquiring the deceased's assets at their market value at death, but without involving a disposal by the deceased (*TCGA 1992, s 71(1)*). If a value is 'ascertained' for IHT purposes, that will be the base cost for future CGT purposes. If such a value is not ascertained, (eg where covered by the spouse exemption or by 100% reliefs for agricultural or business property or within the nil rate band), it is a matter of agreeing with HMRC the value of the asset following the ultimate disposal, whether by the PRs or by the beneficiary – if indeed such disposal takes place. For example, the beneficiary could well retain the asset until his own death, when the same CGT-free uplift to market value would occur.

Transfers to legatees

12.9   Where PRs dispose of property to a legatee entitled under the will, no chargeable gain accrues. Rather the acquisition of the asset by the PRs is related to that of the legatee, ie he is treated as acquiring the asset at the date of death with a base cost equal to market value at that date (*TCGA 1992, s 62(4)*). Generally speaking, it does not matter when the transfer to the legatee takes place.

Effective dates for appropriation – CGT purposes

12.10   Sometimes, the PRs will have to appropriate assets between various beneficiaries. Suppose that there are two equal beneficiaries of residue. To achieve absolute equity, each asset in the estate, after legacies, taxes and other liabilities have been paid, would simply be divided down the middle. This may not be fair, however, and some assets might in entirety go to one beneficiary and other assets to the other. The date on which assets are valued for this appropriation purpose is the date of appropriation. It has already been said that the value date for CGT purposes is the date of death. There could, therefore, be a mismatch between appropriation values and base costs for CGT purposes (which relate back to the date of death).

Residence

12.11   The residence of PRs for CGT is different from the income tax rule (*FA 1989, s 111*). The residence of the PRs follows that of the deceased (*TCGA 1992, s 62(3)*). If the deceased was non-UK resident at his death, disposals by the PRs (even if themselves UK resident) will attract no CGT liability. By contrast, if the deceased was UK resident, disposals by the PRs will be subject to tax. If the deceased was UK resident but non-UK domiciled, no remittance basis is available to the PRs, as they are not individuals.

Example 12.3—Value for appropriation purposes

There are two residuary beneficiaries of the estate, one of them resident in the UK (ie personally subject to CGT) and the other resident in Switzerland (ie not personally subject to UK CGT).

The residue comprises shareholdings in four companies, A, B, C and D. Values at date of death and one year after death, when the PRs decide to appropriate the shares, are as follows:

Company	Value at death	Value at appropriation
A	£40,000	£50,000
B	£50,000	£60,000
C	£60,000	£50,000
D	£70,000	£60,000

Because one beneficiary is non-UK resident, it would be helpful for him to have assets showing a gain and for the other beneficiary assets showing a loss since death. In order to achieve equity between them, the values at the date of appropriation are taken.

Accordingly, the PRs might appropriate shares in companies A and B to the Swiss resident beneficiary and shares in companies C and D to the UK resident beneficiary (subject always to their respective wishes and of course to Swiss taxation).

THE RATE OF TAX AND THE ANNUAL EXEMPTION

Rate of tax

12.12   Any chargeable gains realised by PRs over and above the annual exemption are subject to CGT at 18%.

Annual exemption

12.13   For the year of death, the deceased is entitled to the whole of his annual exemption of £9,600 (for 2008/09) or £10,100 (for 2009/10). For the balance of the year of death, the PRs are also entitled to the individual's annual exemption as well as for the following two years of assessment. If the estate administration continues beyond 5 April following two tax years after the end of the year in which death occurred, they receive no annual exemption at all. So, assuming a death on 1 September 2006, the PRs have an annual exemption of £8,800 for 2006/07, £9,200 for 2007/08 and £9,600 for 2008/09. If the administration continues beyond 5 April 2009, no exemption is available to set off against gains made in 2009/10 or subsequently. They do not get the trustees' exemption because they are not trustees.

Computing the gain

12.14 Gains of the PRs are worked out in the normal way, ie deducting from the gross sale proceeds the base cost, which is the market value at date of death, less allowable expenses. There is an alternative acquisition expenditure available to PRs intended to compensate them for the costs of acquiring title to the asset. As an alternative (not an addition) to the actual allowable expenditure incurred, they can claim the allowance set out in Statement of Practice 02/04, for expenses incurred by personal representatives and corporate trustees. The expense is greater for smaller disposals, less on larger estates. The scale is set out below.

Capacity at the date of any sale

12.15 Because the trigger date for CGT purposes is an unconditional contract under *TCGA 1992, s 28(1)* (rather than completion), one should think carefully about who owns the asset, ie whether it is an executor sale or whether the asset has been released from the estate and it is owned by one or more of the beneficiaries. This would be relevant to the availability of annual exemptions. Where it is stocks and shares that are concerned, typically held in nominee names with the stockbrokers or investment managers, consideration should be given before the sale to the matter of what instructions have been given to them as to the nature of the beneficial ownership.

Statement of Practice 02/04

12.16

Gross value of estate	*Allowable expenditure*
A. Not exceeding £50,000	1.8% of the probate value of the assets sold by the PRs.
B. Over £50,000 but not exceeding £90,000.	A fixed amount of £900, to be divided between all the assets of the estate in proportion to the probate values and allowed in those proportions on assets sold by the PRs.

Gross value of estate	*Allowable expenditure*
C. Over £90,000 but not exceeding £400,000.	1% of the probate value of the assets sold.
D. Over £400,000 but not exceeding £500,000.	A fixed amount of £4,000 to be divided as at B above.
E. Over £500,000 but not exceeding £1 million.	0.8% of the probate value of the assets sold.
F. Over £1 million but not exceeding £5 million.	A fixed amount of £8,000 to be divided as at B above.
G. Over £5 million.	0.16% of the probate value of the assets sold, subject to a maximum of £10,000.

CGT MAIN RESIDENCE RELIEF

Agreeing the gain

12.17   It may happen that property is sold during the administration of the estate but, say, within a year after death, at a price higher than that submitted for probate. Straightforwardly, the factual issue is simply whether the value of the property at the date of death was that submitted for probate or at the higher sale price: did indeed values move in the interim? At face value, if any additional amount would attract IHT in a fully taxable estate at 40%, whereas CGT for 2008/09 and 2009/10 is charged at just 18%, it might seem preferable to argue for a lower, rather than a higher, base cost at death and, ideally, one would like to be able to show changed market circumstances since death which would justify any increase in value.

However, remember that the two taxes 'do different things': CGT charges gains realised over the period of ownership whereas IHT charges transfers of value. In particular (for 2009/10):

	CGT	*IHT*
Exempt band	£10,100	£325,000
Rate of tax	18%	40%
Possible exemptions or reliefs	Main residence relief	Spouse exemption/nil rate band/agricultural property relief

What matters is the ability to establish a proper market value at death. If a market value has already been agreed with a district valuer, that will be the value, even if a higher value is achieved on a subsequent sale. If the value has not yet been agreed, the matter should be raised with HMRC with arguments as to why, if the lower value is maintained for market value at death, values have changed in the interim.

Main residence relief

12.18 PRs are not trustees and therefore the extension of main residence relief to trustees (see **5.25–5.27**) will not apply where executors realise the family home at a gain.

There is a limited concession, now enacted by *FA 2004* in *TCGA 1992, s 225A*, where PRs dispose of a house that both immediately before and after the death was used as the main residence of beneficiaries entitled under the will or intestacy to all, or substantially all (ie 75% plus) of the net proceeds of sale, whether absolutely or for life. The PRs must make a claim to benefit from any private residence relief under this now enacted concession.

The moral is: think hard well before executors sign a contract for sale.

Example 12.4—Achieving CGT efficiency on main residence sales

Bill died owning 'Blackacre'. Its market value at death is thought to be around £200,000. About one year after death a purchaser is prepared to pay £300,000 for the property. There are good arguments as to why the increase in value has occurred over this brief time. It is thought possible that a market value at death of £200,000 can be sustained.

If the house is sold by the executors in 2009/10 then disregarding allowable expenditure, the tax would be as follows:

Sale proceeds	£300,000
Less cost	(£200,000)
Gain	£100,000
Less annual exemption	(£10,100)
Taxable gain	£89,900
Tax @ 18%	£16,182

Vesting the property in the four adult beneficiaries before sale would have some beneficial effect, though, quite apart from the gain, their incomes make each of them a higher rate taxpayer.

The chargeable gain would be as above, though deductible from it would (if available) be four annual exemptions of £10,100, viz £40,400, making the taxable gain £59,600, with tax payable @ 18% of £10,728. It is probably unrealistic to expect all four of the beneficiaries to occupy the property as their main residence, as each has their own home and family. Supposing, however, just one of them was prepared to do so. They could together vary the will to create a will trust of residue, perhaps discretionary or life interest under which the beneficiaries would be the four children and also spouses, their own children, etc (see **13.1–13.4**). The one child, call him Alan, who was prepared to go and live there with his family would, say, nine months after death, take up residence for a decent period of at least six months and preferably more, perhaps letting his own property. A year and a half or so after death, the trustees of the will trust would sell the property at a gain of £100,000. However, since because during their period of ownership, in fact less than 36 months, the house has at some time been occupied by a beneficiary as his only or main residence, the whole of the gain is exempt, even though there are other beneficiaries who live elsewhere. There is a potential tax saving of around £16,000 (rather less than what it would have been before 2008/09). Clearly, so as not to invoke anti-avoidance principles, the trust should not simply be wound up and the proceeds distributed to the four children following the sale of the house by the trustees. It would be useful if there could be established a continuing family reason for having an ongoing trust.

Chapter 13

Deceased estates: post-death rearrangements

WRITTEN VARIATIONS

13.1   A beneficiary (or indeed all the beneficiaries taken together) can rewrite the provisions of a will (or intestacy) as long as they do so in writing within two years after the death. For deeds made since 1 August 2002, the deed must simply contain a statement by all the parties that the IHT and/or CGT reliefs are intended to apply. Generally, the effect of such a variation is to regard for IHT purposes the terms of the variation as written into the will; see Example 13.1 (*IHTA 1984, s 142*). The Conservative government tried to repeal this facility in 1989, though the offending Finance Bill clauses were withdrawn. Five years later, the Labour Party said that when elected they would reintroduce such a repeal. To date, the Labour government has not done so, however.

Example 13.1—A simple variation illustrated

Under James' will there is a nil rate band gift to a discretionary trust with residue left to his wife. The trustees appoint within two years after James' death £50,000 to each of James' children, Bill and Ben. Bill wishes to benefit his own children, Thomas and Serena, and transfers the £50,000 to them again within two years after his father's death. It is open to Bill to make a variation under *s 142*, within six months after the transfer to his own children. This will have the effect of avoiding a gift for IHT purposes by Bill and treating the gift to Thomas and Serena as made direct to them under their grandfather's will.

Some points to watch

13.2

- The deed of variation will not be effective if it purports to take away value from minors or unborn beneficiaries.

- The deed will be ineffective if made for consideration, ie there must be a genuine gift from the original to the new beneficiary (*IHTA 1984, s 142(3)*).

- If the effect of the deed is to create a life interest trust, that trust must last for at least two years, unless terminated by death of the beneficiary (*IHTA 1984, s 142(4)*).

Passing on growth, tax free

13.3   The value of the whole estate, or perhaps that of one or two assets may increase in the two years following death. Such value could be passed under variation to chargeable beneficiaries; see Example 13.2.

An election made for IHT purposes will ensure that the value of the asset at the date of death is treated as passing under the will to the new chargeable beneficiary. That will also be the acquisition cost for CGT purposes.

Income tax and CGT

13.4   A variation has no effect for income tax or CGT. Although it is possible to make a CGT election, this has the simple effect of avoiding the variation itself from being a disposal. However, all the other consequences of the CGT legislation will apply. The particular point here, for both income tax and CGT, is that if the original beneficiary by the variation creates a settlement under which they or their spouse can benefit, the settlement will be 'settlor-interested'. (See **4.26–4.29** for the income tax implications.)

Example 13.2—Securing IHT freedom for post-death appreciation

Marcus died on 1 December 2008, with an estate of £1 million all of which is left to Antonia, his wife, who survives him. Twelve months after his death, the value of the estate has increased to £1.5 million, the whole of which increase is attributable to quoted shares worth £312,000 at his death. Antonia could make a deed of variation under which there is a specific gift of those shares, either to her children, or to a nil rate band discretionary trust.

Alternatively, if perhaps Marcus had made chargeable transfers of £312,000 in the seven years before he died, the deed of variation could have Antonia take a legacy of £1 million with residue to the children. The effect of the IHT legislation would be to attribute the whole of the estate to the exempt specific gift to Antonia.

277

In either case, the result would be to have the uplift in value of £500,000 passing to the children free of tax.

DISCLAIMERS

13.5   A disclaimer is a slightly curious animal, which can apply to any property, but which is particularly apt to wills. It is not enough for a gift to be made, it has to be received. Suppose a will leaves Blackacre to X, and X turns round and says, 'I don't want it': there is no obligation on him to receive Blackacre, and the will is effectively read as if X had died before the testator. The effect is that Blackacre falls to be divided as part of the residue of the estate. If instead, X had been entitled to part of residue and had disclaimed that, the disclaimed share of residue would fall into intestacy. If X had been entitled to receive income under a will trust and had disclaimed his right to income, the will trust would be read as if the next succeeding life interest (or an outright capital gift) came into being.

The IHT effect

13.6   Where the disclaimer is made within two years after the death, the property is treated as passing under the will to the person entitled under the disclaimer (*IHTA 1984, s 142*).

The no benefit rule

13.7   The important point with disclaimers is that an asset cannot be disclaimed if a benefit has already been taken from it. Further, there is no right to disclaim in part unless the will (or other instrument) gives power to do so.

Disclaimers can be of use in simple cases. They came into their own in 1989 when everyone thought that the Finance Bill provisions outlawing deeds of variation (and incidentally, appointments under two-year discretionary will trusts) would be enacted. When the threat passed, people got less excited about disclaimers.

Where more than two years have elapsed

13.8   Like a variation, a disclaimer, to be effective, must be made within two years. If more than two years have elapsed since the date of death, and no benefit has been taken from the asset concerned, there is a possible line of escape if it is desired to avoid a particular asset coming into a beneficiary's estate for IHT purposes. There is a separate provision (in *IHTA 1984, s 93*) that deals with settled property. Generally, a person given a right under a trust who has taken no benefit from it can disclaim that right whatever length of time has elapsed and the trust deed will be read as if he had never become entitled.

Example 13.3—Using a disclaimer

A will gives to Benedict all the furniture in the testator's house and a life interest in residue. The will provides that, subject to Benedict's life interest, residue is to be divided equally between Benedict's two (adult) children. Benedict wants to take neither of the benefits under the will. He can, therefore, execute a disclaimer. The effect of the disclaimer will be:

- to pass the legacy of the furniture into residue, viz subject to the trust; and

- to treat the interest of Benedict's children as coming into effect immediately, ie to presume Benedict to have died.

Accordingly, given notice of the disclaimer, the executors can simply distribute both the furniture and the residue of the estate direct to Benedict's two children.

DISCRETIONARY WILL TRUSTS

13.9   The provisions relating to deeds of variation and disclaimers are contained in *IHTA 1984, s 142*. There is a parallel, albeit different, provision in *s 144*. This provides that where a person has left all or part of his estate on discretionary will trusts, and the trustees make an appointment out of those trusts within two years after his death, the terms of the appointment are read back into the will with no exit charge under the discretionary trust regime (see **6.34–6.35**). This could apply where there was simply a nil rate band discretionary will trust or a discretionary will trust of residue. The terms of the appointment may be to give absolute interests, or they may create a life interest.

It is vital (for deaths before 22 March 2006) that the trustees do not make their appointment within three months after the death; this was established by a Court of Appeal decision in a case called *Frankland v IRC* [1997] STC 1450. The appointment, therefore, must be made at least three months, but less than two years, after the death. However, for deaths on or after 22 March 2006, *IHTA 1984, s 144(3)* has generally cured the problem, at least with settled appointments, though not with outright gifts to a surviving spouse or to charity.

This device is commonly used in circumstances where a testator does not know exactly what the circumstances as to assets and/or children are likely to be at the date of his death, but anticipates leaving a surviving spouse. He might choose to write the whole of his estate under a discretionary will trust giving power to the trustees to make an appointment before probate has been granted or residue ascertained. Given survivorship by his wife, the idea would be that at the same time as putting in the Inheritance Tax Account, the trustees would make and submit their appointment, which would set up a nil rate band discretionary trust giving residue to the surviving spouse, either for life or absolutely. In other words, there would be no IHT charge on the death because the will would be read as though the terms of the appointment were the provisions.

Capital gains tax

13.10 Note that if the effect of the appointment is to create an absolute interest in residue on the part of the surviving spouse and there has been significant growth in the value of the assets since death, the whole of the growth will be assessed on the trustees at 18%. In other words, although assets are coming out of a discretionary trust, there can be no hold-over of the gain under *TCGA 1992, s 260* (see **9.6**) because *s 260* requires there to be a chargeable transfer and this is expressly precluded by *s 144*. By careful ordering of events, however, there may be a way round this problem: see the example below.

Example 13.4—Applying the chose in action principle

Suppose that Gerald dies on 1 June 2009 leaving an estate worth £600,000 at his death. His will is written under discretionary trusts. He is survived by his wife and three minor children. The trustees intend to make an appointment under *s 144*, creating a nil rate band discretionary trust as to £325,000, the beneficiaries to include the widow, three children and their future spouses and children and give residue to the widow absolutely (perhaps an odd thing to do in the light of the transferable nil rate band – see **11.19–11.22**). When they are considering this, a year or so after the death, the assets earmarked for the widow have appreciated by £100,000. If, therefore, they simply proceed with their plan, they will, on distributing the assets to her, make a gain of £100,000. Deducting the annual exemption of £10,100, this gives rise to a taxable gain of £89,900, which with tax @ 18% produces a tax bill of £16,182. The point is that, once the executors transfer Gerald's property to the trustees, it is the trustees' base cost and acquisition date which are related back to the date of death. The CGT implications of any appointments by the trustees within two years after Gerald's death will follow normal principles (without any ability to hold over the gain, except where defined business assets); see the next paragraph.

We have said already that a beneficiary under a will has no right to specific assets, only the 'chose in action' described at **2.15**. The beneficiary of the estate is the trustee, albeit to hold on the trusts provided in the will. The conventional order of things is that the PRs wind up the estate by distributing the £600,000 (now worth £700,000) to the trustees to use as they see fit. Suppose on the other hand, that, before the distribution of the estate, the trustees make their appointment on the nil rate band trust and the gift of residue to the surviving spouse. HMRC helpfully take the view that at that stage nothing happens for CGT purposes. As and when the PRs appropriate the assets in the estate to the trustees and bring the administration to an end, the trustees are bound by their appointment. They hold assets worth £325,000 on the discretionary trusts, and the balance now worth £375,000 they hold for the widow as 'bare trustees'. Normally, it would be the acquisition date and acquisition cost of the trustees that would be related back to the date of death. In this case, however, it is the acquisition circumstances of the widow who is the ultimate beneficiary, which are related back to the date of death. Accordingly, there is no chargeable gain, no tax to pay and she is simply treated as having inherited assets now worth £375,000, with a base cost of £275,000, ie an inherited gain of £100,000, but at least with time to plan the disposals in a tax-efficient manner.

IHTA 1984, SECTIONS 142 AND 144 INTERACTION

13.11 A decided case called *'Russell'* in 1988 (*Russell v IRC* [1988] 1 WLR 834) established that you cannot vary the same property twice, ie you cannot have two bites at the same cherry. However, there is no reason in principle why within the same estate there should not be two or more variations.

Section 144 followed by s 142

13.12 An appointment by trustees under *s 144* can also in principle be the subject of a subsequent variation under *s 142*. See Example 13.5.

Example 13.5—Appointment followed by variation

Jeremy, a bachelor, has just died, leaving his entire estate subject to a discretionary trust. A year after Jeremy's death, the trustees make appointments within *s 144* passing the whole trust fund absolutely to Jeremy's three nieces. One of the nieces varies her entitlement, within two years after her uncle's death, into an accumulation and maintenance trust for her children. Subject to claiming the benefit of *s 142* in the deed of variation, the transfer into trust will not be a PET made by the niece, but will be treated as a new will trust made by Jeremy. Hence, if the niece settlor were to die within seven years after the settlement was made, there would be no IHT implications of her death for the will trust.

Section 142 followed by s 144

13.13   This situation envisages the original beneficiary, say the surviving spouse who is left the whole estate, varying her interest to create a nil rate band trust including herself as a beneficiary. This would be on the footing that the property put into the trust was within the nil rate band. If subsequently, the assets concerned turn out to be worth rather more than originally envisaged, the trustees could, within two years of the death, appoint back to the widow the excess over the nil rate band reducing the chargeable value on death to nil. See Example 13.6.

Example 13.6—Variation followed by appointment

Malcolm dies in 2009/10, leaving his estate worth £400,000 to his wife, Jill. Jill varies the will to put specific assets worth, as she thinks, £300,000 into a nil rate band discretionary trust. It turns out six months later that the assets put into the trust are in fact worth £350,000. This produces an IHT liability in Malcolm's estate of £25,000 × 40% = £10,000. Given that Jill is a beneficiary under the trust, the trustees could, within two years after Malcolm's death, appoint £25,000 back to her to restore the *status quo* and to restrict the chargeable transfer on Malcolm's death to £325,000, viz the nil rate band.

Chapter 14

Deceased estates: stamp duties

14.1   The scope of stamp duties is now restricted to (broadly) shares and land: see **3.21–3.22**. Personal representatives of a deceased estate are very unlikely to be acquiring shares or land (though, if so, they would be treated just as are trustees: see **7.1–7.5**).

More likely, their involvement with shares or land is to distribute them to beneficiaries entitled under the will.

SHARES

14.2   The transfer of shares by personal representatives to a beneficiary may be certified as exempt from stamp duty by certificating the relevant stock transfer form, the appropriate category under *The Stamp Duty (Exempt Instruments) Regulations 1987*:

- Specific Gifts: Category B.

- Specific Intestate Property: Category C.

- Satisfaction of General Legacies and Intestacies: Category D.

- Transfers of Residue: Category E.

LAND

14.3   The transfer of land to a beneficiary entitled will be exempt from SDLT unless the beneficiary gives consideration *(FA 2003, Sch 3, para 3A)*. Interestingly, in this case assumption of secured debt by the beneficiary does not constitute consideration (whereas it does in a trust case). For land transactions before 12 March 2008, a transfer document is self-certified with form SDLT 60, which is provided by the beneficiary to the Land Registry to enable his re-registration as beneficial owner. Where the transfer takes place on or after 12 March 2008, *FA 2008* has dispensed with the need for form SDLT 60: re-registration is procured by delivering to the Land Registry the assent by the personal representatives, together with Land Registry transfer form TP1.

Example 14.1

Under the terms of her father's will Fiona is entitled to shares worth £100,000. This is a specific testamentary gift and the transfer forms are certified by the executors with Category B of the *1987 Regulations*, enabling Fiona to be re-registered in the books of the relevant companies.

Her brother Gerald is, as the residuary beneficiary, entitled to Black Horse Farm burdened with debt of £100,000 which Gerald is happy to take over. There is no liability to SDLT, being within the nil-rate threshold of £150,000 for non-residential transactions, but Gerald as the 'purchaser' must still within 30 days of the assent to him by the personal representatives submit form LTR1 to HMRC Stamp Taxes (as the debt exceeds the *de minimis* of £40,000). Delivery to the Land Registry of Revenue certificate SDLT5 together with the assent will procure Gerald's registration as the new owner.

Appendix

Modernising the income tax and capital gains tax treatment of trusts

Following the announcement in the Chancellor's pre-Budget Statement on 10 December 2003, HMRC published four consultation documents on 11 December 2003. The consultation period ended on 18 February 2004 and HMRC subsequently published the results. Although the original intention appears to have been to introduce a comprehensive new regime to take effect from 2005/06, the exercise clearly proved more difficult than had been anticipated. A further consultation document was issued at Budget 2005 with responses to specific questions requested by 10 June 2005. The four issues concerned were: income streaming, definition of a trust; residence tests for trusts; and sub-fund elections. In the event, draft legislation published on 2 February 2006 and enacted in *FA 2006* covered all of these apart from income streaming.

Accordingly, as at 2009/10, we have the following changes to the earlier regime:

- The rate applicable to trusts (RAT) for the income and capital gains of discretionary and accumulation settlements was increased from 34% to 40% from 2004/05. This is now called the 'special rates' for trusts, viz 32.5% for dividend income and 40% for non-dividend income. It was announced at Budget 2009 that, as from 2010/11, these rates will increase to 42.5% and 50% respectively.

- As from 2004/05 there is a special income tax and capital gains tax regime for trusts with vulnerable beneficiaries (see **4.37–4.40**).

- As from 2005/06 the first £500 (£1,000 from 2006/07) of taxable income is taxed at just the 10% dividend ordinary rate, the 20% lower rate or the 22% basic rate, with any balance over £500 (now £1,000) attracting the RAT (see **4.35–4.36**).

- As from 2006/07 various definitions, including 'settlor' are conformed for income tax and CGT purposes (see **2.5**). The definition of 'settlor-interested' for CGT is also expanded to include cases where the minor unmarried children of the settlor not in a civil partnership can benefit (see **5.21–5.22**).

- As from 2006/07 trustees can make a sub-fund election in respect of the income and gains of a specified part of the settlement (see **5.40–5.43**).

- As from 2007/08 the residence rules for CGT purposes are conformed to the income tax rules (see **5.8**).

This leaves on the table the following main issue, which the author understands was shelved from the 2006 draft legislation for 'lack of Parliamentary time'. Whether it does eventually see the light of legislative day remains uncertain, although HMRC have confirmed that they are still giving it thought.

INCOME STREAMING

The general proposal is that income passed by the trustees to beneficiaries either during the tax year of receipt or on or before the 31 December following should be exempted from the RAT. While the trustees should still pay tax at the basic or dividend rate, income received net of tax would cover the trustees' tax liability. Some tracking mechanism for types of income streamed out would be required, perhaps a *pro rata* system.

A related proposal would abolish tax pools, with the benefit of a three- (or perhaps five-) year transitional period.

Index

[All references are to paragraph numbers]

305